The Inheritance of Wealth

# NEW TOPICS IN APPLIED PHILOSOPHY

*Series Editor*: Kasper Lippert-Rasmussen

This series presents works of original research on practical issues that are not yet well covered by philosophy. The aim is not only to present work that meets high philosophical standards while being informed by a good understanding of relevant empirical matters but also to open up new areas for philosophical exploration. The series will demonstrate the value and interest of practical issues for philosophy and vice versa.

# The Inheritance of Wealth

*Justice, Equality, and the Right to Bequeath*

Daniel Halliday

OXFORD
UNIVERSITY PRESS

# OXFORD
UNIVERSITY PRESS

Great Clarendon Street, Oxford, OX2 6DP,
United Kingdom

Oxford University Press is a department of the University of Oxford.
It furthers the University's objective of excellence in research, scholarship,
and education by publishing worldwide. Oxford is a registered trade mark of
Oxford University Press in the UK and in certain other countries

First Edition published in 2018

Impression: 1

Published in the United States of America by Oxford University Press
198 Madison Avenue, New York, NY 10016, United States of America

British Library Cataloguing in Publication Data
Data available

Library of Congress Control Number: 2017955291

ISBN 978-0-19-880335-5

Printed and bound by
CPI Group (UK) Ltd, Croydon, CR0 4YY

*For my parents, David and Patricia*

# Contents

# Acknowledgements

I first tried to think seriously about inherited wealth some time around 2007, while I was a PhD student in Stanford University's Philosophy Department. I wrote a scruffy paper on inheritance and distributive justice, which I sent to my advisers, Joshua Cohen and Debra Satz. They took the trouble to read through it and helped me appreciate its shortcomings while advising me that the merits of the topic made it still worth pursuing. For better or worse, I wrote a dissertation on a different theme. Having moved on from graduate school, I have come back for another go at working out what to say about inheritance. This book is the result.

I have accrued many debts during the two years or so that it has taken to write this book. Much early momentum was gained from a series of conversations with Elizabeth Anderson in Michigan in November 2014. I'd like to thank Liz for her valuable guidance and encouragement when I was still trying to get this project off the ground. In early 2015, Guido Erreygers allowed me to examine his Rignano archive in Antwerp. Around the same time, discussion with Jens Beckert provided another valuable source of early inspiration. Peter Momtchiloff at Oxford University Press took an interest in the project from the start and remained patient throughout its slow development.

I got the first full draft completed during a semester's sabbatical leave in 2015, most of which was spent at Warwick University's Centre for Ethics, Law, and Public Affairs. This was probably the best intellectual community I could have found in which to work on this project. Thanks especially to Matthew Clayton, John Cunliffe, Clare Heyward, Hwa Young Kim, Andy Mason, Helen McCabe, Tom Parr, Mark Philp, Adam Swift, and Victor Tadros, all of whom helped a great deal by reading draft chapters and/or offering their thoughts in many useful conversations.

I spent the rest of 2015 and much of 2016 on getting the draft up to a higher standard. We were lucky to have Samuel Fleischacker visit Melbourne in August 2015, and I'd like to thank him for taking the trouble to read a draft of chapter 2 and providing valuable feedback.

Later on, I was fortunate enough to have the manuscript subjected to extended scrutiny at two outstandingly helpful workshops. In May 2016, Georgetown University's Institute for the Study of Markets and Ethics hosted me as part of their series of Junior Faculty Manuscript Workshops. Thanks here to Jason Brennan, Michael Douma, John Hasnas, Peter Jaworski, Michael Kates, Govind Persad, and the three invited commentators: Anne Alstott, Richard Arneson, and Heidi Hurd. In October 2016, I got a similar treatment at the Australian National University. Thanks here to Christian Barry, Geoff Brennan, Devon Cass, Bob Goodin, Serene Khader, Seth Lazar, Chad Lee-Stronach, Shmulik Nili, Fabienne Peter, Luke Roelofs, and Lachlan Umbers.

Various ideas from the book were aired as talks at departments and conferences during the past three years or so. Here I thank audiences at the Australian National University, the University of Auckland, Boston University, Canterbury University (Christchurch), Melbourne University Law School, the University of Otago, the University of Utrecht, Victoria University (Wellington), and the University of Western Australia. I thank the University of Melbourne for the sabbatical leave in early 2015 and for research support at other times, which funded some of the travel mentioned earlier. At the end, I'm grateful to Judith Hoover for extremely thorough copyediting.

Many other individuals played a supporting role in this project. I'm grateful to Kok-Chor Tan for providing valuable advice and encouragement at several stages. Nicholas Vrousalis provided excellent feedback on an ancestor of chapter 7. Ben Miller sent comments on the whole manuscript. Many others provided valuable conversations, email exchanges, and the like. Here I also thank Andrew Alexandra, Ralf Bader, Luc Bovens, Michael Brady, Harry Brighouse, Gillian Brock, Trevor Burnard, Rutger Claassen, Steve Clarke, David Coady, Tony Coady, Ben Colburn, Roger Crisp, Charles Delmotte, Tom Dougherty, Patrick Emerton, Luara Ferracioli, Samuel Freeman, Johann Frick, Barbara Fried, Gerry Gaus, Alberto Giubilini, Axel Gosseries, Catherine Gough-Brady, Karen Green, Amanda Greene, Jesse Hambly, Keith Hankins, Matthew Harding, Karen Jones, Hugh Lazenby, Holly Lawford-Smith, R. J. Leland, Colin Macleod, Colin Marshall, Helen McCabe, Brad McHose, Francesca Minerva, Fidelius Most, Sara Mrsny, Kieran Oberman, Janine O'Flynn, Theron Pummer, Cameron Rider, Ingrid Robeyns, Sagar Sanyal, David Schmidtz, Anne Schwenkenbecher, Shlomi Segall, Assaf Sharon, Bob Simpson, Peter

Singer, Dale Smith, Jiewuh Song, Daniel Star, Cindy Stark, Karen Strojek, John Thrasher, Dave van Mill, Philippe van Parijs, Han van Wietmarschen, Lulu Weis, Stuart White, and Gabriel Wollner. All remaining errors are my own but would be more numerous were it not for the influence of each of these individuals.

As is discussed at length in the following pages, parents benefit their offspring through a variety of means besides the transfer of wealth. Whether or not I have handled this fact properly when developing the arguments of this book, I am among those fortunate enough to have experienced it first-hand, and I'd like to thank all members of my family for helping me get this far.

To Jessie Belcher, I owe very special thanks. Her support helped me enormously, especially in getting the project over the line at the end. But in addition, I would like to express my gratitude for the many other great things she does.

# 1

# Introduction

## 1.1 Undermining Justice Gradually

This book tries to identify the conditions under which inherited wealth undermines social justice. It asks whether, to reach a more just society, we would have to greatly restrict the right of individuals to pass wealth 'downwards' in their family tree. Many of us feel conflicted about this subject. The idea of a right to bequeath or transfer wealth, especially to one's own children, enjoys a certain level of intuitive support. Such support can be found among people who have no great wealth to pass to their children, and even among people who are childless. At the same time, many of us suspect that inheritance, and the way in which it selectively confers advantage on some people but not others, is bound to lead to some sort of injustice if nothing at all is done to control it. This book aims to illuminate this conflict and to grapple with it.

Over the following pages, I will gradually develop one focused concern, amongst others. This is about the relation between inherited wealth and what I call *economic segregation*. Segregation of this kind occurs when an individual's life prospects, and/or social status, depend on his or her group membership—specifically, membership of a group that possess greater wealth than other groups. Inherited wealth undermines social justice when it helps maintain group-based wealth inequalities over time, so that one's prospects in life become dependent on the fortune of being born into a family that already possesses substantial wealth, which it has managed to retain through the passing of its generations. Properly developed, this approach gives some vindication to certain ideas about the role of inheritance in perpetuating class systems and restricting social mobility, though with some qualifications. Importantly, however, it also leads to some explanations for why inherited wealth is not always an objectionable thing. Small, first-generation inheritances may help reduce segregation by expanding the middle class, or at least by stopping it from shrinking. Larger, second-generation inheritances may threaten to create further class distinctions in ways that increase economic segregation.

Another central goal of this book is to use the problem of inherited wealth to illuminate long-standing theoretical disagreements between competing theories of social or distributive justice. Thinking about inherited wealth enables some examination of egalitarian, utilitarian, and libertarian theories, based on how well they advance thinking about this topic. I shall argue that some otherwise quite promising contemporary conceptions of justice get into trouble when probed for their implications about the regulation of intergenerational wealth transfers.

Conversations about inherited wealth quickly become conversations about taxation. Often it is assumed that the taxation of intergenerational transfers will track the *size* of such transfers, in terms of financial value, and little else. In other words, it is assumed that an inheritance tax will work much like a progressive income tax: as a transfer gets larger, its liability to taxation gets larger still. Admittedly, most jurisdictions protect certain bequests from taxation, such as donations to charity, and in this way reflect judgements of common-sense morality. But such exceptions merely qualify what remains an implicit commitment to taxing wealth transfers according to how *much* wealth is being moved around. This book seeks to resurrect an alternative or supplementary proposal about how to calculate the tax liability of intergenerational transfers: inheritance should be taxed not simply in accordance with how much wealth is actually passed on but also in accordance with the wealth's *age*, assuming this can be measured. As such, this book aims to renew the case for what was once called "progressivity over time".[1] More specifically, it aims to renew the case for taxing second-generation inheritance at higher rates than first-generation inheritance.

Writing at the end of the twentieth century, Ronald Dworkin claimed that "equality is the endangered species of political ideals".[2] Restriction of inherited wealth is a subspecies that is among the most critically endangered. The taxation of inheritance ceased in Australia and Canada during the 1970s and in New Zealand in the early 1990s. Sweden, often viewed as a natural habitat for egalitarian ideals, taxed its last intergenerational

---

[1] The phrase is from Eugenio Rignano (see chapter 2).
[2] Dworkin (2000: 1).

wealth transfer around 2014. Little other habitat remains. The demise of inheritance tax may have been hastened by the growing ability of wealth to influence the political process, particularly the design of tax law.[3] Such trends probably represent an injustice in their own right.[4] But unjust procedures can (in principle) result in policy outcomes that are otherwise just. There could be good moral reasons for not taxing intergenerational wealth transfers even if such reasons have not motivated recent legislation that has hacked away at inheritance taxes. At any rate, some burden of proof lies on those who want to say otherwise.

According to John Rawls, there are some types of injustice that arise slowly over time. In particular, Rawls was concerned about the persistence of what he called "background justice" in the distribution of property and political influence. He saw the erosion of these conditions as a hazard faced by any long-running system of social cooperation and something that might occur in spite of nobody really trying to bring it about.[5] Rawls regarded the cumulative effects of inheritance and bequest as among the more significant factors that, without careful regulation, might account for the wearing down of background justice over time. He did not venture a defence of why intergenerational wealth transfers should be thought especially threatening to social justice over time. (Such an attempt is ventured in this book.) What can be said about inherited wealth is that it, along with its influence, is a shadowy sort of thing: flows of wealth down the generations, no matter how large, undergo their movements largely hidden from view, if not from the tax authorities, then at least from most citizens. For this reason, the problem of inherited wealth lacks the drama of many other social phenomena that moral and political philosophers try to study, such as war, immigration, and punishment. Other, not quite so dramatic subjects are at least highly visible, and therefore hard to ignore, like justice in education, healthcare,

---

[3] Such has been the case, at any rate, in the United States. For an extensive account, see Graetz & Shapiro (2005). For brief discussions, see Friedman (2009: ch. 9) and Murphy & Nagel (2002: 142–5).

[4] A number of political philosophers have written on the problem of money in politics. See for example Christiano (2012) and Joshua Cohen (2001).

[5] Rawls (1993: 265–8). Rawls is not really concerned to make a particular point about inherited wealth but rather a more general point for which he is well known, namely that "The role of the institutions that belong to the basic structure is to secure just *background* conditions against which the actions of individuals and associations take place" (emphasis added).

and gendered divisions of labour. The impact of inherited wealth is easier to forget, or even hide or misrepresent. Such facts establish nothing on their own, of course, about whether intergenerational wealth transfers undermine or preserve justice. But Rawls's remarks about the background conditions to social cooperation should help remind us of the potential for injustice to occur slowly and become deeply entrenched without this being especially obvious.

What is needed, therefore, is a careful inquiry into what moral foundations support the individual right to transfer wealth and property and what moral considerations favour its restriction. The role of political philosophy is to provide such foundational inquiries. This falls short of the naïve claim that political philosophy can 'come to the rescue' and sort out the real world's political controversies or turn around prevailing political forces. But any attempt to grapple with such matters can benefit from having a bit of theoretical substance behind it. This book is an effort at supplying some of that substance.

## 1.2  The Main Arguments in Brief

What to do about inherited wealth should be treated as an open question across various general perspectives in political philosophy. This book engages with various theoretical perspectives at different points in the following pages. But the more ambitious parts of the book seek to advance an egalitarian case for restricting intergenerational wealth transfers.

Stated very roughly, the egalitarian complaint with inherited wealth is that it helps keep the life prospects of individuals unjustly dependent on being born into families that possess substantial wealth. Ultimately, this is a concern about group difference being maintained when it shouldn't be. Important work has recently been done on why the segregation of social groups tends, in general, to be incompatible with egalitarian justice. Here are some recent remarks from Elizabeth Anderson:

Segregation of social groups is a principal cause of group inequality. It isolates disadvantaged groups from access to public and private resources, from sources of human and cultural capital, and from the social networks that govern access to jobs, business connections, and political influence. It reinforces stigmatizing stereotypes about the disadvantages and thus causes discrimination.[6]

---

[6]  Anderson (2010a: 2).

These remarks appear in a book about racial segregation. But, as their very general formulation suggests, they could be applied to segregation along other dimensions, such as economic position. Accordingly, it can be said that inherited wealth is unjust when its effects are powerful enough to maintain any of the conditions highlighted in this passage from Anderson. If inherited wealth does not do this, or can be regulated so that it does not have such effects, then it becomes harder to explain why justice (or at least the pursuit of equality) requires any further restriction on it.

The idea of social segregation, economic or otherwise, is subject to certain ambiguities. Taken in isolation, Anderson's remarks leave it open as to whether social segregation is itself an injustice or just prone to cause more specific injustices, perhaps defeasibly. (As philosophers often say, it is unclear whether segregation is *normative*.) I shall postpone more detailed discussion of what economic segregation amounts to, and why it matters, until later chapters. For now, I want to emphasize that being concerned about segregation does not presuppose any particularly precise conception of equality. The idea that there is something unjust about people being born into more or less privileged groups can be defended by appealing to more general views about the injustice of some people being worse off than others through no fault of their own. But it can also be made sense of in terms of the hierarchical character of interpersonal relationships that can result when different groups are cut off from each other or made to interact in certain ways that would not occur under conditions of greater integration.[7] In spite of their differences, both conceptions of equality will get some application in this book. Where the problem of inherited wealth is concerned, I shall argue that neither approach works especially well if used alone but that they work well when combined in the right way. This means reconsidering the relationship between what are often regarded as sharply opposing conceptions of equality.

To be concerned about inheritance is to be concerned about one aspect of the *movement* of wealth. This is distinct from being concerned about the sheer distribution of wealth or about ways in which wealth can be used, particularly when gaining access to important institutions. One might wonder why we should focus on the *transfer* of wealth in particular

---

[7] Influential here are Young (1990: ch. 1) and Anderson (1999).

rather than developing one of these other concerns. It can seem as if inheritance acts as a very minor force in maintaining economic segregation, compared to factors other than wealth transfers. After all, one gets an inheritance largely because of one's group membership, not the other way round. Receiving an inheritance is not usually an early life event. One's inheritance, if it ever comes at all, typically arrives too late to make any real difference to one's group membership. One's social position tends to be influenced by what happens early in life, which has much to do with the way institutions are designed so that wealth already possessed can influence one's access to them. Inheritance and the replication of inequality could easily prove to be *joint effects* of the other factors at work. Inheriting may be a consequence of enjoying membership in a certain economic group. But it is not, strictly speaking, what gets you entry into any such group. An egalitarian who insists that inheritance taxes will combat segregation may begin to sound like the salesperson who tells you that people purchasing their more expensive health insurance tend to live longer.

Ultimately, however, it is a mistake to discount the significance of inherited wealth on grounds that it occurs 'too late to matter'. This book seeks to explain why. The impression of inheritance as a largely inert factor—an effect rather than a cause of social segregation—stems from the habit of thinking of wealth transfers as relatively isolated events. Individual transfers are often mere iterations in chains of transfers that extend down the generations. Important here is the distinction between the immediate effects of intergenerational wealth transfers and their more delayed or cumulative effects. This distinction is important in this book. Sure enough, inheriting wealth probably makes little difference to the social position of the immediate inheritor. But it acts as an important enabler and enhancer of that inheritor's ability to confer subsequent advantage on his or her children, either through additional formal transfers or through a wide range of more informal practices. It is *this* fact that grants inheritance some causal priority as a long-run cause of economic segregation. Developing the reasoning behind these claims is one way to defend Rawls's suggestion that unchecked inheritance undermines background justice in the long run.[8]

---

[8] Though not in ways that depend very much on accepting a particularly Rawlsian outlook.

All of this can be applied to how inheritance should be taxed. The assumption that inheritance taxes will be progressive in the traditional fashion seems to endure whether inheritance is being defended or attacked. But traditional progressivity is not the only way to calculate tax liability. According to the *Rignano scheme*, inheritance can be taxed at a greater rate when it rolls over—when it gets passed down more than once. The scheme owes its name to an Italian theorist, Eugenio Rignano, who helped promulgate it around the early twentieth century. Today, the Rignano scheme is not very often discussed.[9] But multiple arguments can be offered in its favour. One argument for imposing stiffer taxes on second-generation inheritance relies on the way in which parental conferral of advantage compounds over successive generations, and connects this idea with economic segregation. Families that have been wealthy for longer possess a greater range of powers that keep their children privileged. The case for being relatively soft on first-generation transfers may draw some strength from the idea, already mentioned, that new flows of inheritance may help disperse wealth around the population, whereas older flows of inheritance may work more to concentrate wealth within a smaller subset of the population.[10]

Of course, the proposal can be fleshed out in stronger and weaker forms. A very strong Rignano scheme would make transfers entirely free from taxation in the first generation before conferring very high liabilities in the second or third generation. This is a very aggressive degree of progressivity over time. Such a strong view might not be the most

[9] I do not want to exaggerate: the Rignano scheme has been kept alive by some important work by economic historians and by some political philosophers. Here I have in mind works such as Beckert (2008), Cunliffe (2000), Erreygers & Di Bartolomeo (2007), and Cunliffe & Erreygers (2013). This formulation of this book's project, as well as its execution, has been much guided by these valuable works.

[10] The value of making wealth and capital more widely dispersed features prominently in the approach to egalitarian justice known as property-owning democracy. See especially the papers collected in O'Neill & Williamson (2012). While proponents of this approach typically endorse stiff inheritance taxes and wealth taxes on the largest fortunes, the emphasis is very much on government programs as the mechanism to get the wealth dispersed more widely. It is worth asking whether there is a strong case for singling out inheritance taxation rather than other sorts of taxes on capital, such as a land value tax (see Kerr 2016). For more general criticisms of the broader arguments for preferring a property-owning democracy to a welfare state, see Vallier (2015). I suspect, however, that the approach might benefit from relying on small first-generation inheritances as a means of keeping wealth dispersed without having to rely on the machinery of government.

plausible refinement of Rignano's general proposal: a more defensible scheme may be a weakened one on which age does not make such a sharp difference and where liability is still somewhat sensitive to monetary value. Rather than settle on any final word about how much a strong Rignano scheme should be preferred to progressive taxation, this book aims to get clear on what reasons might pull in either direction.

I shall seek to give the non-egalitarian arguments a hearing, and partial defence, as well. It was none other than Robert Nozick who (eventually) conceded that inheritance should "not cascade down the generations", even if could be justly passed on once or twice.[11] Rignano's original defence of the scheme was a sort of utilitarian argument about optimizing incentive structures, influenced by the work of John Stuart Mill. While I will highlight some problems with this defence, an appeal to incentives may still help show why progressivity 'over time' may be superior to progressivity 'over size'. Another appeal of the Rignano scheme lies in its capacity to accommodate a number of broadly libertarian ideas about the moral importance of freedom of bequest, and perhaps the more general power to transfer property to someone else. The scheme helps make these concerns compatible with an egalitarian outlook on inheritance.

## 1.3 Inherited Wealth and Inequality Today: Some Comments on the Empirical Evidence

It is worth saying something about the current social realities of inherited wealth. In this book I will try to connect the largely philosophical argument with real contemporary trends, albeit in a somewhat limited way. I'll use this section to quickly comment on some recent empirical work on the current state of inherited wealth and its social impact, so that I can return to it at points later on.

The first question is of how much inherited wealth is currently at large. Very recently, three substantial economic studies of inherited wealth have attempted to provide answers. Of these, the best known is Thomas

---

[11] Nozick (1989: 31). Nozick's endorsement of this claim is apparently motivated by the view that unrestricted inheritance is unfair, encouraging an egalitarian interpretation after all. I say more about what Nozick might actually have been arguing later on, in 7.3.

Piketty's review of data from France.[12] Comparable in importance, though less famous beyond the academic community, is Edward Wolff's examination of the situation in the United States.[13] Anthony Atkinson has provided a shorter assessment of inherited wealth in the United Kingdom.[14] These economists are generally trying to measure inherited wealth as a fraction of total private wealth within an economy. So their primary question is what portion of current wealth came to be possessed as a result of intergenerational transfers, and what fraction has been newly created through labour and other means.[15] An important additional question for these economists is the extent to which inheritance is dispersed among the population or concentrated into a particular wealthy subset of it. It is worth being explicit that these are primarily questions about the existence of inherited wealth and how it can be measured. Care is required when deciding what sort of moral conclusions can be drawn from their answers.

Piketty's contention is that inherited wealth is in the early stages of a massive comeback. The narrative he extracts from his data is that inheritance flow was at a very high level prior to the early twentieth century, after which it declined rapidly due to various shocks that broke up private capital, such as the world wars. During the decades immediately after the Second World War, individuals were able to increase their level of wealth without inheriting thanks to economic growth and its impact on wages. It has now been some time since such a large shock occurred, and wages have stagnated. This has enabled capital to start displacing labour as a major source of national income.[16] Since capital can be inherited, it will remain concentrated in the families that own it until some shock destroys it or spreads it around. The important conclusion for Piketty is that high inheritance flows make it impossible for those who do not inherit to catch up with those who do, where wealth

---

[12] Piketty (2014).

[13] Edward Wolff (2015). Batchelder (2009) also reviews much recent data.

[14] Atkinson (2013).

[15] Piketty: "In all societies, there are two main ways of accumulating wealth: through work or inheritance. How common is each of these...? This is the key question" (2014: 379).

[16] The larger point here is that returns to capital exceed the growth rate of the economy. Inheritance allows this to perpetuate because it keeps the capital in private hands, whereas a successful inheritance tax might either reduce the return or spread the capital around, changing its moral significance.

accumulation is concerned. This leaves us with a rentier society, in which those with wealth seek to invest it chiefly in ways that allow them to extract money from other people rather than in ways that stimulate new wealth. The economic fate of individuals will depend not on what they do to create wealth but on whether members of prior generations choose to transfer it to them. To use Piketty's evocative phrase, "the past devours the future". An interesting question is whether inheritance violates requirements of social justice before this sort of extreme rentier scenario gets reached. (This book argues that it does.)

Similar conditions seem to exist in Great Britain, according to Anthony Atkinson. This may not be surprising, since Britain shares France's history of exposure to the economic shocks of the early twentieth century, as well as the more distant history of a feudal era and the high inheritance flows that it enabled up until the world wars.[17] Edward Wolff's study of inheritance in the United States relies mainly on data from the late 1980s up to the present day. As such, his study is more of a snapshot view than Piketty's and does not venture any strong claims about whether the United States is reverting to some earlier state in which inheritance looms large.[18] This gives his approach some virtues: Wolff is rather more attentive than Piketty to very recent economic events, which may be morally instructive. In many ways, though, the *current* situation in the United States appears to be very similar to that in Europe. American inheritance flow is very much concentrated among a small minority of very wealthy households. It has become slightly more concentrated over the past few decades.[19] Of those who inherit wealth, the amount received has climbed slightly during this time, but Wolff reports that inheritance has actually *fallen* as a proportion of the total wealth enjoyed by the set of the population that inherits at least something. To the extent that inheritance is making a 'comeback' in the manner associated with France and Britain, Wolff's findings lead him to conclusions that are rather more moderate than Piketty's.

---

[17] See Atkinson (2013). See also the remarks in Piketty, concerning Britain (2014: 426–7). Also useful is Hood & Joyce (2017), which notes similar trends.

[18] In any case, the economic history of the United States is very different to that of Western Europe. This is detailed throughout Beckert (2008).

[19] As Edward Wolff notes, this is true insofar as the share of households reporting a wealth transfer has fallen slightly during this time (2015: 134).

Each of these three economists recommends some increase in taxation to reduce inheritance flow in the country he has studied.[20] But it is not always clear what moral diagnosis is being made. Piketty often uses language that implies he is not just measuring inheritance flow but highlighting injustice. This is evident in such claims as "meritocratic values imply that one might want to tax inherited wealth more than self-made wealth".[21] This idea has some philosophical substance, and I shall come back to it at various points in chapter 2 and more fully in section 4.5. What also seems to matter to these economists is the unequal distribution of inheritance. Atkinson is especially explicit in saying that inheritance would present no real moral problem if everyone received roughly the same. Piketty and Wolff both claim that large economic inequality is a bad thing, particularly when it replicates itself down the generations. But this leaves much unexplained where the moral reasoning is concerned. Several commentators have complained that, irrespective of how well his empirical claims hold up, Piketty's presentation of the subject as having deep moral significance is not properly articulated or defended.[22] I should add that this is no great criticism of the overall contribution that has been made, namely the impressive effort of having mined the data and done the measuring. Completing the moral diagnosis just requires a more prolonged engagement with relevant ideas in political philosophy.

To reach any conclusions about inheritance as a source of injustice, we need to rely on more than some measure of its fractional prominence as a source of private wealth. What really matters is the causal connection between the inheritance flow and the degree to which the fate (opportunities, social status, etc.) of a generation's individual members is tied to that of their parents, or indeed their parents' parents. There is wide agreement among economists and social scientists that inequality's

---

[20] Piketty actually recommends an annual wealth tax rather than a wealth *transfer* tax (2014: 515–39). I discuss this proposal in section 8.5. Edward Wolff makes the more modest claim that the United States should lower the threshold at which inheritances incur tax liability and increase the rate of taxation (2015: 239). Atkinson takes a similar view about the UK (2015: 192–6).

[21] Piketty (2015: 641).

[22] For criticism, see Clark & Cummins (2015). Compare Piketty's later reply (2015: 644). Also see McCloskey (2014), but compare Pressman (2016) on Piketty's behalf. For a more sympathetic discussion of Piketty's normative perspective, written by a philosopher, see Murphy (2015).

replication down the generations is considerable and that it might have been underestimated until quite recently.[23] As I have said, however, there are many mechanisms other than intergenerational wealth transfers that could account for this replication. The fact that inherited wealth is on the rise doesn't change this.

The bad news is that there is not yet a wide consensus as to the mechanisms by which status and economic inequality persist from one generation to the next. But there are various points of agreement and disagreement worth commenting on. There is good evidence that genetic inheritance, such as the transmission of IQ, has less effect than often assumed.[24] A greater effect, according to the experts, is due to the range of informal practices through which parents transmit various determinants of status and economic success.[25] These findings have begun to influence important work in moral and political philosophy.[26] The crucial question is whether such observations really confirm that inherited wealth occurs 'too late', so to speak, to make any contribution to the relevant sorts of intergenerational replication. It is notable that while studies tend to discount the *direct* effect of intergenerational transfers, they leave it open whether there might yet be some indirect effect.[27]

Many people think of inherited wealth in terms of the metaphor of getting a head start. I have already said that you don't normally get an inheritance at the start of life. Metaphors alluding to one's position in a race also encourage the sense that, in terms of wealth accumulation, people are generally moving forward rather than backwards. But this picture of general forward movement (equal or otherwise) cannot be taken for granted. As I have noted, many industrialized countries experienced a historically high period of growth in private wealth during the second half of the twentieth century. This happens to be the period during which much currently influential political philosophy, particularly on equality and distributive justice, was written. But the wealth of young

[23]  On this point see Mazumder (2005).

[24]  See Bowles, Gintis, & Groves (2005: 12), also Harding et al. (2005: 105–7) on the defeasibility of other genetically inherited factors besides IQ.

[25]  See for example Bowles, Gintis, & Groves (2005: 19).

[26]  Particularly the work of Harry Brighouse and Adam Swift, on which I draw heavily in chapters 5 and 6.

[27]  See especially the formulation in Bowles, Gintis, & Groves: "[I]t seems unlikely that for *most* of the population a substantial degree of economic status is transmitted *directly* by the intergenerational transfer of property or financial wealth" (2005:19, italics added).

households declined massively in many such countries after the global financial crisis of 2008. This was particularly true in the United States, where a relative lack of state-provided services (such as free healthcare) made its significance even greater.[28] In short, some people are heading backwards. This complicates the metaphor of head starts.

The point I want to stress is that when private wealth is generally contracting, rather than expanding as it did during the late twentieth century, we might be led to slightly different conclusions about the morality of intergenerational transfers. Since older households suffered less in the global financial crisis, inheritance has been a mechanism through which the older generation has 'rescued' some members of the younger generation. We should be open to thinking of inheritance not as a head start but as a safety net. Careful work is needed to establish what, if anything, follows from this. It may be concerning, for example, that young adults have become more financially dependent on their parents at an age when they did not expect to be. One British social scientist claims, "a whole generation is now growing up with a financial interest in their parents' early death, so that they can inherit a deposit for a mortgage".[29] This state of things may give parents undue power over their children. But it may also indicate something problematic about taxing away the private wealth even further. To put it crudely, inheritance might be helping to keep the middle class alive after an economic crisis that has robbed the younger generation of private wealth and earning potential. An inheritance tax that did not make allowances for this could have a 'feudalizing' effect, accelerating a shift towards a binary inequality between the super-rich and a propertyless mass. State policies aimed at promoting home ownership in the 1980s were sold on the ambition of creating "a nation of inheritors".[30] Even if the ambition was never realistic, it may be objectionable to reverse what limited success it has had. It is important to stress that this concession may apply mainly to first-generation inheritances. Parents who purchased homes in the late

---

[28]  Edward Wolff (2015: 49–51). Some economists suggest that the global financial crisis merely accelerated a decline of the middle class that was already apace due to the changing nature of labour markets. On this see Cowen (2013: esp. 37–40).

[29]  Dorling (2015: 105). See also Hood & Joyce (2017).

[30]  This phrase was used by Nigel Lawson, Britain's chancellor of the exchequer, when defending the selling of state housing so that tenants could become owners. For some discussion see Hamnett (1999: esp. ch. 6).

twentieth century, who are now entering old age, may be in a position to bequeath substantial wealth for the first time in their family's history. These cases may be distinguished from the inheritance of much larger family fortunes that may have endured for somewhat longer.

Edward Wolff draws particular attention to the role of inherited wealth following the global financial crisis. The impact of the global financial crisis has been so strong that inheritance increasingly has an equalizing effect on overall wealth inequality, at least in the United States.[31] This claim needs to be understood carefully. Intergenerational transfers have their equalizing effect due in large part to the simple fact that parents tend to be wealthier than their children (something that the financial crisis has exacerbated through its disproportionate impact on younger households). Economists measure wealth inequalities across *households* but do not adjust for the age of people in households. No adjustment is made for the age differences or biological relationships between households. If we were to look at wealth inequality across family lines rather than households, the equalizing effect may decrease or disappear. This is on top of other well-known problems with treating households as the relevant wealth-bearing entities for measurement purposes. For example, when adult children move back in with their parents, this can create a richer household and contribute to an overall reduction in measured inequality even though it occurs only because young adults have got poorer. Another point is that any equalizing effect of inheritance on *overall wealth inequality* is quite compatible with inherited wealth being *itself* unequally distributed across family lines (chains of households over time), something that Wolff is quite explicit about.

What, then, does the current empirical scenario suggest about how to execute the philosophical project? Many of the more influential philosophical accounts of distributive justice were not designed to take into account the idea of a shrinking middle class or other ways in which contractions of private wealth might matter. Broadly speaking, theories of distributive justice developed in the latter half of the twentieth century typically assumed that society was generally moving forward in an economic sense. Taking Rawls as an example, the concept of justice

---

[31] Edward Wolff (2015: esp. 134–40). There may also be an equalizing effect in Britain, though this is marginal enough to depend on some specifics of how wealth is measured. See Karagiannaki (2015) and Crawford & Hood (2016).

was always taken to be a matter of fair terms of cooperation. It was, and has been, taken for granted by philosophers that the cooperative scheme at least succeeds in maintaining its total output and preserves or enlarges the total stock of private wealth. Events such as the global financial crisis should encourage philosophers to develop theories of justice that include some sensitivity to the possibility that cooperative schemes can suffer shocks and undergo failures that result in the destruction of what they are supposed to create.

Taking these methodological considerations seriously may mean a return to doing political philosophy in the manner that was popular during the nineteenth century. After Rawls, political philosophy became more preoccupied with making progress via the discussion of abstract examples rather than cases from real life.[32] At the other extreme, there is a real danger of making political philosophy excessively subordinate to the empirical context in which it gets produced and from which it draws some of its motivation. One way to approach the problem of inherited wealth is by seeking a very precise measure of the impact of intergenerational transfers relative to other factors. This could then be paired with a similarly precise expectation of what would happen if inheritance were taxed, compared with other sorts of policies designed to bring about similar effects via different mechanisms. Equipped with all this, it would be possible to perform a comprehensive cost–benefit analysis of an inheritance tax. There are various reasons for not taking such an ambitious approach in a philosophy book. First, there is the fact that the empirical demands facing such an account are incredibly high. Edward Wolff himself claims that fully isolating the difference made by intergenerational wealth transfers lies beyond the powers of realistic scholarship.[33] A second, less concessive response is that things are never static. A cost–benefit analysis depends on a very precise set of empirical claims at a given time. This may prove useful in its moment but become outdated very quickly. Overall, political philosophy should aim to take some notice of the facts, but seek to supply some theoretical substance whose relevance can endure (to a degree) over somewhat changeable social and economic conditions.

---

[32] Here I follow Jonathan Wolff, who makes a similar assessment about political philosophy since the 1970s (2010: 340–1).

[33] Edward Wolff (2015: 100).

## 1.4 Outline of the Book

The remaining chapters of this book can be divided into three parts. The first (chapters 2 and 3) assembles various views on inheritance and bequest from the early liberal and classical utilitarian positions. Apart from historical interest, the point of these chapters is also to identify which of these older arguments have the most contemporary application. They seek to identify which arguments are now outdated, even if they were plausible at the time their authors made them, and which arguments may be adapted so that their force is as great as (or greater than) at the time at which they were first put forward. Here there is some scope for uncovering certain egalitarian themes among some of the early liberals, themes that are sometimes overlooked when these works are discussed in the context of other questions about political philosophy.

Chapters 4, 5, and 6 focus on more contemporary egalitarian views. Chapter 4 is a set of largely negative arguments against various egalitarian views that make little or no use of ideas about segregation or group difference. These include, principally, versions of the large body of 'luck egalitarian' views, as well as egalitarian ideas that emphasize the value of reciprocity as a way of giving content to equality as a political ideal. This chapter might be skipped by readers more interested in getting to the book's positive arguments and less interested with a review of alternative conceptions of egalitarian justice. Chapters 5 and 6 then expand on the main argument about segregation and parental conferral of advantage. This retains some of what is attractive in the luck egalitarian project but owes a certain amount to the alternative 'social' or 'relational' egalitarian project.

The third section moves away from ideas about equality and towards questions about property rights and taxation. Its two chapters are rather self-contained. Chapter 7 examines libertarian views in a somewhat piecemeal fashion. Here there is discussion of Lockean libertarianism (in both its 'left' and 'right' guises), as well as the sort of classical liberal views that attach less foundational significance to self-ownership or private property. Some libertarian arguments are rejected, while others are endorsed as ways of demonstrating the wider appeal of the Rignano scheme. Chapter 8 is an attempt to arrive at some more practical claims about tax policy. This is in the spirit of making what I hope are useful suggestions rather than robustly derived conclusions of a level of detail sufficient to meet all the demands of public policy. This is also an opportunity to review some philosophically interesting policy proposals that might be unfamiliar to readers. Overall, the chapter aims to emphasize ways in which the evaluation of inheritance taxes should be highly comparative, especially at the policy level, if not the philosophical level too: since some taxation is both inevitable and morally defensible, what gets said concerning the feasibility of an inheritance tax should be measured against the feasibility of other sorts of taxes. I close with some remarks about how the ideas in this book might serve as 'consciousness raisers' in a depressingly one-sided political narrative that maintains the illusion that all inherited wealth is newly produced. The Rignano scheme helps draw attention to this rather damaging way in which the political classes of various nations continue to mislead their electorates.

## 1.5  Further Remarks on the Study of Inheritance within Contemporary Political Philosophy

I have already suggested that extended discussion of inheritance is currently rather scarce. Views about inheritance and justice tend to be expressed by way of tangents or afterthoughts attached to larger discussions whose main focus is on something else. Conclusions about inheritance tend to be reached given efforts to extend theoretical frameworks not necessarily designed with a view to being applied to this problem. Some other influential contributions to justice and equality simply don't get round to mentioning inheritance at all.[34] This tendency can be traced to two prevailing forces that, for a few decades now, have been powerful influences over how political philosophy gets done. These concern the scope of inquiries into social justice and their methodology.

An enduring view in political philosophy is of a liberal "division of labour" between individuals and institutions. The idea here is that principles of justice regulate only certain sorts of institutions, principally laws and policies. John Rawls, a major source of the idea's current

---

[34] I have not found a single reference to inheritance or bequest in all of the writings of G. A. Cohen.

influence, called this set of institutions "the basic structure" of society.[35] This idea is not as simple as it may sound, and there are different ways of filling it out.[36] Accepting this division of labour might make it hard to approach the topic of inheritance and bequest. On the one hand, inheritance looks like the stuff of institutions. As Alan Ryan has pointed out, inheritance and bequest are partly *constituted* by various regulated institutional frameworks (banks, law firms, the tax office, etc.).[37] Very large wealth transfers, and particularly bequests, cannot happen down back alleys and must rely on cooperative action (or inaction) from such institutions. Similar remarks apply to large gifts, trust funds, and the like. At the same time, inheritance is not *wholly* internal to the sorts of institutions that normally get included within the scope of liberal principles of justice. Restricting the right to bequeath is clearly going to have ramifications for the internal workings of families.

I suspect that these facts have made it harder to locate the topic of inherited wealth within existing frameworks. David Miller has suggested that political philosophy needs to produce different sets of rules for different "spheres". The spheres he envisages include economic activity, community activity, and (perhaps) individual activity.[38] The problem with inheritance, says Miller, is that it doesn't fit neatly into any of these spheres.[39] I believe that *part* of the reason for why inheritance gets approached less often, or at least less directly, is simply that political philosophers like to work on topics that don't pose this sort of complication.

---

[35] The basic structure is mentioned at various points across Rawls's corpus. A widely quoted formulation is at (1999: 47). See also Rawls (1993: ch. 7) and (2001: 10–12). Another influential discussion of the liberal division of labour is Nagel (1991: ch. 6). Scepticism about the basic structure as the subject of justice can be found in Murphy (1998) and Cohen (2000: ch. 9; 2008: ch. 3); compare Scheffler (2005).

[36] Most salient might be the broad distinction between neutrality and perfectionism as interpretations of liberalism. Raz (1986) is still perhaps the most prominent defence of the perfectionist project. For a thorough discussion of the neutrality approach, see Patten (2012).

[37] Ryan (1987: 62).

[38] Pluralism of this sort is similar to the liberal division of labour, but not entirely the same thing. Roughly, the division of labour is about a unified principle of justice being constrained by independent reasons limiting its scope. Pluralism is about multiple principles of justice constraining each other's scope.

[39] Miller (1999: 25–37).

Such complexities, however, can be overcome. Families and privacy may be important, but their importance is quite compatible with getting serious about restricting intergenerational transfers.[40] Favouring the regulation of inheritance and bequest is perfectly compatible with maintaining that principles of justice must avoid certain intrusions into family life. I will later defend the claim that restricting the right to bequeath is actually among the more minor ways in which legislation can disrupt the family. None of this requires rejecting the liberal division of labour or anything similar. At most, it requires acknowledging that the distinction between private and public spaces is not completely sharp. In the case of the family, it is ultimately quite implausible to suggest that its internal workings are wholly off limits to a theory of justice.[41] More plausible is that principles of justice need to tread carefully and that certain aspects of family life might be beyond regulation. But that is a much weaker requirement, as should become clearer later on in this book.

Writing in 1991, Eric Rakowski remarked that egalitarians had become preoccupied with questions about what people owe to their contemporaries, to the exclusion of questions about what might be owed to people who don't yet exist.[42] In effect, Rakowski was highlighting an important methodological limitation of the sort of work being done on distributive justice in the late twentieth century. More specifically, there was, and still is, a tendency to view distributions as 'snapshots' rather than iterations within long processes that see generations of people enter and exit them, and in which the general stock of wealth or resources sometimes shrinks instead of expands. In the twenty-five years since, there has been a good deal of work on intergenerational justice, which has corrected for the particular disparity that Rakowski perceived. Much of this work discusses what whole generations *must* do for subsequent ones, not on what individual persons *may* do for subsequent individuals.[43] Because of this difference, Rakowski's assessment is still true

---

[40] Alstott (2008) and (2009) provides what I take to be a more general defence of this claim.

[41] The best-known case for this claim has to do with the injustice of gendered divisions of labour that are (at least historically) integral to family life. Okin (1989) is the classic text on this.

[42] Rakowski (1991: 149).

[43] This is not *quite* right, as the intergenerational justice literature contains important questions about whether certain groups within generations (e.g. wealthy industrialized states) must bear heavier obligations to mitigate harms to future persons. But such

for the study of individual, as opposed to collective, entitlements and obligations.

One way or another, most contemporary work about distribution can afford to make two kinds of simplifying assumptions about its subject matter. It can either treat distributions as noncumulative, 'snapshot' populations of a fixed set of people, or it can distinguish generations while ignoring distinctions between their members. The topic of inheritance might be the only topic for which neither of these simplifications is available. It requires engagement with the fact that distributions are not snapshots of a single generation, while facing up to the other fact of important relations between contemporaries. This has made the problem of inheritance difficult to approach from within these currently strong methodological frameworks. This may further account for the scarcity of recent work on inheritance, in spite of the generally large output of work on equality and distributive justice more generally.

I am not the first to complain about the snapshot approach. Philosophers with utilitarian or libertarian leanings sometimes criticize egalitarians by pointing out that distributions are not just groups of persons who are in a position to be given something.[44] Whatever might be distributed to meet the supposed entitlements of current persons often required work or activity of other persons, including earlier generations. Focusing on recipients is open to the objection that it ignores the past and future stages in a cumulative process. Those who make this sort of criticism are often in favour of strong freedom of bequest or transfer. Libertarians sometimes say that "recipient-oriented" egalitarians are preoccupied about inheritance while forgetting about the right to bequeath, precisely because they ignore the historical aspects of distribution. In more recent work, Christopher Freiman has suggested that when egalitarians present us with "one-off distributions of a fixed sum of goods" they are describing the problem in ways that make intuitions in favour of equal distribution emerge more readily than they might otherwise.[45] I want to concede that the non-egalitarians are right about

---

distinctions remain at a relatively macro level, not approaching the micro level of inter-generational transfers between specific individuals, characteristic of inherited wealth.

[44]  Most famously by Robert Nozick (1974: 167–8).

[45]  On this point see Christopher Freiman (2014).

the methodology, at least where the study of inheritance is concerned. But this settles nothing as to who is ultimately right about the substance.

In sum, various recent methodological trends have made many topics somewhat easier to approach for egalitarians while making inheritance more difficult to approach. So long as this remains the case, it will be easy for opponents of egalitarian views to make it look like such views are set up to get things wrong when applied to the problem of inheritance. Consequently, I have tried in this book to come to terms with the way in which distributions are cumulative effects of many earlier distributions. This introduces complexity but also makes it easier to eventually propose answers. Indeed, the main positive proposals developed later in this book depend on the way in which distributive trends develop and endure over time.

## 1.6  Inheritance and the Moral Foundations of Capitalism

An evaluation of capitalism's moral foundations is never going to be complete until some effort is made to come to terms with the problem of inheritance and bequest. This represents another important motivation for this book.

I take the moral foundations of capitalism to include (at least) two central components. These are, on the one hand, the importance of individual economic rights, principally property and contract, and the comparable importance, on the other hand, of robust conditions of competition. In various respects, these commitments come into conflict with each other: among the tasks of any philosophical defence of capitalism is an explanation of how to balance the noninterventionist demands of economic rights with the more interventionist demands of maintaining competition. Although not everyone will want to characterize capitalism in precisely this way, my way does not say anything new or controversial. It is plausible, for example, to model the commitments to economic freedom and competition as respective applications of more general sets of liberal, deontological principles about individual rights and some combination of utilitarian and egalitarian principles that may provide a degree of support for the infringement of such rights. On this view, this internal problem about the defence of capitalism is simply a local instance of a deeper theoretical conflict already familiar in moral and political philosophy.

It should be clear that capitalism needs to be understood in terms of the pillars of freedom and competition if it is to be distinguished from alternative ways of arranging social life. Imagining any society containing one of the pillars without the other will make this clear. Communist societies, for example, fail to enforce individual economic rights but usually impose plenty of competition on their citizens. Such competition will be of an artificial sort where the state decides what goals should be set and what fates should be allocated to the winners and losers. But the intention is still usually to get people to be more productive. Individual economic freedom by itself doesn't produce capitalism either. Plenty of noncommunist societies purport to support capitalism when protecting freedom of contract and property, but failure to preserve competition is manifest in the sorts of nepotism, plutocracy, and other ills that plague societies that profess a reliance on markets to get things done. Strictly speaking, these societies are not properly capitalist either.

Proponents of capitalism often talk about 'spontaneous order' that contrasts with the artificial order of societies organized around centralized economic planning. Roughly, spontaneous order emerges when individual freedoms lead to certain structured forms of progress without any of the participants really knowing what is going on and without there being any overall controller or designer who oversees things. But no economic order worth having is *fully* spontaneous. The most desirable orders are those that are in some sense spontaneous yet coordinated, where the coordination is maintained partly by rule of law and the right set of coercively enforced policies.[46] Achieving such order depends in large part on how to define and restrict rules of private property, including the transfer of property from one generation to the next.[47] The problem of what to do about flows of inherited wealth, especially once they become large, counts as one of the more important points of

---

[46] For a more extended development of this point and an explanation of its significance, see Satz (2010: ch. 1). It is of course possible that coordination can come about partly through custom in the sense of being not reliant wholly on coercive law. But no sensible view discounts the role of legal coercion altogether.

[47] Here I am suppressing the theoretical question of whether bequest is merely a way of using one's property or is in some deeper sense essential to having that property at all. On this, see section 7.2.

conflict between individual freedom and the maintenance of competition. Large inheritance flows allow one generation to exercise freedom with respect to what they own but may have profound effects on how members of the next generation compete with each other.[48]

The founders of the moral case for capitalism—a group that included early liberal political philosophers—recognized the importance of the inheritance question in roughly this way. They raised the question of how much inheritance was too much. As I will argue in chapter 2, they gave some partial answers that were quite plausible as far as they went, given certain empirical assumptions they were able to make at the time about the nature of private capital and the ways it could be put to productive use. My own suspicion is that the moral case for capitalism has become too much associated with the moral significance of individual freedom at the expense of the attention paid to the moral significance of competition. At least, the relative scarcity of work on inheritance in contemporary political philosophy marks a notable decline relative to the prominence it had between the late eighteenth and early twentieth centuries, when competition was taken seriously alongside economic freedom. This book is, in part, an attempt to restore the topic to something closer to the status it used to enjoy.

Ideologically, and to some extent philosophically, capitalism is finding itself somewhat on the defensive nowadays. Outside of political philosophy there is much talk, often highly moralized, of why we need efforts to 'tame' capitalism, or similar. Much of this talk simply assumes that capitalism is representative of the political status quo in most developed countries. But it is unclear whether that has ever been the right thing to say. Early phases of capitalism struggled to escape from the mixture of imperialism and feudalism that preceded them, and the escape is probably not complete. John Stuart Mill said that "the system of private property has never yet had a fair trial in any country...the laws of property have never yet conformed to the principles on which the justification of private property exists".[49] Mill's claim was true at the time and has probably remained true ever since. And its truth is partly

---

[48] Here I am following the line taken in Haslett (1986). Earlier works make a similar point, particularly the views of John Stuart Mill that I discuss in chapters 2 and 3.

[49] Mill (2004: II.iii.7). The omitted middle part of the quote contains an explicit reference to the "conquest and violence" associated with Europe's precapitalist past.

due to our failure to put in place a set of laws and policies reflecting a plausible philosophical view about how to deal with inherited wealth.

The moralized defence of markets is enjoying something of a qualified resurgence in political philosophy. Much of this is being carried by attempts to update the classical liberal tradition and associated ideas about spontaneous order. Classical liberalism differs from the 'hard libertarianism' familiar to most political philosophers. Its case for small government does not rest on attaching some fundamental importance, or absolute strength, of individual property rights. Instead, small, relatively noninterventionist government is favoured in large part because classical liberals regard state power as being vulnerable to regulatory capture, rent-seeking, along with tendencies towards warmongering, both abroad and at home (e.g. through an oppressive militarized police force and the so-called war on drugs). These concerns motivate the importance of economic freedoms but explain this importance with reference to other values rather than treating them as theoretically basic. So construed, classical liberalism has a certain proximity to, and capacity to accommodate, concerns held by egalitarians but normally rejected or set aside by hard libertarians (e.g. that taxation may be a way of pursuing justice). The language of 'big versus small' government may prove to be a misleading way of framing the debate. Being in favour of small government, whatever that may mean, could include strong endorsement of some particular things that government does. Certainly any attempt to update and defend classical liberalism requires something to be said about inherited wealth, but its proponents have not yet provided this.

Importantly, a pro-capitalist or 'market-affirming' political philosophy is not thereby a pro-inheritance political philosophy. Intergenerational wealth transfers are asymmetric exchanges in a sense that distinguishes them from standard market exchanges. Bequests are largely 'gratuitous' acts, which is to say that they involve a transfer of wealth based on someone's mere desire to give it to someone else rather than as compensation for something that has been supplied in return. This suggests that unregulated patterns of bequests may disrupt ideal conditions of competition. And ultimately, market-affirming philosophies do not amount to forms of anarchism. They accept *some* significant market regulations and permit some taxation. This means they have reason to consider accepting inheritance taxes, if only as a way of providing citizens with relief from other forms of taxation. D. W. Haslett once claimed that, once the moral foundations of capitalism are properly understood, inheritance should be abolished.[50]

While pro-market does not entail pro-inheritance, neither does anti-market entail anti-inheritance. Certain strands of egalitarian thinking are explicitly anticapitalist. G. A. Cohen famously wrote that a market society relies on "fear and greed".[51] Even such a strident antimarket position might yet not be committed to including an anti-inheritance position. Since inheritance is not a market exchange, it is therefore not clear whether a general egalitarian fear of markets should immediately extend to inheritance. So egalitarian objections to inherited wealth are probably not best construed as parts of more general objections to capitalism. This point should alert us to the possibility that some egalitarian frameworks, designed to address market-induced distributive inequalities, might struggle to generate a strong stance against freedom of bequest. The risk is that such frameworks have been designed in ways that can't condemn inequalities induced by factors that aren't symmetric in the manner of market exchanges. Indeed, the asymmetric status of bequests may create special trouble for some types of egalitarianism.[52]

This chapter has aimed to provide the reader with a sense of what is to come. But it has also made a case for approaching the problem of inherited wealth with an open mind, regardless of one's preferred theoretical perspective in political philosophy.

---

[50] The reasoning for this is laid out in Haslett (1986) and (1994: 238–57). Exceptions are made for spousal inheritance, orphaned children, and bequests to charities. Haslett's view of the moral foundations of capitalism is not quite as simple as the combination of freedom and competition, but it comes close.

[51] Cohen (2001: 66).      [52] See chapter 4, especially.

# 2

# Inheritance in Early Liberal Writings

## 2.1 Antifeudalism in the Origins of Liberalism

The problem of inheritance and bequest looms large in political philosophy during the period running from the late seventeenth to the late nineteenth century. This chapter cannot cover all of this period. Instead I focus on five philosophers taken from what might be called the early liberal tradition: John Locke, Adam Smith, Thomas Paine, William Godwin, and John Stuart Mill. I have chosen these five because they offered the most developed arguments about inheritance. Apart from that, there isn't necessarily anything that unites these authors as a 'tradition' strong enough to distinguish them collectively from other writers of their times. Quasi- or nonliberals such as Edmund Burke, Georg Hegel, and Jeremy Bentham each had things to say about inheritance as well, but their discussions remained rather undeveloped, and their views will be confined to footnotes and passing mentions. There is also a notable French tradition, which I have had to overlook.[1]

The main point of this chapter is to convey something of the origins of philosophical debate about inherited wealth. Historical surveys can be helpful at bringing together ideas that otherwise lie strewn across large bodies of text. I have also sought to survey these works with a view to recovering some insights that remain relevant to the contemporary

---

[1] Included in this group are Rousseau, Montesquieu, Constant, and de Tocqueville. Rousseau apparently had some support for progressive inheritance taxes; see Neuhouser (2008: 165). For some further comments on inheritance in the French philosophical tradition see Beckert (2008: 26–9, 121–2). A general treatment of French political thought in this era can be found in de Dijn (2008).

problem of inheritance. Some care is required to separate what is relevant in historical material from what might no longer be. There is sometimes a temptation to resurrect arguments from the history of political philosophy without checking that they have proper potential for life. I have tried to 'control' for this by being explicit about where a philosopher's position on inherited wealth, or some connected issue, may have had its force overtaken by economic events.

The authors discussed here span a relatively large period of time, in which very important changes occurred to the nature of the economy and of wealth itself. I will place some emphasis on the fact that Locke and Smith both wrote at a time when the vast majority of capital was in the form of agricultural land. This meant that the bulk of any inheritance flow consisted in the transfer of landownership from one generation to the next. This had significant implications for how the problem of inherited wealth was understood. The preoccupation with inherited land, and indeed with land as a dominant form of capital, began to diminish in the writings of later liberals such as Mill, who wrote after the onset of the Industrial Revolution. Hence, authors may appear to disagree with predecessors when, so far as normative commitments are concerned, they need not. Through the early liberal period it is possible to see a sort of evolution of argument from one author to the next. It is perhaps worth remembering that the idea of philosophical inquiry as divorced from political economy—something highly abstracted from sociological and other empirical considerations and more directed at analysis of concepts helped by simplified fictional examples—was not nearly as mainstream as it became in the second half of the twentieth century.

The early liberal writings exhibit a strong and at times passionate antifeudalism.[2] Rejecting the feudal order required a particular sort of defence of the capitalist alternative and a particular perspective on inherited wealth. Philosophers writing at this time realized that inheritance was central to the maintenance of feudal society but that the right to transfer wealth might yet be harnessed, through the right regulation, as part of a successful and more just market society. This gave rise to some important insights and proposals, as well as a certain amount of indecision on the part of some writers. If there is any sort of enduring theme to

---

[2] Overviews of the origins of liberal thinking against its feudalist background can be found in Freeman (2011) and Tomasi (2012: chs. 1 & 2).

these early discussions, it occurs from Adam Smith onwards. This is the explicit opposition to the long-standing practices of entail and primogeniture. Entail laws allowed one to bequeath wealth to heirs and also exercise the power of limiting how those heirs could bequeath it subsequently; they ensured that estates would not fragment with the ageing of a family line. Primogeniture operated alongside legal entail by directing that all or nearly all of an estate was to be inherited by the eldest male heir. These conventions had the effect (very much intended) of preventing inherited wealth from dispersing around the population. Indeed, they deprived owners of any real discretionary freedom of transfer. Nowadays, these practices feel like historical relics, the stuff of Jane Austen and Anthony Trollope novels. Philosophically speaking, entail might be compared with slavery—an obvious injustice but, perhaps just because of its obviousness, not very interesting. Closer examination of the actual arguments against entail that are made in early liberal texts suggests otherwise.

One point I want to stress about early liberal opposition to entail is that, in spite of appearances, entail is not the strict target of early liberal complaints. The concern is not really with the legal mechanism of entail itself but with the broader idea of hereditary concentration of wealth. The problem was with the concentrated *flow* of wealth down family lines, not simply with the *legal enforcement* of that flow. While entails may be a thing of the past, large inheritance flows decidedly are not, as is confirmed by recent economic studies such as those mentioned in chapter 1. The rejection of entail was perhaps a prototype for a concern to eliminate social hierarchies similar to those that might be maintained by the replication of very large distributive inequalities down the generations. Admittedly, the concern about enduring inheritance flow was partly about its economic inefficiency, which need not presuppose a concern about oppressive aspects of aristocratic hierarchies and associated segregation of different economic classes. In highlighting this, I aim to join some other scholars in identifying egalitarian strands in the writings of some early liberals. But I am not trying to argue that the early liberals were more egalitarian than many have understood them to be or that the egalitarian elements in their work are somehow more representative of their fundamental normative commitments than, say, the utilitarian strand that runs through the writings of Smith and especially Mill. Bringing out more fully the link between inheritance, social hierarchy, and segregation takes a certain amount of extra work, which the early liberals were not in a position to make and might not have endorsed. Still, the egalitarian element in these writings partly accounts for why they are worth reading today.

## 2.2  Locke on Property versus Political Authority

There are various reasons to begin with the treatment of inheritance in the political writings of John Locke. There is, first, the fact that Locke provided an extremely influential treatment of the moral foundations of private property. The bulk of this treatment occurs in his *Second Treatise on Government*, to which political philosophers devote most of their attention. Less time is given to Locke's *First Treatise*, whose point was to refute Robert Filmer's attempt to defend the divine authority of kings. This makes some sense. Political philosophers don't take hereditary monarchy very seriously, and so the *First Treatise* is usually regarded as the less interesting of Locke's political writings. Locke's response to Filmer is, however, where the bulk of his thinking on inheritance gets articulated. This is because Filmer claimed that kings were entitled to absolute power as part of their inheritance from Adam, who had been granted such power by God. Locke was concerned to show that Filmer's case was poorly argued (which it was). But in so doing, he formulated a number of broader positive views on inheritance whose interest goes beyond the disagreement with Filmer.

Locke claimed that there is no right to bequeath political *authority* even if there is a right to bequeath private *property*. Locke gets to this claim by first discussing the right of children to inherit. According to Locke, parents generally have a moral obligation to care for their children in ways that include provision of resources. While Locke recognized that such an obligation is embedded in "common practice", he also saw it as commanded by God.[3] But a child's right to inherit is restricted to a right in the parent's *property* and does not extend to the parents' political

---

[3] Here Locke says, "[W]here the Practice is Universal, 'tis reasonable to think the Cause is Natural.... Men are not Proprieters of what they have merely for themselves, their Children have a Title to part of it, and have their Kind of Right joyn'd with their Parents.... That Children have such a Right is plain from the Laws of God" (I.89, 2009: 207).

office, since property is enough to provide for "subsistence and comfort". By grounding the morality of inheritance in the rights of children, Locke separated children's entitlement to a degree of material provision from the less plausible idea that they're entitled to a parent's power and authority:

> The Right a Son has to be maintained and provided with the necessaries and conveniences of Life out of his father's Stock, gives him a Right to succeed to his Father's *Property* for his own good, but this can give him no Right to succeed also to the *Rule*, which his Father had over other Men. All that a Child has Right to claim from his father is Nourishment and Education, and the things nature furnishes for the support of Life: But he has no Right to demand *Rule* or *Dominion* from him.[4]

Locke clearly believed that there had to be some limit to the right to inherit. Indeed, he suggested that, were it not for the weak and vulnerable position of children, we might think that bequests should move 'upwards'. That is, if children were not so dependent for their survival on parental provision,

> it would be reasonable, that the Father should Inherit the Estate of his Son, and be preferr'd in the Inheritance before his Grand Child. For to the Grand Father, there is due a long Score of Care and Expences laid out upon the Breeding and Education of his Son, which one would think in Justice ought to be paid.[5]

This is an interesting suggestion.[6] As to the main point that children have a limited right to inherit property, it might be noted that Locke wrote during a time when life expectancy was much lower than it is in the developed parts of today's world and when state institutions for taking care of children's health and education were almost absent.[7] In the *Second Treatise*, where the topic of inheritance makes a brief reappearance, Locke adds that children's right to parental support does indeed diminish once the children are able to "provide for themselves".[8] It is quite

---

[4] (I.93). Similar thoughts are repeated soon after at (I.97).      [5] (I.90).

[6] For some useful discussion of precisely what Locke might have been getting at here, see Kendrick (2011: 155–8).

[7] Of course, much education still takes place within the family. Locke was working with a sense of 'education' that was far broader than that of academic education. For relevant discussion of Locke's wider views on family morality, see Simmons (1992: ch. 4). For some comment on the idea that financial provision may be among the essential roles of parenting, see Alstott (2008: 19–21).

[8] (II.78).

possible, then, that Locke's views would not support a very strong right to inheritance in contemporary developed society in any cases where the children of the deceased had reached adulthood. At any rate, a right to inheritance may be wholly subordinate to a parent's right to decide what happens to his or her property, which includes the power to disinherit as well as the power to bequeath. On this view, the right to inherit may have little force except in cases where a parent dies intestate, in which case a child's right to inherit acts as something of a tie-breaker. This is hardly a strong right at all.

A weak right to inherit is compatible with a donor's having a very strong right to bequeath or transfer. Locke was a natural law theorist, which means (roughly, and among other things) that he saw morality as a set of commands originating in God, although partly left for humans to interpret through their own reasoning.[9] This provides a foundation of sorts for private property, since property rights provide a means through which humans can become better cooperators, and thus improve the world rather than merely consume its raw materials, as the beasts do.[10] This gave Locke a starting point from which to formulate his principles about the original acquisition of property in land, including the constraints governing it. It is important to note, though, that Locke is not normally read as having drawn any implications from natural law concerning freedom of bequest, even if a child's right to inherit might be a natural right. One view is that rights of bequest or transfer are among the uses of property that *lack* a natural law justification but might in principle be given other forceful justifications.[11]

Unfortunately this is more or less as far as Locke got. His ideas can be adapted so as to inspire more elaborate claims about inheritance. The distinction between property and authority might have more in it than Locke spelled out. Intuitively, property is in some way inclusive of *some* form of authority, namely authority over what happens to the asset that

---

[9] This is meant as a description of Locke as a natural law theorist, not as a general definition of natural law that might cover the diverse range of its historical proponents.

[10] Here I follow the interpretation that property rights solve certain collective action problems, particularly commons tragedies. This interpretation differs from readings of Locke that see the foundation for private property in self-ownership and may enjoy less textual evidence. For more on this version of Lockean foundations for property, see Schmidtz (2008).

[11] Here I follow the interpretation in Neal Wood (1984: 80), also Waldron (1981: 47–8). For a dissenting view, articulated by a careful handling of Locke's text, see Kendrick (2011).

is owned. When the asset in question is an organization, such as a business, authority over the asset becomes harder to separate from a degree of authority over other people, such as the power to affect the lives of employees. Locke claimed that no matter how much competence a person may show when exercising authority, there is no guarantee that his or her offspring will possess anything like it. This claim may be just as applicable to executive control over a business as it is to formal political office. This suggests that Lockean ideas about the illegitimacy of inherited authority could be adapted into an argument against the inheritance of family businesses.

To summarize, Locke's overall view on inheritance remains somewhat indeterminate. Some of his readers continue to ask why he didn't regard his case against inherited power as extendable to inherited property.[12] Such indeterminacy may be understandable given that Locke's aim was primarily to defeat Filmer, which limited his intellectual ambitions concerning inheritance even though his ambitions regarding the wider concept of property were substantial. It is also difficult to state with precision how much Locke thought children could claim by right of inheritance, and how much of a right of discretionary bequest might remain once this claim had been satisfied.[13] Locke's enduring influence on contemporary views lies in attempts to use his ideas about self-ownership and the acquisition of worldly resources as foundations for more complete views about how to regulate the distribution of property. Such views are typically more determinate than Locke managed to be where inherited wealth is concerned, though the Lockean project can be taken in different directions regarding this matter. More in chapter 7.

## 2.3  Adam Smith on Entails and "the Progress to Opulence"

Adam Smith is best known for two works, the economically focused *Wealth of Nations* and the *Theory of Moral Sentiments*, whose focus is more on personal agency and ethics. His discussions of inheritance and bequest occur in the third book of *Wealth of Nations* and in a largely

---

[12]  See for example Grant (1987: 59–64).
[13]  For more general discussions of Locke on this topic, see Duff (2005: 24–8), Kendrick (2011), Sreenivasan (1995: 104–6), and Waldron (1988: 241–7).

parallel discussion in his lesser-known *Lectures on Jurisprudence*. Smith's opposition to entail appears as a mixture of two different concerns. The first is a sort of scepticism about the strength of posthumous interests, as articulated in this passage from the *Lectures*:

Upon the whole nothing can be more absurd than perpetual entails.... Piety to the dead can only take place when their memory is fresh in the minds of men. A power to dispose of estates for ever is manifestly absurd. The earth and the fulness of it belongs to every generation, and the preceeding one can have no right to bind it up from posterity. Such extension of property is quite unnatural. The insensible progress of entails was owing to their not knowing how far the right of the dead might extend, if they had any at all.[14]

These claims get repeated, with perhaps more egalitarian language, in the *Wealth of Nations*.[15] Smith's remarks leave it as to whether he thinks posthumous interests are simply nonexistent or just too weak an interest to justify the entail of property. Possibly the latter: Smith seems reluctant to rule out the possibility that the dead have a stake in what happens after their departure but doesn't seem quite prepared to rule it in either. What to say about posthumous harms and benefits is rather hard philosophical work, so perhaps Smith's indecision is forgivable.[16]

More can be said about the second of Smith's two concerns, which is the one more representative of his broader views on both economic productivity and social hierarchy. Smith granted that laws of entail may have promoted security during the medieval era, when the fragmentation of large estates would have weakened the nobility's ability to

---

[14]  *LJ* 1766/168–9, 1978: 468.
[15]  "They [entails] are founded on the most absurd of all suppositions, the supposition that every successive generation of men have not an equal right to the earth, and to all that it possesses; but that the property of the present generation should be restrained and regulated according to the fancy of those who died perhaps five hundred years ago" (*WN* III.ii.6, 1999a: 486). The egalitarian thought that the fruits of the earth need to be equally divided among members of each generation has its modern representative in the left-libertarian project, discussed in chapter 7. My use of the quote from *LJ* suggests that Smith's view on posthumous interests can be separated from any view about joint ownership of the earth.
[16]  In part the problem is of how to specify the limits of posthumous interests without arbitrariness: Smith writes that "the difficulty is to find at what period we are to put an end to the power we have granted a dying person of disposing of his goods" (*LJ* 1762–3/165, 1978: 70). For a contemporary discussion of posthumous interests as a foundation for the right to bequeath, see Braun (2010) and Lamb (2014). Posthumous harms are discussed alongside other contemporary puzzles about death and well-being in Bradley (2009: esp. ch. 1).

constrain a tyrannical monarch.[17] This point is worth noting as evidence of how Smith saw the regulation of economic production as something that might vary with changes in social context. Also plausible is the suggestion that the evolution of such regulation might lag environmental change. Smith tells us that "Laws frequently continue in force long after the circumstances which first gave occasion to them, and which could alone render them reasonable, are no more." Entail was a case in point. The emergence of Parliament and rule of law had, by Smith's day, removed the need for an aristocratic check on royal power. Having outlived their original purpose, entails had become an undesirable relic of the medieval past.

Specifically, the problem with entail was that it kept land in ill-productive hands:

Entails are disadvantageous to the improvement of the country, and these lands where they have never taken place are always best cultivated. Heirs of entailed estates have it not in their view to cultivate lands and often they are not able to do it. A man who buys land has this entirely in view and in general the new purchasers are the best cultivators.[18]

Smith wanted to stress that feudal arrangements, with large bodies of land owned by a relative few, grossly impeded agricultural productivity. Those who actually work the land (the tenants) have no real incentive to maximize its potential, since they did not get to keep the profits gained from selling its produce. Any attempt to improve the land would simply increase the amount they had to pay their feudal landlords in rent.[19] Smith was disdainful of the vast swathes of crown and aristocratic land set aside as "forests", i.e. as hunting grounds for frivolous sport.[20] Feudalism needed to give way so that individual tenants could gain ownership or extended lease of the land they worked, or at least some share of the profits from its production and relief from liability to large rents.[21] Only

---

[17] Smith III.ii.1–6, 1999a: 484–6. For more on the origin of entail, see Beckert (2008: 115–17), also West (1908: 185–6), who notes that the history of inheritance taxation dates back as far as ancient Egyptian society.

[18] LJ 1766/171, 1978: 469, also 1762–3/166, 1978: 70. Note also the earlier remark that "primogeniture hinders agriculture" at 1766/163, 1978: 466.

[19] See especially the discussion in WN, I.xi, 1999a: 247–9.

[20] WN V.ii.19, 1999b: 414. Note the archaic use of "forest", evidenced by Smith's observation that some forests contain no trees.

[21] WN III.ii.14–17, 1999a: 491–3.

then would they make the "best cultivators". The same ideas helped guide Smith's condemnation of slavery and sharecropping.[22]

It is well known that feudal societies were oppressively hierarchical. But on the reconstruction I've given, Smith's is not an overtly egalitarian, or even moralized, condemnation of feudalism. The actual text, nevertheless, is full of egalitarian sentiments. Most explicitly, Smith's criticism of entails in continental Europe slips into an explicit claim that the convention of making inheritance a necessary condition for civil or military seniority is to combine a first "unjust advantage", i.e. that of such inheritance itself, with a second.[23] Such claims would be superfluous if Smith's point had *only* been that entails were a massive inefficiency.[24] Smith describes the lot of the feudal poor not just in terms of absolute poverty but as "servile dependency upon their superiors".[25] He doesn't hide his dislike of the "tyranny of the feudal aristocracy" as something separate from their mere indolence.[26] At best, tenants of feudal landowners were little different from servants.[27] Smith's concern about the oppression of the common people extended to the sphere of political influence. Smith suggested that landlords lacked the intellectual powers to understand politics in any case. However, the employer class (owners of capital other than land, such as merchants and manufacturers) far exceeded the dim country gentlemen in their powers to manipulate and capture any attempt at market regulation, to the detriment of illiterate workers.[28] Even if landowners were not oppressing tenants, granting landownership to tenants would be a route out of their oppression by others. Overall, Smith was in favour of a market society, based on the conviction that markets and private property could emancipate the feudal poor from domination by the aristocratic and merchant classes. But there is more going on in Smith than an endorsement of the way in which production can be increased when property is dispersed. Smith takes frequent swipes at the landed gentry, emphasizing their idleness,

---

[22] *LJ* 1766/289–95, 1978: 522–5.    [23] *WN* III.ii.6, 1999a: 486.

[24] Smith may also have been deliberately holding back, given the reasonable expectation that those privileged enough to be able to read his work may not take kindly to a moralized, as opposed to economic, criticism of a system in which they were a beneficiary. On this, see Fleischacker (2004: 14).

[25] *WN* III.iv.5, 1999a: 508.    [26] *LJ* 1766/294, 1978: 524.

[27] *WN* III.iv.7, 1999a: 509.

[28] See especially the closing paragraphs of *WN,* I.x, 1999a: 245–7.

ignorance, and tendency to covet trinkets and luxuries as a substitute for more worthwhile pursuits.[29] Smith was astutely aware of the way in which those with great wealth gained a kind of bogus esteem, and critical of the way in which industry could be misdirected towards supplying superfluous luxuries for rich people. The security afforded to the gentry is enjoyed on top of the benefit of the "tranquillity" of a country life funded by land rents, one of the most risk-free sources of revenue, compared with the trials of being a merchant or trader, or for that matter a tenant farmer.[30] Again, if these points communicate something of substance, it is that wealthy inheritors are not entitled to their superior holdings while others work harder and take more risks. Overall, while the text contains no greatly extended articulation of an egalitarian point of view, the frequency of egalitarian sentiments conveyed in more briefly stated points makes for a substantial body of accumulated evidence.[31]

Let me make some concluding points about what should be taken from Smith's treatment of inheritance. As mentioned earlier, the *target* for Smith is clearly the practice of entail as a means of concentrating the ownership of *land* in a small number of hands. I have stressed that if Smith had lived in a world in which entail was not legally enforced, and landowners simply *chose* to bequeath whole estates to the eldest son, then the same inefficiency would exist. The crucial point is that the inefficiencies associated with entail depended solely on the *concentration* of large inheritance flows into small pockets of the population. The legal enforcement of such practices was causally significant in preserving them, since it gave incumbent landowners little choice but to go along with this way of doing things. But the real problem, as I mentioned at the beginning of the chapter, is with the flow itself rather than the coercive enforcement of the flow.

---

[29] See also the discussion of wealth and happiness in *TMS* IV.i, 2009: 209–18.

[30] *WN* III.i.3, 1999a: 481.

[31] For more on how the various elements of Smith's views can be given an egalitarian interpretation, see Anderson (2016a) and Rothschild & Sen (2006: esp. 334–7 on inheritance and the hierarchies of feudalism). Buchanan (1976) argues for the proximity of Smith's views to the later thinking of Rawls. A helpful discussion of Smith's attitudes towards the position of the poor, and of how a better appreciation of their position should guide public policy, is given in Gilbert (1997). Egalitarian perspectives on primogeniture and entail can be found in some of Smith's followers, such as the Scottish legal theorist John Millar, whose anonymously published writings on inheritance are discussed by Knud Haakonssen (1996: 169–73). To say that Smith had an egalitarian 'side' is not to say, of course, that his other 'sides' should be downplayed. How to weigh Smith's egalitarianism against his libertarianism or utilitarianism is something I leave to his more expert readers.

Smith does not have a developed view about how to regulate the inheritance of wealth other than land. The most that might be said is that his general caution with regard to taxation would probably count against a very aggressive tax on small inheritances. It bears emphasizing that Smith formulated his views before the Industrial Revolution had really taken hold. He was therefore unable to appreciate the extent to which land would gradually lose its importance relative to other types of capital. This suggests that his argument against large inheritance flows may now have been somewhat superseded. There is less reason, on grounds of efficiency, to care much about the inheritance of land now that efficiencies can be secured through what is done with other sorts of capital. In the right conditions, a society can flourish even if most of its citizens do not own any land or even their own homes. Some level of inheritance flow might even come at no cost to overall efficiency.[32] For sure, wealthy people living off capital gains may be quite idle, and Smith might disapprove of this. Some of today's super-rich continue to pursue activities that look a bit childish and frivolous. But financial capital is typically controlled by persons who do not own it and who have incentives to put it to good use. Of course, much may depend on how the relevant financial industries are (un)regulated, but that's a separate topic.[33] Nor is there any point, necessarily, in worrying about the extent to which such wealth is concentrated. Smith wanted estates to fragment so that relatively small portions could be held by a relatively large number of individuals, each with an incentive to improve his or her smallholdings. But, again, modern capital is of a sort where incentives can be generated without the fragmentation of ownership. I shall make further use of this point in section 7.5, where I explore its potential to feature in contemporary opposition to inheritance taxes.

To summarize, there may no longer be a good Smithian argument for the *inefficiency* of large flows of inherited wealth. Indeed, there may be no very extensive 'residual' interpretation of Smith that can say anything much about how inheritance ought to be regulated in a postindustrial society. Other readers of Smith detect a similar indeterminacy about

[32] See for example the remarks of Harding et al. (2005: 131–2).
[33] Here I am suppressing the complication, highlighted by Piketty, that inheritance flows can become so large that they eventually suppress incentives to work *simply* because the returns from work are so outstripped by the returns on capital. In any case, the early liberals would not have foreseen this way of arriving at such a problematic situation due to the low rate of return on capital during their times.

what regulatory framework should remain once entails are gone.[34] But this does not show that Smith's views have become wholly irrelevant. The evaluation of contemporary inheritance depends more on what connection might exist between such flows and social hierarchy. Smith saw the moral importance of this. At the same time, it is worth recalling that Smith had certain aversions to taxation and that a restriction of the right to bequeath might therefore need to be tempered accordingly. His most explicitly pro-bequest remark perhaps occurs when he says it "would be cruel and oppressive" to tax inheritors in cases where the death of a testator has already made the bereaved parties considerably worse off. Here he mainly has children in mind, especially those young enough to be still living under their parents' roof. Like Locke, Smith lived in the era before the state provided support for children. He was no great sup- porter of state-controlled redistribution as the best means of helping the poor. Smith was, after all, a classical liberal who was sceptical about centralized power. This goes for state power as much as feudal power.[35] But then again, 'pro-redistribution' views, let alone redistributive institu- tions, were not prominent during Smith's times. Again, the project was to articulate antifeudalism as opposed to mount a case against the modern welfare state. This makes it difficult to know exactly how Smith would have viewed contemporary redistributive policies and institutions, particularly given his belief, noted earlier in connection with medieval entail, that the set of defensible policies and institutions may vary from one economic era to the next. What can be stressed, however, is that Smith was strongly against the economic mechanisms through which hierarchical societies might replicate themselves. There is nothing in Smith that counts against any attempt to apply this concern more fully to inherited wealth.

## 2.4  Paine on Land and Compensatory Taxation

Locke famously proposed that persons acquire property in worldly resources by "mixing their labour" with them. The point of this is that labour improves the raw materials with which it is mixed. I improve a

---

[34]  See for example the summary in Fleischacker (2004: 197–200).
[35]  For a clear account of the role of decentralization in Smith's work, see Otteson (2016).

wild boar by killing it and turning it into sausages, or by ploughing unused land and then cultivating crops on it. Inevitably, the supply of nonacquired raw materials becomes scarce as new generations of persons arrive.[36] Wild boar went extinct in Britain in the thirteenth century, which Locke might have known about. Although animals, like some other resources, can be renewed, land is the paradigmatic zero-sum good. This is a significant complication for any view on which everyone is supposed to get a chance to acquire private property. Although Locke discussed both inheritance and the idea that acquisition must leave behind "enough and as good" for others, he did not connect them. And yet restricting intergenerational transfers of any resource could be one way of returning it to an unowned state to be reacquired by others. It was Thomas Paine who saw this connection more clearly. In doing so, he was able to develop some of the earliest proposals about the role of taxation in pursuing justice.

Paine's most significant writing connecting inheritance with taxation is contained in his pamphlet *Agrarian Justice*, which builds on some more isolated discussion of inherited wealth in his larger work, *The Rights of Man*.[37] Paine stays close to Locke when he speaks of the "inseparable connection" between humans' ability to improve land and their ownership of it.[38] He also sought to develop Locke's claim that land, and other natural resources, had been created by God for mankind in common:

It is a position not to be controverted that the earth, in its natural uncultivated state was, and ever would have continued to be, *the common property of the*

---

[36] One view is that there is no such inevitability, so long as one is prepared to understand acquisition to include such things as the creation of intellectual property. This point had little or no force in the era when land was the dominant sort of capital. But it has some relevance to contemporary Lockean proposals. See section 7.4.

[37] The remarks in *Agrarian Justice* are in some respects the more ambitious but are limited to a fairly narrow condemnation of the system of property as one that has led to widespread poverty. *The Rights of Man* contains a much more vehement attack on the ills of hereditary power, parts of which extend to the inheritance of land. See especially Paine's reaction to Edmund Burke's approval of primogeniture and entail (2000: 222), and the defence of a progressive estate tax (242–8), which is peppered with complaints about the undesirable effects of entail.

[38] These remarks occur in *Agrarian Justice*, very close to the quoted passage (2000: 325). One needs to be careful, however, not to overestimate the similarity between Locke's and Paine's views once all aspects have been taken into account. Here I have been helped by Lamb (2015: 33–4, 129–34).

*human race*. In that state every man would have been born to property. He would have been a joint life proprietor with the rest in the property of the soil, and in all its natural productions, vegetable and animal.[39]

Locke was not himself so explicit that the earth's unowned resources start off jointly owned, such that there is a problem with any subsequent distribution of ownership being less than perfectly equal. Locke often says that the earth was "given" or "provided" to "all in common". But it is not obvious that this should be interpreted as a claim in favour of joint ownership. Creating something for someone else's *benefit* is, strictly speaking, not the same thing as giving or transferring it to him or her.[40] Resources might start off as *unowned* and can become privately owned by individuals willing to mix their labour in ways that benefit their fellows, according to God's intentions in having created these resources in the first place. If this is what Locke thought, then Paine thought something different when asserting that the world starts off as "common *property*". The difference may be due to Locke's more thoroughgoing theism compared to Paine. Contemporary attempts to secularize Locke's views can easily miss this difference between benefiting from a thing's existence and benefiting by *receiving* that thing, precisely because they take divine creation out of the story. Whether or not everyone gets to own part of the world may not matter for Locke, so long as God's plan gets carried out in ways that benefit us all, including those who do not seek to mix their labour to improve what God gave us. Paine may not have been an atheist, but *Agrarian Justice* is less prominently theistic than Locke's writings.[41] And he makes no bones about inheritance having done most of us out of our share in a commonly owned earth.

---

[39] Paine (2000: 325).

[40] Locke does say, once, that the earth and its fruits "*belong* to mankind in common" (II.26, italics added). So the textual evidence is not conclusive. The point I want to stress is only that Paine is more explicit than Locke on this matter. I leave the final interpretive answer to others more qualified than myself.

[41] Locke's claims that God "hath *given*" the world to human beings in common require only the weaker idea that all humans have a right to acquire property by appropriating parts of the world, not the stronger idea that they own any part of it (apart from their bodies) already. Here I follow the interpretation of Matthew Kramer (1997: 106–9). Locke's views about the acquisition of property may rest on more deeply theological convictions: humanity has been created with the purpose of interacting with the world so as to improve it rather than merely consuming it, as the beasts do. This might explain why humans need to become owners rather than starting off as such. On this, and the theological aspects of Locke more generally, see Waldron (2002: 159–60). Paine does not have anything like such an elaborate

Paine did more than Locke to face up to what happens to the distribution of private property once acquisition of land has begun to have an effect. Again the point is that the stock of unclaimed resources becomes depleted over time, and property concentrates into a small number of hands, as per the feudal way of things. Given the actual history of human development, land became owned by a minority of individuals seeking to pass it on to a comparably small number of heirs. And so "the common right of all became confounded into the cultivated right of the individual".[42] In making these claims, Paine wanted to stress that human development has its upsides:

Cultivation is at least one of the greatest natural improvements ever made by human invention. It has given to created earth a tenfold value. But the landed monopoly that began with it has produced the greatest evil. It has dispossessed more than half the inhabitants of every nation of their natural inheritance, without providing for them, as ought to have been done, an indemnification for that loss, and has thereby created a species of poverty and wretchedness that did not exist before.[43]

In other words, inheritance of land may be unjust, but it does not *follow* that the ownership of productive land should be simply torn up. To jeopardize its productive output in this way would be to throw the baby out with the bathwater. Clearly there is an egalitarian thought animating Paine here. One can interpret Paine as expressing misgivings about allowing gains in efficiency to trump losses that come in the form of inequality or absolute deprivation. It is good to make the pie bigger, but only if each individual share is bigger.[44]

---

theology, and his religious views were idiosyncratic for their times, although apparently well worked-out and compatible with his political agenda; see Lamb (2015: ch. 6).

[42] Paine (2000: 326).

[43] Paine (2000: 326). Paine's sense of private property's downsides might have been influenced by Rousseau. On this point see Lamb (2015: 117–18). Alan Ryan (1987: 97) has identified ways in which Rousseau's lengthy discussion of status inequality makes at least some mention of the added injury of its being inherited. Anderson (2016b) has much to say on Paine's views about private property, taxation, and distributive justice.

[44] In this way, Paine's views about permissible inequality bear some resemblance to parts of Rawls's theory of justice, particularly his 'difference principle'. Rawls, perhaps curiously, made no extended reference to Paine's writings. (The difference principle may be more demanding than anything Paine had in mind, given its demand that inequalities are just only when *necessary* to *maximally* benefit the least advantaged.) Other readers of Paine, e.g. Little (1999), have suggested that *Agrarian Justice* might be better read as articulating a more humanitarian concern to compensate those otherwise condemned to poverty. Such a

Locke required that ownership come with constraints against mis-management, such as letting an asset spoil.[45] He said nothing explicitly in favour of taxation to compensate those who hadn't managed to become owners. Again, this might support the interpretation that Locke didn't see ownership of the world as key to being a beneficiary of its productive potential. Unlike Locke, Paine sought to distinguish ownership of an acquired resource from ownership of the improvements one might confer on it. For Paine, you never own land; you own only what you get the land to produce. Those who mix their labour with land merely gain permission to *occupy* the land while owning the fruits of its cultivation. Paine is explicit that the "additional value made by cultivation" belongs wholly to the cultivator and is not part of the common property.[46] The problem, instead, is not that those who own land become unduly wealthy but rather that they are sitting on something that belongs partly to someone else. Assuming this view is defensible, it clearly puts pressure on the idea that land can be transferred to some other party via bequest.

Paine didn't draw the conclusion that land should be simply tossed back into the common stock at the death of its owner/occupier. Again, this would be to throw the baby out with the bathwater. Instead, he proposed that landowners should pay a land tax used to compensate disinherited future persons. This tax, or "ground rent", was supposed to represent the precultivation value of land—the part that land occupiers never really own. Paine believed that this would usually be around one-tenth of its market value, conveniently allowing him to propose that ground rents be set at 10 per cent of the value of improved land.[47] This bald assertion is one of the bigger problems with his project. Such calculations are very hard to make. Paine did not trouble himself to show how he made this calculation. He was probably correct to see

concern may fall short of the stronger requirements associated with contemporary liberal egalitarianism.

[45] Locke's opposition to spoilage can be reconstructed with different degrees of theological commitment. See Waldron (2002: 171–2) and Simmons (1992: 285–8), respectively.

[46] Consider Paine's remark: "I am a friend to riches because they are capable of good. I care not how affluent some may be, provided that none are miserable in consequence of it" (2000: 332).

[47] On this see Cunliffe (2000: 7–10). One important observation made here is that Paine stands aside from other agrarian radicals, many of whom preferred the actual redistribution of land itself.

financially equivalent compensation, funded by taxation, as superior to the direct strategy of land redistribution and the associated disruption to agricultural output. And in any case, the fact that the quality of land varies from one place to another may mean that calculating everyone's natural share of the land is no easier than calculating its separate values before and after cultivation.

Paine's proposal did not get fully worked out, but his influence was substantial, particularly on the founding of the United States. Thomas Jefferson managed to ensure that the American republic began without the impediment of entails. His efforts probably owe something to Paine's thinking.[48] Paine was considerably ahead of his time—his proposals about the taxing of inheritance are far more precise than anything else that emerged before Mill. His foundational claims about unifying individual rights to property with egalitarian ideas about the common ownership of the world remain fertile: *Agrarian Justice* is really an early defence of a universal stakeholder grant, an idea that continues to attract much interest in contemporary political philosophy.[49] Discussion of these views in chapter 7 will provide an opportunity to grapple more fully with the questions raised by Paine's ideas.

## 2.5 Godwin on Aristocracy, Segregation, and Well-being

William Godwin's largest contribution to political philosophy is his *Enquiry Concerning Political Justice*. It is on this that I will focus, leaving aside his various literary works.[50] Godwin was in various respects an anarchist, a utilitarian, and an egalitarian, though there is controversy

---

[48] For more on inheritance and the American founding, see Beckert (2008: 71–5) and Chester (1982: ch. 3). Paine's relationship to Jefferson in particular is discussed by Mark Philp (2013a: ch. 7).

[49] For a prominent contemporary defence of stakeholder grants, see Ackerman & Alstott (1999). Closely related to stakeholder grants are the various proposals in favour of universal basic income. See van Parijs (1992: 11–14) on how these proposals connect with Paine's earlier writing.

[50] For a recent summary of Godwin's complete writings, including his works of fiction, see Philp (2013b). The novel *Caleb Williams* is full of ideas associated with social egalitarianism, such as the rigging of legal systems in favour of the elite, the stereotyping of the poor, and the domination of employees by bosses.

amongst scholars as to how he should be categorized.[51] Unlike the other liberals discussed in this chapter, he can't be viewed as making efforts to develop moral foundations for capitalism. Much of Godwin's thought was driven by his apparently perfectionist theory of well-being, according to which human flourishing depended on access to intellectual improvement.[52] An important contention in Godwin is that we shouldn't take it for granted that the state can fix things so that such access is forthcoming. Systems of government cannot help but hold back human mental improvement, while encouraging blind obedience and servility.[53] Government, for Godwin, was "abstractly taken, an evil, an usurpation on the private judgment and individual conscience of mankind".[54] Even democracy left people at the mercy of demagogues.[55]

None of this disqualifies Godwin as a liberal of some sort. He held a substantial dislike for the feudal history of Britain and desired to see a social arrangement that did more to unlock the potential of each individual than protect the position of a privileged few. To this extent, his views overlap with those of the other liberals. Nevertheless, his stance on inheritance is distinctive and of some philosophical interest in its own right. Godwin's contribution goes substantially beyond the efforts of Smith when it comes to elaborating on the injustice of entails.

Aristocracy turns the stream of property out of its natural channel, and forward with the most assiduous care into the hands of a very few persons. The doctrines of primogeniture, as well as the immense volumes of the laws of transfer and inheritance which have infested every part of Europe, were produced for this purpose.[56]

If the "natural channel" has anything to do with making property work efficiently for wider society, then Smith would agree. Apart from this passage, Godwin's sole explicit reference to inheritance comes a few pages earlier, when he tempers his condemnation of Roman aristocracy by pointing out that primogeniture was not part of it. But Godwin spends

---

[51] For some discussion of these disagreements, see Lamb (2009).
[52] Here I follow the interpretation developed by Philp (1986: 85–9). See also Lamb (2009: 135–6).
[53] See especially Godwin (2013: III.vi, III.vii, IV.i, V.x).
[54] Godwin (2013: V.i). The qualifier "abstractly taken" reflects Godwin's willingness to accept that toleration of government was better for humankind than resort to violent revolution, tempering his anarchism (IV.ii).
[55] Godwin (2013: V.xiv).     [56] Godwin (2013: V.xiii).

many pages, and develops many interesting ideas, in explaining why an aristocratic society is profoundly unjust. This bears on how we should understand his position towards inheritance, given the role of intergenerational transfers in sustaining the aristocracy.

The key ideas are the various relations that Godwin saw between virtue, human well-being, and equality. He thought these went together as part of a "natural" balance, which aristocracy pulled apart. For Godwin, possession of virtue (and hence well-being) depended on the benefits of education, which included moral and practical knowledge as well as academic.[57] His description of the education of princes bemoans the promotion of flattery and mollycoddling over the exposure to the sort of hardship necessary to build fortitude and, importantly, the ability to empathize with the suffering of others.[58] Without such virtue, true happiness is unattainable, and a society of virtuous people will have the greater tendency towards a social harmony built around mutual esteem and trust.[59]

Godwin makes some remarks that appear to favour the pursuit of distributive equality. He denounced apologists for aristocracy as labouring under a sort of 'class essentialism', according to which people were not born with an equal capacity to be improved through education.[60] And he realized that excessive distributive inequality "deprives us of all intercourse with our fellow men upon equal terms, and makes us prisoners of state, gratified with baubles and splendour, but shut out from the real benefits of society and the perception of truth".[61] These are

---

[57] See especially Godwin (2013: IV.iv). Note also the remarks, made earlier in the *Enquiry*, that "virtue demands the active employment of an ardent mind in the promotion of the good. No man can be eminently virtuous, who is not accustomed to an extensive range of reflection" (I.vii).

[58] Godwin (2013: V. ii). Here Godwin may have been influenced by Smith: see the rather evocative remarks in *The Theory of Moral Sentiments* on the way in which poverty causes the poor to hide out of shame, and the rich to "turn their eyes away" (I.3.2.1). I might point out, on the other hand, that the sole reference to Smith is in Godwin's reference to the pin factory example toward the end of the *Enquiry* (VIII, vi). Godwin's reaction is to condemn the onset of divided labour as a means of adapting the labouring classes so as to "gild over the indolent and the proud". In this way, he overlooks the fact that the increased production of pins may benefit those outside of the aristocratic classes.

[59] Godwin (2013: IV. ix).

[60] See Godwin (2013: IV.v). Godwin's more general opposition to innate differences in human potential is laid out early in the *Enquiry* (I.iv–vi and II.iii).

[61] Godwin (2013: V, ii).

extremely intriguing remarks. They may certainly go beyond Smith's concern that wealth suppresses its possessor's labour and productivity, which is not explicitly about wealth's role in maintaining segregation.[62]

Godwin used his theory of well-being to draw a second conclusion: in an aristocratic society, persons of all ranks stand little chance of reaching an optimal level of well-being. Again this draws on the way that equality and well-being interact:

In such a state [of aristocracy] it is impossible that eminent virtue should not be exceedingly rare. The higher and lower classes will alike be corrupted by their unnatural situation.... The situation that the wise man would desire for himself and for those in whose welfare he was interested, would be a situation of alternate labour and relaxation that was in no danger to degenerate into indolence. Thus industry and activity would be cherished, the frame preserved in healthful tone, and the mind accustomed to meditation and reflection. But this would be the situation of the whole human species, if the supply of our wants were equally distributed.[63]

In other words, aristocratic systems, as Godwin saw them, prevent anyone from achieving the balance between work and rest that is needed to achieve genuine flourishing. Everyone is either utterly overworked or wholly lazy. Thus, "the dissolution of aristocracy is equally the interest of the oppressor and oppressed. The one will be delivered from the listlessness of tyranny, and the other from the brutalizing operation of servitude".[64]

In sum, Godwin wanted to emphasize that rampantly concentrated inherited wealth gives us a segregated society, in which mutual esteem and proper intellectual development are impossible. Godwin was not opposed to some people being more esteemed than others, but believed that ability rather than wealth should be the decisive factor. These claims closely resemble those made by contemporary proponents of social egalitarianism (see chapter 5). The important question, of course, is of how plausible they are. Godwin's views have their weaknesses. His attempt to derive a condemnation of aristocracy from a perfectionist theory of well-being is intellectually inventive but rather hard to follow. Perfectionism of any sort is controversial in the first place, and Godwin fails to anticipate rival theories of well-being that remain popular

---

[62] See the remarks in *WN* (III.iv.10). See also the discussion of luxury goods ("trinkets of frivolous utility") in the *TMS* (IV.1.6).

[63] Godwin (2013: V, xiii).        [64] Godwin (2013: V, xii).

today.[65] Godwin is forced to overstate perfectionism's implications in order to make his desired point about the evils of aristocracy. In particular, it is rather hard to accept that total abundance of wealth and leisure time would induce vice-like levels of slovenliness. The privileged classes have always contained members who have used their time and money to undertake projects that most perfectionist theories would treat as conducive to increased well-being. One might think it unfair when only the very wealthy get to travel the world in comfort, learn to fly helicopters, and so on, but these are hardly signs of a wasted life. Godwin's recognition of the importance of leisure time is an important piece of political philosophy in its own right.[66] But his view of the structure of social hierarchy has an implausibly binary character. Economic social hierarchies are rather more complicated nowadays. Ultimately, Godwin was right to suspect that distributive inequality might cause and maintain hierarchies of social status, but any confirmation of this suspicion requires more argument than he was able to supply.

Godwin is an unusual figure in the context of the group I have selected for this chapter. His views on inheritance come apart, in interesting ways, from the efficiency-based objections to entail offered by Smith before him and Mill afterwards, and from the sort of concerns grounded in common ownership that animated Paine. Godwin's strategy is adventurous in identifying the injustice of massive inheritance flows as the driving force behind oppressive class systems. His claims about the social bases of esteem and the causal power of material distribution remain intriguing. I have said that Godwin didn't provide a compelling argument for the position he took, even when measured against the social realities of his own times, but his views are suggestive enough that we may value them as a precursor to the sort of arguments that get their hearing in later chapters.

## 2.6  Mill on the Limited Right to Bequeath

John Stuart Mill's landmark discussion of inheritance and its taxation is laid out mainly in books 2 and 5 of his *Principles of Political Economy*,

---

[65] An influential summary of contemporary theories of well-being, including perfectionism broadly construed, is the one found in Parfit (1984: 493–502).

[66] For a modern expression of this idea, see Rawls (2001: 179).

with a brief return to the subject in his later *Chapters on Socialism*.[67] Mill widens his inquiry beyond the narrower preoccupation with entail that one finds in Smith and Godwin, focusing additionally on the individual right to bequeath or transfer wealth that one has actually produced. Mill's more sophisticated understanding of capitalism, including his discussion of inheritance, reflects the fact that the Industrial Revolution was well under way by the time of Mill's thinking. There remain, however, important continuities between Mill's thinking and Smith's.[68]

Unfortunately, whereas many aspects of the nature and regulation of property receive a dedicated chapter, the treatment of inheritance and bequest is rather spread across the lengthy *Principles*. So one has to exercise care when putting together a reconstruction of Mill's views. His clarity and relative consistency of thought nevertheless make this task easier. Mill joins the early liberals in expressing a clear disdain for primogeniture and entail. But he goes beyond his predecessors by grappling more fully, if not quite completely, with the problem of how to regulate intergenerational wealth transfers short of the extremes of doing nothing at all and of abolishing them entirely. This section will focus more on Mill's background views and how they help provide a sense of how he characterized the problem of inheritance in the first place, in ways that differ from how it was approached by his pre-industrial predecessors. His views on how to actually solve the problem will get their hearing in chapter 3.

Mill was highly sensitive to the objections made by capitalism's early socialist opponents. His defence of capitalism aimed to accommodate such concerns without abandoning the role of private property and individual enterprise in social progress. As I indicated in chapter 1, the core of Mill's response to the socialists of the early nineteenth century

---

[67] The *Chapters on Socialism* observes that it is perfectly possible to have a system of private property in which there is no right to bequeath what one owns. This occurs as part of Mill's effort to say that however well founded socialist complaints about status quo capitalism might be, they can be addressed by regulating capitalism rather than abandoning it. The restriction of bequest is given, here, as an explicit example of this. The relevant passages are in Mill (1989: 275–6).

[68] Mill thought very highly of Smith: the preface to Mill's *Principles* describes it as an attempt to update, rather than criticize, Smith's programme in *The Wealth of Nations*, as Mill understood it.

was to urge that capitalism had not yet been properly implemented. Mill's point here was partly a methodological one about the dangers of comparing an idealized version of one system (in this case socialism) against nonideal representations of a rival (in this case capitalism).[69] But he also wanted to make the valuable point that the idea of property "is not fixed but variable".[70] There is no such thing as a wholly free market, but rather different sets of regulations that enable as well as constrain the market's role in producing and allocating goods.[71] The final chapter of *Principles* lays out a lengthy explanation of why the most defensible form of capitalist is not laissez-faire.

Mill's thoughts about entail are summarized in a longish but representative passage in book 2:

Whether the power of bequest should itself be subject to limitation, is an ulterior question of great importance. Unlike inheritance *ab intestato*, bequest is one of the attributes of property: the ownership of a thing cannot be looked upon as complete without the power of bestowing it, at death or during life, at the owner's pleasure: and all the reasons, which recommend that private property should exist, recommend *pro tanto* this extension of it. But property is only a means to an end, not itself the end. Like all other proprietary rights, and even in a greater degree than most, the power of bequest may be so exercised as to conflict with the permanent interests of the human race. It does so, when, not content with bequeathing an estate to A, the testator prescribes that on A's death it shall pass to his eldest son, and to that son's son, and so on for ever. No doubt, persons have occasionally exerted themselves more strenuously to acquire a fortune from the hope of founding a family in perpetuity; but the mischiefs to society of such perpetuities outweigh the value of this incentive to exertion, and the incentives in the case of those who have the opportunity of making large fortunes are strong enough without it.[72]

---

[69] Consider especially Mill's claim that "we must compare communism at is best, with the regime of property, not as it is, but as it might be made" (2004: II.iii.8).

[70] See the closing section in the *Chapters on Socialism* (Mill 1989). It is also possible to detect the same view in *Principles* and to see this as enabling Mill to approach the problem of inherited wealth as an open question. On this see Schwartz (1968: 198–203).

[71] Again, there are contemporary versions of this claim, e.g. Satz (2010: ch. 2).

[72] Mill (II.ii.27) The passage continues with the following, also interesting, thought: "A similar abuse of the power of bequest is committed when a person who does the meritorious act of leaving property for public uses, attempts to prescribe the details of its application in perpetuity." Here Mill may be making a point about intellectual modesty, similar to those made later in *On Liberty*.

Salient here is Mill's preoccupation with the incentive effects of large inheritance flows. Entail is particularly bad for encouraging bad habits in its beneficiaries:

The heir of entail, being assured of succeeding to the family property, however undeserving of it, and being aware of this from his earliest years, has much more than the ordinary chances of growing up idle, dissipated, and profligate.[73]

So far, Mill's line is not very different from Smith's. The same goes for his observation that bequest tends to allocate a productive asset less efficiently than its sale.[74] Mill went so far as to suggest that the very idea of property in land becomes hard to justify when it comes to be held by someone unable to improve it.[75]

Like Godwin and Smith, Mill disliked the indolence of the aristocratic classes, although it is unclear to what extent this came from his views about human flourishing or via ideas about the fair division of labour in a society.[76] Again like Godwin, Mill attributed considerable importance to leisure time and solitude as conducive to personal development.[77] Mill allowed that some material inequality was a tolerable side effect of the progress enabled by capitalism.[78] But equality of status cannot be so readily sacrificed. Mill's condemnation of slavery includes reference to its incompatibility with equal status or "fellowship".[79] A much more extended commitment to status equality guides Mill's overall line of argument in *The Subjection of Women*. This work gives much prominence to the complaint about women's subordinate position being maintained partly through their exclusion from private property, though of course other factors played their part. Indeed, Mill was more explicit than any of his predecessors in condemning the role played by primogeniture in the oppression of women. Similar claims about status equality and servitude

---

[73] Mill (V.ix.11).    [74] Mill (V.v.5).    [75] Mill (II.ii.6).

[76] Mill: "I do not recognize as either just or salutary, a state of society in which there is any 'class' which is not laboring" (IV.vii.1).

[77] Mill (IV.vi.2). Special approval is reserved for "solitude in the presence of natural beauty and grandeur".

[78] Mill: "The inequalities of property, which arise from unequal industry, frugality, perseverance, talents, and to a certain extent even opportunities, are inseparable from the principle of private property, and if we accept the principle, we must bear with these consequences of it" (II.ii.4).

[79] Mill (II.ii.7). Slavery's limits as a means of securing *productive* labour are discussed in (II.v).

may be found in his discussion of the lot of the labouring classes. Mill contended that the hereditary replication of the division between workers and their (nonlabouring) employers maintained a hierarchical relation of master and dependant between both parties. He took this to be incompatible with relations of civic equality.[80] The *Principles* makes a strong case for workplace democracy and even expresses sympathy for market socialism that might secure "the association of labourers on terms of equality".[81] Mill expressed approval for the eventual "putting an end to the division of society into the industrious and the idle, and effacing all social distinctions but those fairly earned by personal services and exertions".[82] He thought the behaviour of those who had merely inherited great wealth could corrupt the poor by setting a worse example than those who show the road to self-improvement by earning their fortune through labour.[83] The point here is about the dangers of hierarchical separation of groups, given members' tendencies to form judgements about those in the other group. This can be viewed as an early warning about social segregation as a source of pernicious stereotyping, less explicit but perhaps more sophisticated than Godwin's. Certainly there is some truth in the contention that people tend to mimic the economic behaviour of those at higher income levels in ways driven partly by, while reinforcing, anxieties about social status.[84]

Many of the passages in *Principles* that allude to status equality make no explicit reference to inheritance. But they are strong evidence of the way in which Mill regarded the pursuit of status equality as a legitimate foundation for the restriction of private property rights. Mill's various references to the "unearned advantage"[85] enabled by inheritance suggest some affinity for the idea that the uneven distribution of fortune creates a problem for social justice. Overall, Mill's progress left much work for others to do.

---

[80] Mill: "If the rich regard the poor, as, by a kind of natural law, their servants and dependents, the rich in their turn are regarded as a mere prey and pasture for the poor." Further on, Mill writes, "The aim of improvement should be not solely to place human beings in a condition in which they will be able to do without one another, but to enable them to work with or for one another in relations not involving dependence" (IV.vii.4).
[81] Mill (IV.vi.6).     [82] Mill (IV.vi.6).     [83] Mill (V.ix.2).
[84] I make use of this point later, in connection with arms races in positional consumption; see 6.4.
[85] See the longer quotation in 3.1.

## 2.7 Some Generalizations

Before concluding, I should reiterate what I claimed at the outset of this chapter, that the liberal authors discussed here do not exhaust the supply of views on inheritance made during their times. The practice of entail had its proponents among conservative thinkers who regarded aristocracy and hereditary privilege as an important pillar of a stable society. Edmund Burke adopted something approximating the sort of 'class essentialism' denounced by Godwin and Paine, according to which the nobility possess a sort of 'hereditary wisdom' which favours the preservation of aristocracy. And so Burke suggested that "some decent, regulated ... preference given to birth is neither unnatural nor unjust".[86] Hegel was conservative in a different way and suggested that the owner of property may in some cases be the family itself rather than individuals within it, meaning that inheritances are not really transfers and therefore shouldn't be taxed as such.[87] There is a certain version of this view that has something to be said for it, and I will revisit it in section 7.3.

I have tried to make it clear that some of the more central ideas in early liberal thought are now obsolete. Any attempt to condemn large inheritance flows on grounds of their inefficiency will now have to come to terms with substantial changes in the nature of capital, as well as rates of return that are high enough to cast doubt on the early liberal assumption that merely fragmenting an estate at the point of bequest would be enough to ensure that none of its inheritors could live a life of idleness. Overall, though, it is the more moralized concerns that are most worth examining. In conclusion, three important themes in early liberal discussions continue to have relevance for the contemporary evaluation of inherited wealth.

First, there is the distinction between the intergenerational transmission of ownership and the transmission of executive power. This concern is particularly acute in jurisdictions that continue to protect inheritance

---

[86] See *Reflections on the Revolution in France* in Burke (2014: 53) Consider especially Burke's suggestion that entails helped preserve resources for posterity (99).

[87] The relevant passages are sections 178–80 of his *Philosophy of Right*. I do not wish to advance any claims as to how to best interpret the claims here. It is worth noting that Hegel's view of the family had notable influence on German inheritance law, which upheld entails for longer than most other European jurisdictions; see Beckert (2008: 52–4). Further mention of Hegel's views on inheritance can be found in Ryan (1987: 118).

of family firms. From a theoretical point of view, the relationship between ownership and executive control is quite complex.[88] This is partly because the question of how to understand property in the first place is itself quite fraught. Property rights are nowadays usually understood as clusters of various 'use rights'. It is quite coherent to insist that the power to transfer includes the transmission of the right to profit from an asset but not always the right to control other things about it, or that the power to transfer is limited in some way.

Second, there is the concern about the way in which inherited wealth promotes idleness. The objection here is not always made clear. While Godwin attempts to provide a principled explanation in terms of his theory of well-being, there is a lingering suspicion that the disapproving remarks about indolence found in Mill and Smith are in part driven by Protestant values rather than by a wholly secular rationale. Nevertheless, the idleness point remains very interesting and can be reconstructed with the help of contemporary egalitarian concerns about reciprocity and freeriding. I shall focus on such prospects for reconstruction in section 4.5.

Third, there is the worry about the role that large inheritance flows might play in causing or maintaining inequalities relating to group difference or some sort of social class hierarchy. This concern is the more complex one, philosophically speaking, but remains promising. Again, this concern is somewhat subordinate in Smith and Mill, relative to the main line about inefficiency. But it possesses even greater potential than the concern about idleness. Chapters 5 and 6 are my attempt to realize this potential. Overall, there is much in early liberal writings whose reappearance can be detected later in this book.

---

[88] Distinguishing executive control from merely 'beneficiary' ownership is important with regard to various contemporary questions that have much to do with inequality without relating directly to inheritance. The distinction is brought up at various points in Atkinson (2015).

# 3

# The Utilitarian Case against Iterated Bequests

## 3.1 Mill on Taxation and Incentives

It is sometimes said that anglophone political philosophy entered a kind of wilderness era after John Stuart Mill, which ended only when John Rawls's writings began to appear some seventy years after Mill's death. This gloomy assessment is rather misplaced with respect to philosophical work on inherited wealth. Representative authors from this period include the Italian utilitarian philosopher Eugenio Rignano and British thinkers such as Hugh Dalton, R. H. Tawney, and Josiah Wedgwood. The early decades of the twentieth century witnessed considerable interest among policymakers regarding the taxation of intergenerational wealth transfers, though such interest died down as the century wore on. This chapter aims to review the ground that was covered between Mill and the emergence of Rawls and those he influenced. In particular, I want to get clear on the sort of defence that Rignano offered for his proposal, so that it might be distinguished from arguments that I will develop later on.

Before doing this, I need to finish discussing Mill. The idea that regulation of property should seek to improve incentives runs throughout Mill's thinking on taxation. While there is no profoundly general expression of this idea, there is solid textual evidence regarding particular applications of it. Mill was very clear, for example, that taxation should target unearned income over earned income.[1] Indeed, he blamed the

---

[1] Here's the quote in full: "To tax the larger incomes at a higher percentage than the smaller is to lay a tax on industry and economy; to impose a penalty on people for having worked harder and saved more than their neighbours. It is not the fortunes which are earned, but those which are unearned, that it is for the public good to place under

decline in Asian prosperity on (rightly or wrongly) the excessive taxation of voluntary industry.[2] These claims were guided by the more general conviction that capital could expand only if the population were to become disposed to saving their wealth rather than spending it.[3] Once the project of formulating tax principles is understood in this way, it becomes clear why Mill regarded inheritance as a special and difficult case: the prospect of being able to bequeath one's wealth was an important source of motivation to produce wealth in the first place. Such productive activity delivers benefits to other persons (given the right regulations for other aspects of the economy) and ought to be promoted. At the same time, the expectation of inheritance will have the opposite effect on its beneficiaries, who will tend to become idle. This is bad for subsequent productivity, setting aside any independent reasons for disapproving of idleness. Inheritance, then, generates a significant sort of dilemma: An unconstrained right to bequeath generates a large incentive at the cost of comparable disincentives later on. Abolishing the power to transfer altogether would simply destroy the incentive for the sake of removing the disincentive, which is not obviously preferable. Somehow, a balance needs to be struck.[4]

All of this sets up an interesting way of viewing the problem. Mill's solution appears in the following passage:

> With respect to the large fortunes acquired by gift or inheritance, the power of bequeathing is one of those privileges of property which are fit subjects for regulation on grounds of general expediency; and I have already suggested, as a possible mode of restraining the accumulation of large fortunes in the hands of

limitation. A just and wise legislation would abstain from holding out motives for dissipating rather than saving the earnings of honest exertion" (Mill 2004: V.ii.14).

[2]   Mill (2004: V.viii.2).

[3]   This gets stressed throughout book 1 of the *Principles*; see especially (2004: I.v and I.xi). It is worth noting, though, that the right to bequeath gets no explicit mention as a source of the individual motivation to save. Plausibly enough, Mill seems to have regarded the culture of saving as dependent on a variety of factors, including confidence in prolonged national security and a government that could be trusted not to arbitrarily appropriate one's wealth.

[4]   Like Locke, Mill makes it clear that the right to bequeath does not entail a beneficiary's right to *inherit* (2004: II.ii.3). Note that Mill qualifies this claim shortly after having made it: "The law ought, no doubt, to do for the children or dependents of an intestate, whatever it was the duty of the parent or protector to have done." The more general thing to remember is that, in claiming that a right to inherit is not part of property, there remains room for such a right to exist upon other moral foundations. The remainder of the section contains various reflections on why the rights of children might be limited. See also (V.ix.1).

those who have not earned them by exertion, a limitation of the amount which any one person should be permitted to acquire by gift, bequest, or inheritance.... The principle of graduation (as it is called,) that is, of levying a larger percentage on a larger sum, though its application to general taxation would be in my opinion objectionable, seems to me both just and expedient as applied to legacy and inheritance duties.[5]

These remarks make it clear that Mill favoured the progressive taxation of inherited wealth.[6] The other important claim, expanded on after this passage, is the idea of a cap on receipts. Mill says "no one person should be permitted to acquire, by inheritance, more than the amount of a moderate independence".[7] Taking these two ideas together, Mill's proposed scheme is best understood as including two parameters: a progressivity parameter and a cap specifying some absolute level of inheritance, above which liability jumps to 100 per cent. Mill's view might be quite radical, depending on where this threshold is located. Nothing jumps out as especially strange or mysterious about Mill's proposal. But it does not actually accommodate any distinction between inheritance that has been newly produced and inheritance that is already generations old. The idea of an upper bound on receipts may yet do much to break up dynastic fortunes, but in doing so it fails to grant any relaxed liability for bequests resulting from (and thus incentivizing) an individual's own industry rather than his or her mere preservation of an earlier inheritance. As such, Mill's proposal is at best a heuristic: tax *all* large inheritances, and you'll tax the old ones. Like chemotherapy that attacks the patient's healthy cells along with the cancerous ones, Mill's proposal appears rather indiscriminate.

I'll close with a couple of other observations. First, Mill's proposal was tailored to the socio-economic context of his day. Mill may have believed substantial inheritance flows would not exist in an ideal society. His discussion of the stationary state, which he admired as a

---

[5]  Mill (2004: V.ii.14).

[6]  An interesting historical point is that Mill may not have fully endorsed the principle of diminishing marginal utility, even though it is a natural source of support for progressive taxation in general. Mill in fact expressed some hostility towards the use of mathematical principles in political economy, and particular hostility towards the emerging 'marginalist' school of economic thought. On this, see Schwartz (1968: 238–9). Also interesting is the fact that Mill favoured the progressive taxation of inheritance but not of income. For discussion of this, see Ekelund & Walker (1996).

[7]  Mill (2004: V.ix.2).

possible 'end point' of economic development, has as one of its elements "no enormous fortunes, except what were earned and accumulated during a single life-time".[8] This is an important claim, which reflects Mill's appreciation of industrial society as an evolving process that may face great changes in years ahead. Political philosophy of the pre-industrial, agrarian era was less well placed to see this. Second, Mill was reluctant to express his approach to taxation as a mere exercise in calculating efficiency: the connection between inheritance and moral concepts like fairness and desert is emphasized strongly in the following passage:

[T]hose who have inherited the savings of others have an advantage which they have in no way deserved.... I strenuously contend, that this unearned advantage should be curtailed, as much is consistent with justice to those who thought fit to dispose of their savings by giving them to their descendants.[9]

Overall, Mill's position remains somewhat incomplete. This is not a criticism. It should be said that his position was among the more sophisticated of those that emerged from classical utilitarian writings.[10] Mill's distinction between fortunes that are inherited and fortunes accumulated within a lifetime gestures at a more general distinction between merely intragenerational distributive inequalities and inequalities that are able to replicate themselves from one generation to the next. A more general distinction of this sort has much potential to shape the taxing of inherited wealth, perhaps even more than the other idea about inheritance being a provider of undeserved advantage. But it was left to Mill's later followers to develop his proposals in this direction.

---

[8]  Mill (2004: IV.vi.2).

[9]  Mill (2004: II.ii.2). The remarks are repeated at (V.ii.3).

[10]  There is a chapter-length discussion of inheritance in chapter 7 of book 1 of Henry Sidgwick's (1891/2012) *Elements of Politics*. Here, Sidgwick repeats the appeal to incentives made by his utilitarian predecessors. Sidgwick is more concerned than Mill about the prospect of parents using the threat of disinheritance to influence the life choices of their offspring (104). But apart from this we find a fairly strong aversion to bequest beyond the idea of a consanguinity rule allowing higher taxation of bequests to more distant relatives. A yet briefer discussion in Sidgwick's *Principles of Political Economy* (1887: 581–2) adds the caveat that incentives will be reduced less than by a tax on incomes, and that bequests to charities should be wholly exempt from an estate tax, for the sake of the benefit to the community.

## 3.2 Rignano's Proposal and Its Context

The world does not divide neatly into pure inheritors and pure testators. Many people who inherit also pass it on to their own heirs at some point, either later in life or posthumously through bequest. Inheritance exists not as isolated transactions but, very often, as an iterated flow down a family line. Although Mill did not emphasize these facts, they bear significantly on what incentive effects might be introduced by the taxation of intergenerational transfers. Beneficiaries' incentives are shaped partly by the expectation that they will inherit, but partly also by the expectation that they may bequeath their inheritance to their own heirs later on. The key is to design a tax scheme that can accommodate both of these considerations simultaneously.

Eugenio Rignano was born in 1870, in Italy, where he lived and worked until his death in 1930.[11] He began his professional life as an engineer but was somehow able to gain expertise in a variety of other disciplines, becoming involved in the editing of various scientific journals. He wrote ten books, many of which have not been translated into English. Of these, just two focus on political philosophy. One, a lengthy early work on the moral foundations of socialism, is among those that remain untranslated.[12] The bulk of Rignano's thinking on inherited wealth is contained in a later, short monograph titled *The Social Significance of Death Duties*, which was translated during the 1920s.[13] On his death, Rignano bequeathed a substantial amount of his wealth to fund prizes to be given to academic work on the topic of inheritance.[14]

---

[11] For a fuller account of both Rignano's life and the salience of inheritance taxes in the policymaking contexts of the 1920s, see the excellent Erreygers & Di Bartolomeo (2007). Selections from Rignano's work are reprinted in Vallentyne & Steiner (2000a).

[12] This is *Di un Socialismo in accordo colla Dottrina Economica Liberale*. This book contains some elements of the ideas later worked out in *The Social Significance of Death Duties*. See Erreygers & Di Bartolomeo (2007: 609). Rignano's main ideas also appear in a short (1919) article, written in English, in which both the utilitarian and quasi-Marxist arguments (distinguished below) feature.

[13] There were two such translations made, one in Britain and one in the United States. I have worked mainly from the British translation made by Josiah Stamp, i.e. Rignano (1925). The other translation appeared in 1924, by the American William Schultz (under the different title of *The Social Significance of the Inheritance Tax*). The two translations are not wholly identical: the introduction to Schultz's version notes that he has gained Rignano's permission to make several modifications so as to "make it fit American conditions" (1924: 11). For some comment on this, see Chester (1976: 72–8).

[14] The fate of these funds remains unknown.

Rignano distinguished between two kinds of wealth transfers: those that involve the passing on of wealth produced by the donor, and those that involve the passing on of what the donor received as the beneficiary of some earlier transfer. The point of this distinction is to separate first-generation bequests from older fortunes that are being 're-bequeathed' by a party who just sat on the wealth rather than produced it. In this distinction Rignano saw a solution to Mill's puzzle. Newly accumulated wealth, being bequeathed for the first time, could face little or no taxation, thereby incentivizing the industry necessary for the creation of the wealth in question. But inheritance coming from prior inheritance, being passed on for the second or third time, could be made liable to greater levels of taxation, so that those fortunate enough to inherit would still have the incentive to be productive. In other words, by making inheritance taxes "progressive over time", Rignano's proposal was intended to optimize the incentive effects of an inheritance tax, by making sure that everyone, whether they inherit or not, had better get productive if they want to pass something on to the next generation. I will call this proposal the *Rignano scheme* and will also use this label for variations on it. In naming such schemes after Rignano himself, I don't want to give the impression that he was the first person to conceive of the idea of linking tax liability to a fortune's age as opposed to its monetary value. Other European authors conceived various similar schemes during the late nineteenth century.[15] Apparently, these authors formulated their proposals largely in ignorance of each other. Robert Nozick went on to propose a version of the Rignano scheme in the 1980s, again apparently without any familiarity with these older writings.[16] Rignano's scheme made greater reference to earlier landmark works in political philosophy, Marx as well as Mill, and received the most attention after its emergence.[17]

---

[15] Of considerable note here is the Belgian industrialist Ernest Solvay, who in 1897 (just ahead of Rignano) proposed a "re-iterated inheritance tax" whereby liability was to increase with the number of generations between the creator of a wealth and its inheritor. For discussion see Erreygers (1998). Even earlier, the French philosopher Francois Huet proposed an unlimited right of bequest in 1853 for newly accumulated wealth, with total confiscation of inheritance on the death of its owner (see Erreygers & Di Bartolomeo 2007: 614–16).

[16] I discuss Nozick's formulation, briefly, in 7.3.

[17] The best recent scholarship on proposals similar to the Rignano scheme can be found in Erreygers & Di Bartolomeo (2007) and Cunliffe & Erreygers (2005). Also useful, though less detailed, is Chester (1982: 62–73).

Before spelling out the Rignano scheme in more detail, let me say a little about its social and economic context. Rignano's writings gained prominence at a time when European policymakers were under substantial pressure to increase tax revenues. (Such pressure came partly from the need to pay debts accrued when fighting the First World War.) In these times income tax did not have the sort of 'default' status as a principal tax base that it has come to have since. Nowadays, the moral evaluation of other taxes usually labours under the lazy assumption that the prior taxing of incomes is a done deal—as evident in the common complaint that inheritance tax counts as "double taxation".[18] In Rignano's time, however, no such view about the relative standings of different tax bases was widely held, and inheritance tax was thought to have considerable potential. This was in part due to the substantial inheritance flow that remained in place, though this had been considerably diminished by the war.[19] The shared struggle imposed on the wider population by the war had done a certain amount to arouse socialist feelings.[20] Policymakers in various European countries were therefore quite well disposed to giving the Rignano scheme serious consideration. For a time, the scheme had some prospect of being implemented as real policy in Great Britain. In the end, however, the scheme's prominence proved short-lived. Rignano's influence was largely countered by the objections raised by Josiah Wedgwood at the end of the 1920s, just a few years after the translation of Rignano's *Social Significance of Death Duties*. So far as I can tell, no jurisdiction has worked a Rignano scheme into its tax legislation, although Rignano-type proposals did resurface in some reviews of tax policy later in the twentieth century.[21] Certainly the scheme has never gained very much extended philosophical attention since Wedgwood, much less a proper defence.

[18] For discussion of this rhetoric see Murphy & Nagel (2002: 143–4).

[19] Measured as a fraction of national income, inheritance flow in Europe began to decline after peaking around 1910, with the First World War accelerating that decline considerably. For a presentation and discussion of the relevant data, see Piketty (2014: ch. 11).

[20] Rignano had his own way of pointing this out: "No revolutionary propaganda could ever have intensified and broadened the class consciousness of the laboring masses as did this war, this tragedy of blind nationalistic imperialism" (1925: 30; see also 44–5).

[21] Perhaps the best chance for the proposal's implementation was Hugh Dalton's eventual appointment as Britain's chancellor of the exchequer under Clement Attlee's 1945 government, though Dalton's later writings suggest that this would have been politically unfeasible. For more discussion, see Erreygers and Di Bartolomeo (2007: 631–2).

Since this is a book about political philosophy, I note these contextual facts for the sake of interesting historical background about a figure largely unknown in current philosophical circles. But the significance attaching to the Rignano scheme goes well beyond its historical interest. Rignano's broad proposal has strong philosophical credentials that are enhanced by recent developments in egalitarian theorizing. The objections that were made to Rignano's scheme during the time of its influence owe their force largely to the mainly utilitarian foundations that Rignano happened to use when defending it, which he took from Mill. Once the Millian framework is changed for a more egalitarian set of assumptions, the Rignano scheme can eventually be made more attractive. In the meantime, I shall spend the rest of this chapter laying out the utilitarian rationale and its limitations, before offering some sympathetic suggestions about how much force it might retain.

## 3.3  Progressivity Over Time

The core point of the Rignano scheme is that an inheritance tax should be sensitive to a fortune's age rather than its monetary value alone. There are multiple ways of adding precision to this idea. Rignano's own refinement is represented by the remarks in the following passage:

Up to the present, the principle of graduation has been applied to death duties according to two criteria—the size of the estate, and the degree of relationship of the beneficiaries. But there is a third criterion which would admit of graduated rates, and this is the *relative age*, if one may name it thus, of the different portions of the estate left by the deceased—or more exactly, the *number of transfers* in the way of succession and donation that the different portions of the estate have undergone before coming into the possession of the deceased. By the application of this criterion...the right of the testator would vary with the different increments of his estate. Over the wealth which he had himself created or saved he would have complete or almost complete control; his rights would be more restricted over the wealth which he had inherited directly, and would grow proportionately less according as the original accumulation was more remote by reason of repeated transfers.[22]

---

[22]  Rignano (1925: 37–8). Some of Rignano's contemporaries provided summaries of his proposal as well. See for example Dalton (1920: 132–3, 316–17; 1936: 114–18), Wedgwood (1929: 254–5).

Note that Rignano begins by suggesting that his own proposal be compared with the alternative of traditionally progressive taxation, that is, progression according to monetary value rather than time. The point of this may be to discourage evaluation of his proposal in isolation and to encourage its comparison with alternative tax schemes instead. This is an important methodological claim that went largely unnoticed by Rignano's critics.[23] Tax proposals are probably best evaluated in comparison with each other rather than in isolation. This is a claim I shall defend at greater length in section 8.1. The more central idea in the quoted passage concerns the basic form of the proposal itself. Here, the idea is that any individual bequest can be divided up into different portions according to how much of it has already undergone some number of earlier intergenerational transfers. Inheritance is taxed more when it comes from prior inheritance, and taxed even more when it comes from prior inheritance that itself came from prior inheritance.

It can help to work through a schematic example: Imagine I possess ten million dollars and wish to bequeath or transfer it to an heir. This fortune needs to be separated into portions representing how much I inherited from my parents, how much my parents inherited (let's say collectively) from *their* parents, and how much 'extra' I produced on my own. Let's suppose a refinement of the Rignano scheme imposing a tax rate of 0 per cent for newly produced wealth, followed by 50 per cent for inheritance undergoing its second transfer, and a full 100 per cent for inheritance that is 'third generation', i.e. already passed from a grandparent to my parent, and again on to myself. If my ten million is equal to what I've already inherited, then no fraction of my subsequent bequest will enjoy the 0 per cent tax rate. So far as the Rignano scheme is concerned, I have simply spent my whole life being idle. Whether my transfer is taxed at the 50 per cent rate or the 100 per cent rate depends on how much of the ten million represents the amount that my parents themselves inherited. The optimization of incentive structures is supposed to come from the fact that I can always pass on more wealth when I've produced it myself, regardless of how much I inherited. So, the idea goes, I have every incentive to be productive, irrespective of whether I've inherited a large fortune or nothing at all, or indeed anything in between.

---

[23] Here I am expanding on a similar point made by Barbara Fried (2000: esp. 395).

As Rignano tried to make clear, the scheme is merely a framework that is subject to considerable indeterminacy or, depending on how one sees it, flexibility. He emphasized that the proposal could be weakened in favour of more heuristic versions that could prove more politically feasible. Rignano himself proposed that implementation might be made more realistic by scrapping any sensitivity to inheritance that had already passed down twice, leaving only a single distinction between the portion of a bequest that has been saved or produced and that which has been inherited at least once before.[24] The scheme might also be supplemented with various qualifications, exemptions, and so on, as is the case with most taxation schemes. My selection of 0 per cent as a rate for the transfer of newly produced wealth was chosen for illustrative clarity and is otherwise arbitrary.[25] The real point of the proposal is that the liabilities attaching to the first, second, and third transfers simply increase to some degree. The degree of difference could be sensitive to the finer features of any context in which the scheme were to be implemented. Aside from the problem of setting the rate, there is the problem of setting the base. This boils down largely to whether the tax attaches to estates or receipts: a Rignano scheme may impose a lower rate of taxation on third-generation inheritance, so long as it is dispersed among multiple beneficiaries, depending on what other inheritance these beneficiaries receive. I come back to the distinction between estates and receipts in section 8.2. Yet another question is whether Rignano measured the age of a fortune in the right way when speaking of 'progressivity over time'. Rignano's formulation measures age in terms of what we might call *strict* iteration, which is simply the number of intergenerational transfers in a chain of bequests. This could be modified so as to include or exclude various factors, such as the skipping of generations. A second candidate dimension is sheer time—the length of any period that lies between successive bequests. Clearly this has some significance if the taxing of inheritance is supposed to be a way of improving incentive structures. A short interval between bequests may mean that a donor has had less opportunity to save and accumulate due to an early death. It is harder to

---

[24] See Rignano (1925: 126–34), also Dalton (1920: 320–1).
[25] What Rignano actually says is that "the nation would not levy on the portion [of a bequest] due to his labour and thrift any higher duties than it imposes today" (1925: 38; repeated almost verbatim at 51).

say, in that case, that this person's bequests should still be taxed as if he or she had remained idle. Rignano's own proposal attaches no significance to any dimension besides what I've called strict iteration, and he leaves the case for these other forms of measurement unexamined. The question of how to best measure age comes up in Wedgwood's criticisms, as we'll see shortly.

Since Rignano himself favoured it, I'll comment here on the idea that wealth should eventually be transferred at a rate of 100 per cent. Rignano is explicit that his proposal rests on the utilitarian "axiom" that "the justification of all human institutions, and consequently of the very right of property, should be sought exclusively in their social utility".[26] Going on this quote alone, one might conclude that Rignano had simply adopted utilitarianism, following Mill. And yet Rignano saw fit to devote two chapters of *The Social Significance of Death Duties* to explaining why his proposal offers socialists a superior way of overcoming class hierarchy to the sort of Marxist revolution that (he believed) would destroy individuals' incentives to engage in productive work.[27] The idea is that capital should eventually become nationalized. This is what accounts for the eventual tax rate of 100 per cent. Marxism was perhaps the dominant intellectually respectable alternative to utilitarianism during Rignano's times. But the degree of attention it receives in Rignano's defence of his scheme may be a hangover from his earlier career, in which socialist sympathies featured prominently.[28] By the time he wrote *The Social Significance of Death Duties*, Rignano had apparently settled on the view that the state was generally good at owning and managing the means of production but not innovative enough to create new capital in the first place. Rignano rejected Marx's historical materialism and its essential idea of the inevitable overthrow of capitalism. He believed that a more moralized case needed to be made for the shift to socialism. He stressed the need for a gradual, peaceful transition rather than the more

[26]   Rignano (1925: 36).

[27]   Rignano (1925: 42–8, 83–96). Other passages (e.g. 34–5, 49–50) focus on the division of labour between the state's management of capital and individuals' creation of it. It is worth noting that Rignano might again be following Mill, whose discussion of socialism (2004: IV.vii) exhibits a clear preference for gradual egalitarian reform rather than revolutionary change that violates expectations even if achieved without violence or destruction of the means of production. An excellent discussion of Mill's egalitarian 'gradualism' can be found in Riley (1996).

[28]   See Erreygers & Di Bartolomeo (2007: 610–11).

sudden and violent revolution. The solution was to simply tax the transfer of capital gradually, as it becomes older:

The sole way to achieve an effective and gradual nationalization of private capital without injuring the delicate mechanism of economic production is, in my opinion, for the nation to take a part of all inheritances ... which would combine the advantages of a more intense economic production with those of a more equitable distribution of wealth.[29]

These claims may invite speculation about what sort of egalitarian claims Rignano might have ventured had he not written at a time when relatively little developed egalitarian theory existed. But the case for the 100 per cent rate rests on little more than the view that eventual nationalization of capital is highly desirable. Though I won't try to settle the matter here, I don't find this to be a very plausible view. One does not find endorsement of the eventual 100 per cent rate in subsequent authors such as Dalton and Tawney, who were otherwise sympathetic to a Rignano scheme. I suggest, at any rate, that the Rignano scheme does not need to lead to eventual confiscation of wealth in order to be worth considering.

The most plausible Rignano scheme may not wholly replace traditional progressivity with progressivity over time. Rignano makes this concession himself. More specifically, he stated that the scheme would apply only to bequests whose monetary value exceeded some threshold. Small fortunes, heirlooms and so on, might cascade down a family line unimpeded. Certainly, the exemption of small inheritances accords nicely with common sense but stands in need of explanation. Some views about justice and taxation may do better at explaining it than others, as I shall later emphasize when comparing varieties of egalitarianism. Finally, the receipt of gifts made *inter vivos* would "naturally be treated as hereditary successions".[30] This is actually quite a substantial qualification, since making an inheritance tax inclusive of gifts is really to create a very different and more extensive sort of tax, and possibly more disruption of individual freedom and of families. The case of gifts does, indeed, raise quite a substantial question for any inquiry into the problem of inheritance, and the two cannot be completely disconnected.

---

[29] Rignano (1925: 50). This quote is taken from the chapter that is reproduced (in part) as a free-standing entry in Vallentyne & Steiner (2000a).

[30] Rignano (1925: 52; see also 114–15).

However, it may be that the problems posed by gifts are no more serious or difficult in the context of Rignano's proposal than on any other view favouring the taxation of intergenerational wealth transfers.

Overall it is clear that Rignano regarded his scheme as highly intuitive and inoffensive to common sense. Indeed, Rignano also proposed an analogy between his scheme for taxing inheritance and the familiar principles governing the expiration of certain intellectual property rights.[31] We should keep in mind his own qualification, that his proposal was "no more than a rough draft... which would have to be studied, enlarged and completed before it was capable of realization".[32] The question is how much can be done to build on Rignano's rather limited defence.

## 3.4 Some Problems

Josiah Wedgwood's critique of Rignano remains the best developed among several to have emerged after the 1920s.[33] Although a work in economics, one strength of Wedgwood's treatment is its clear-headedness about how the question of inherited wealth is largely a question about justice. Wedgwood believed that large amounts of distributive inequality carried a burden of justification, going so far as to claim that "a more equal distribution of wealth is at least as important an aim as an increase of production".[34] Still, much of Wedgwood's discussion is not overly moralized or philosophical. Large parts of it are devoted to reviewing data on inheritance flows in Britain at the time, which Wedgwood used to conclude that such flows are composed largely

---

[31] Rignano (1925: 37). It's unclear whether the analogy is supposed to be merely illustrative or to add some force of its own, given the lack of controversy surrounding patent expiration. The point about public domain by 'trivial' nationalization is just meant to imply that while the ownership is public, the state need play no role in managing what is owned.

[32] Rignano (1925: 61).

[33] Wedgwood (1929). The Rignano scheme was also criticized by Frank William Taussig (1921: 269–72), who apparently opposed the scheme for reasons relating to scepticism about the nationalization of capital, while being overall sympathetic to what Mill and Rignano had said about incentives. A useful discussion of Rignano in the tax theory literature is Alan Tait's (1967: h. 10), who raises more or less the same objections (and very concisely put) to those from Wedgwood that I discuss below.

[34] Wedgwood (1929: v). He also remarked that "great inequalities in the division of the product of industry among the individuals concerned are... socially deplorable" (31).

of prior inheritances rather than newly created wealth.[35] On its own, this is hardly a point against the Rignano scheme. Overall, then, Wedgwood was not an opponent of inheritance taxation. But he developed four objections to the Rignano scheme itself that could be upheld by anyone committed to progressive taxation instead. The first two assess the scheme on its own terms, i.e. grant that there's something right about viewing inheritance taxes as an opportunity to incentivize productive activity. The second two objections raise interesting concerns about some of the assumptions behind Rignano's (and Mill's) approach. I shall suggest some replies to these objections once each has been summarized.

Wedgwood first queries Rignano's distinction between inherited and newly produced wealth. Specifically, "Rignano seems . . . to neglect the fact that what a man inherits has considerable influence on his capacity both to earn and save".[36] The point here is that Rignano's distinction is less sharp than he made it appear. Inheriting wealth and producing wealth are not causally isolated from each other: An entrepreneur who inherits wealth can rationally take bigger risks and invest more in his or her education than a would-be entrepreneur who stands to inherit nothing and may face special difficulties securing loans, paying for training, and so on. Generally speaking, 'industry' occurring on top of prior inheritance is at least partly enabled by it. Consequently, the Rignano scheme does not provide any *special* incentive to parties whose 'own industry' genuinely starts from nothing. The people who are really incentivized are those who want to be productive but also get an inheritance windfall. This might not be a gross shortcoming, since any increase in incentives may be a good thing from a utilitarian point of view, even if they're not equally distributed. But the more one wants to accommodate egalitarian ideas of any sort—as both Rignano and Wedgwood apparently did to some degree—the more powerful this objection must become.

Wedgwood's second objection concerns the discrepancy between the value that an asset is judged to have at the point of being transferred across generations and the value that it has at various other times.

---

[35] As Wedgwood formulated his conclusion, "In the majority of cases, the large fortunes of one generation belong to the children of those who possessed the large fortunes of the preceding generation" (1929: 164).

[36] Wedgwood (1929: 256).

Wedgwood's example is of an oil field that is bequeathed and taxed heavily because it is assumed to have great financial value, but then turns out to contain less oil than estimated. Nothing in the scheme's design stands to accommodate such cases. Nor does it notice any effort inheritors might make to overcome subsequent depreciations in the value of their inherited assets. An inheritor who "by dint of hard work and saving, just makes good his losses will be deemed to have saved nothing".[37] In addition to false negatives, there are false positives: it is easy to imagine transfers of assets that appreciate in value after having been passed on, without any help from the party to whom they were given. The scheme treats this sort of fortune as equivalent to creative hard work, which makes little sense. The general point here is that the value of assets can grow or shrink between 'iterations' of being passed between generations, and can do so as a matter of brute luck. Rignano did anticipate this observation but claimed, rather crassly, that the loss of an inherited fortune could only ever be the heir's own fault.[38] Of course, this sort of problem may attach to any scheme for taxing inheritance, so long as it relies on the value of an asset being judged at the point of transfer. But it is much more significant if the justification for the scheme is given in terms of the optimization of incentives, rather than (say) the breaking up of distributive inequality, in which case such fallibility of estimating value may be rather more tolerable.

A third objection alludes to an important distinction between different *kinds* of productive activity. Here, Wedgwood's claim is that economic production, in terms of creating a profitable asset, does not always amount to "a genuine economic service". Sometimes an inheritor may 'accumulate' wealth by choosing to gamble it and getting lucky. Alternatively, inheritors may simply realize that their capital has excellent potential for rents and come to produce more wealth simply by saving the rental income while making no effort whatsoever to improve what they've received. In so doing, the asset may still increase in value, as is common for physical capital such as real estate. Clearly, such ways of accumulating wealth are not always socially useful, especially if they occur on a larger scale because of tax laws that happen to encourage them. Again, Wedgwood might here be making a point about the ills of a

---

[37] Wedgwood (1929: 262).     [38] Rignano (1925: 69–71).

rentier society and the tendency of inheritance to maintain it. At least, Wedgwood is trying to say that Rignano has erred by assuming that *all* production of new capital is equally valuable and that all capital-producing activity should be incentivized to the same extent. Wedgwood is probably right on this point.

A fourth objection questions whether the right to transfer wealth even has very powerful incentive effects in the first place. There are plenty of cases of people who produce valuable capital due to motivations other than conferring material benefit on their offspring.[39] Some very product-ive people remain childless, and may even do so because they suspect that the duties of parenting would make them less productive. Other industrious individuals may have children while believing that there is something morally wrong with bequeathing large sums to them, and may choose to bequeath to other parties, such as charitable organiza-tions, instead. There is also the very simple fact that working hard to amass wealth that one intends to bequeath after death to children may mean spending less time with one's children while alive. Suffice it to say that while the power to transfer may well have an important positive impact on incentives to create wealth, this may be defeasible. In addition, incentives might be stimulated by alternative policies besides taxation.[40] In making these observations, Wedgwood is beginning to press a version of the now well-established view that the bequest motive is extremely difficult to pin down. It is very hard to establish plausible generalizations about what makes people want to bequeath wealth and what connection this has with tendencies to produce wealth during one's life. Wedgwood also pointed out that the supply of new capital is hardly a matter of the choices of isolated individuals. In effect, Wedgwood was disputing what has now become a strong contemporary political narrative: We should reject the view that an economy is driven by an atomistic army of talented 'wealth creators' who ought to be allowed to keep a large slice of their wealth so that the rest of us can benefit from their creative efforts. The reality is that much depends on the role of institutions, which create environments enabling individuals to make what contribution they do. Even entrepreneurs need to go to school, and whatever innovations they

---

[39] Wedgwood makes this point most explicitly at (1929: 227–37). Others have made similar points more recently; see for example Haslett (1986, 1994: 251–2).

[40] I'll come back to the important topic of charitable bequests in 8.4.

have created will probably be better implemented if they can employ people who went to school as well. Generalizing, Wedgwood claims that ensuring future production of capital has much to do with the appropriate institutional design (in both state and private sectors) and perhaps less with what set of restrictions are placed on freedom of bequest. Again, Wedgwood is surely right on this point.[41]

So the first two objections from Wedgwood hold that Rignano's scheme doesn't optimize incentives for production, even accepting the assumption that such optimizing should be the guiding purpose of the regulation of bequest. Wedgwood's second two objections question the appropriateness of this guiding purpose in the first place. The striking feature uniting these objections is that they do not, strictly speaking, target the Rignano scheme itself. Although they are good objections, they are not good objections to the Rignano scheme. Instead, they are objections to the larger set of claims comprising the scheme along with the presuppositions and methodology for defending it created in part by Mill. I have presented Wedgwood's objections in ways that should make it clear that they really target the Millian assumption that inheritance taxes should be judged as incentive optimizers. Had Rignano offered a completely different foundation for his proposal, Wedgwood's objections may have had much less force and may not even have been advanced.

Wedgwood makes only one objection wholly separable from the question of incentives. It is less forceful than the others, but worthy of comment. According to Wedgwood, the Rignano scheme discriminates against heirs whose parents die young. Wedgwood goes so far as to say that this is a way in which the proposal is "regressive", in the sense that children who are orphaned at a young age tend to have greater need for their inheritance than children who lose their parents late in life, meaning that the real burden of an inheritance tax is higher on the very young.[42] Again, this objection exploits the fact that Rignano's scheme pays no attention to what happens to a fortune between successive bequests. The force of this fairness objection is a little obscure. As Wedgwood himself notes earlier, cases of orphaned children who inherit very young, and while needy, are rare. Wealthy persons, the source of large inheritances, tend to live longer than people with no wealth to

---

[41] Wedgwood (1929: 43–7, also 214).
[42] Wedgwood (1929: 248–9) Compare Rignano's remarks at (1925: 61–2).

bequeath. What's more, surviving spouses tend to own substantial property in their own name. Wedgwood actually invokes these very facts early in his book, when dismissing narratives that are invoked to defend inherited wealth by alluding to the cruelty of not allowing the bereaved to inherit.[43] Cases of an orphan left in dire financial straights can in any case be handled by an exemption threshold allowing relatively small bequests to pass untaxed, which Rignano included in his proposal and which may enjoy independent justifications. Granted, some rationale needs to be given for such thresholds, but they provide an effective reply to the sort of objection that Wedgwood makes. With such exemptions in place, any remaining unfairness is confined to that which obtains among beneficiaries who are already quite fortunate in a strictly absolute sense. It is unclear what to say about the significance of such unfairness, if that's what it is.[44] Even if there is something unfair about an inheritance tax that does not make an allowance for the case of early deaths among the wealthy, allowances are easy to make for the most compelling cases.

These points aside, Wedgwood's discussions raise other matters that will be worthy of comment later on. He may have been naïve as to the realities of parental conferral of advantage in ways that led him to miss important insights. On the other hand, some of his insights can be recalled when discussing proposals other than the Rignano scheme. I will come back briefly to Wedgwood's discussions at appropriate points later in the book. The main point I wish to stress here, though, is that his objections to Rignano are not really objections to making inheritance tax "progressive over time". At most, they highlight the valuable lesson that this idea may have its greatest theoretical potential when extracted from the sort of utilitarian rationale that Rignano wanted to give it.

## 3.5  Prospects for Recovering the Rignano Scheme

The principal theoretical advantage of the Rignano scheme is in its main structural feature: it allows the regulation of bequests to be made sensitive to the longevity of inherited fortunes rather than just their sheer size.

---

[43] Wedgwood (1929: 203).
[44] See for example Roger Crisp's discussion of this question (2006: ch. 6).

This is an advantage because it allows the taxation of inheritance to be made sensitive to the cumulative effects of intergenerational transfers. Traditionally progressive taxation will miss this, unless an estate's size is a *very* reliable proxy for its age. The plausible reality is that any such correlation will be highly defeasible and probably weaker than it would have been in the pre-industrial era. At any rate, size will be a poorer way of tracking age than any scheme that actually makes age an input in its own right when calculating tax liability, which is precisely what the Rignano scheme does. These facts, when properly unpacked, show why the Rignano scheme still has potential quite apart from whatever might be said about incentives and the appropriateness of any utilitarian foundation.

I should note, though, that these remarks have no presence within Rignano's actual defence or explication of the case for progressivity over time. The case for the Rignano scheme, along the above lines, depends on arguments that are yet to be made. Rignano's own utilitarian and quasi-Marxist arguments have little to do with the cumulative effects of inherited wealth. I will seek to move away from Rignano's own utilitarian defence of his scheme. But I would like to note that its force is not completely taken apart by Wedgwood's criticisms. As I have said, Wedgwood is largely correct in maintaining that freedom of bequest provides an incentive only alongside various other environmental and institutional factors that might be promoted instead. That said, it is hard to believe that a Rignano-type scheme would not have *some* positive effect on incentives to save and produce. Rignano's own presentation of the scheme suggests that it might not be an optimizer of incentives but merely an improvement over the most familiar alternative proposals for taxing inheritance. Wedgwood would still be right to point out that there are other ways in which productive activity can be incentivized or disincentivized through means other than the regulation of inheritance and bequest. But the Rignano scheme may have better incentive effects than the traditionally progressive taxation of inheritance, and this should not be forgotten.

What deserves more attention is the question of what alternative foundations might be used to motivate and refine a similar proposal. I have said that overall the prospects for recovering the Rignano scheme rest on what potential exists in egalitarian political philosophy for being concerned about the long-run effects of inherited wealth. In particular, what needs to be examined is the plausibility of two related claims: first, that there is an egalitarian reason to be concerned about the ability of distributive inequality to replicate itself from one generation to the next; second, that inherited wealth plays some sort of primary or otherwise important role as the mechanism through which such replication occurs. The first claim is often accepted by egalitarians. The second claim is important, and its truth is often simply assumed by those already persuaded of the egalitarian case for taxing inherited wealth. But its defence needs to proceed carefully. This makes for the work of the next three chapters.

# 4

# Inheritance and Luck

## 4.1 The Intuitive Idea

According to the economist Anthony Atkinson, "there is nothing intrinsically wrong with inheritance. The problem is that inheritance is unequal. If everyone inherited the same amount, the playing field would be equal".[1] Atkinson's suggestion is that inheritance creates injustice when (and only when) some people inherit significantly more than others.[2] A more general claim is that injustice occurs when material inequalities occur as a matter of fortune, when some people simply have better brute luck than others. This chapter examines theories of justice associated with the defence and development of this idea. Chief among these is the cluster of views known collectively as 'luck egalitarianism'.

Luck egalitarians attach great importance to a distinction between personal choice and personal circumstance, as a way of sorting out just from unjust inequalities. There are many ways in which such a distinction can be interpreted and applied. Many involve some attempt to develop the moral significance of closely related concepts, such as luck and responsibility. One can find various summary definitions in the literature. According to Richard Arneson, "the luck egalitarian project is to develop a plausible account of personal responsibility and integrate it into an egalitarian conception of social justice".[3] According to Larry Temkin, justice is achieved when no person is worse off than others unless through some fault of his or her own.[4] In a recent published

---

[1] Atkinson (2015: 170).

[2] Others make similar claims. For example, Philippe van Parijs, paraphrasing Samuel Brittan: "There is nothing wrong with inherited wealth, except that not everyone has it" (1997: 209).

[3] Arneson (2004: 7).

[4] I'm adapting this slogan from the discussion it receives in Temkin (1993: 25).

lecture on the current state of political philosophy, Jeremy Waldron half-jokingly said that luck egalitarianism now comes in "57 varieties".[5] The goal of this chapter is to assess how some of these varieties deal with inherited wealth. I shall argue that, of the versions of luck egalitarianism examined here, none provides a wholly satisfactory account of how to regulate intergenerational wealth transfers. I shall nevertheless conclude that a choice/circumstance distinction must be retained in any satisfactory explanation of what's unjust about unregulated flows of inherited wealth. But this distinction cannot do such work all by itself, or when paired with the supplementations or modifications discussed in this chapter. Instead, the distinction needs to be combined with and constrained by egalitarian ideas normally (though perhaps not rightly) taken to be competitors of the luck egalitarian project. While receiving an inheritance is generally going to be a matter of brute luck, the moral significance of inheritance flows cannot really be understood without reference to economic segregation and group difference.

Luck egalitarianism did not commence with any canonical defences, such as those associated with the liberal or utilitarian traditions. (Even the name 'luck egalitarianism' was coined by one of the project's more forthright critics.[6]) Instead, luck egalitarianism gained prominence through the modifications of some other views in which ideas about luck, choice, and circumstance play a sort of secondary role. The following remarks from Rawls are among the most frequently quoted in contemporary discussions of justice and luck:

> The existing distribution of income and wealth . . . is the cumulative effect of prior distributions of natural assets—that is natural talents and abilities—as these have been developed or left unrealized, and their use favored or disfavored over time by social circumstances and such chance contingencies as accident and good fortune. Intuitively, the most obvious injustice [of this system] is that it permits distributive shares to be influenced by factors so arbitrary from a moral point of view.[7]

Special attention might be paid to Rawls's claim that a distribution is always a *cumulative effect* of preceding distributions—a claim he

---

[5] Waldron (2013: 21). Readers wanting a survey of the luck egalitarian literature may wish to consult the following recent works: Knight (2013); Knight & Stemplowska (2011); Lippert-Rasmussen (2016); Stemplowska (2012).

[6] Anderson (1999).      [7] Rawls (1999: 62–3).

returned to in later writings.[8] There are so many discussions of the passage's significance that it is remarkable how little attention is paid to this qualification. Attention tends to be directed at the passage's later claim that certain effects on distribution are "morally arbitrary", which does not by itself draw attention to the fact that such effects might occur gradually and incrementally across generations. In effect, philosophical development of the choice/circumstance distinction has been an effort at formalizing what separates the morally arbitrary factors from the non-arbitrary ones.

Alongside Rawls, Ronald Dworkin's work has done much to inspire the luck egalitarian programme as well. His distinction between brute luck and option luck is closely related to the distinction between personal circumstance and personal choice. Brute luck is the unavoidable sort, such as being born with a genetic impairment, while option luck is (for Dworkin) in some sense the outcome of making oneself exposed to avoidable risks, for instance when investing money in housing or devoting time to gaining educational qualifications whose value in the labour market is uncertain.[9] Dworkin's actual theory goes beyond this distinction and gets its own section at the end of this chapter. I should say, however, that the influence exerted by Dworkin and Rawls over the luck egalitarian project does not entail that either of these philosophers was, or ought to have been, a luck egalitarian. This is perhaps most obvious in the case of Rawls, since the quoted passage merely claims that some correction to the arbitrariness of fortune is necessary to secure a just distribution, not that it is the sole or dominant criterion. A few paragraphs later, Rawls makes it clear that justice "does not require society to try to even out handicaps as if all were expected to compete on a fair basis in the same race".[10]

---

[8] Here I have in mind the passage in *Political Liberalism* that I quoted in this book's opening section. Recall his remarks about the gradual erosion of background justice over time, citing inheritance flow as one of the important cumulative effects on any distribution having some history. Rawls also suggests that large inheritance flows lead to concentrations of power that undermine what he calls the "fair value" of political liberties. Otherwise, his view is quite permissive: "the unequal inheritance of wealth is no more inherently unjust than the unequal inheritance of intelligence" (1999: 245). See also Rawls's remarks at (2001: 51–3).

[9] Here I am working with the formulations provided by Dworkin at (2000: 73).

[10] Rawls (1999: 86). Rawls is here distinguishing his view from what he calls the "principle of redress", which bears some resemblance to naïve luck egalitarianism. Will

It looks like it should be easy to apply luck egalitarianism to the problem of inherited wealth.[11] After all, receipt of an inheritance looks like a clear case of having one's distributive position influenced by circumstances rather than one's own choices. In short, unrestricted inheritance flows are unjust because they make some people worse off than others, through no fault of their own, setting aside the extremely remote possibility that inheritance flows fall with the same impact on every person. This seems to capture Atkinson's intuition, an intuition which many of us share. But appearances may be illusory. It may yet turn out that the choice/circumstance distinction does not offer a plausible explanation of why unrestricted inheritance is unjust and what ought to be done about it. As I remarked at the beginning of chapter 1, the wealth of literature on justice and luck has not included very much discussion of intergenerational wealth transfers. No luck egalitarian, to my knowledge, has so far worked out the details.[12] So we should be wary of the project's apparent potential.

## 4.2 Naïve Luck Egalitarianism: Some Problems

Atkinson's intuition is most powerful when inheritance flows are *large* and *selective*—that is, when a privileged few inherit lots while others get nothing. Another, complementary intuition is that *small* inheritances aren't much cause for concern. If I inherit my grandfather's old beer tankard, which has minuscule financial value, and you inherit nothing at all, that is still an unequal distribution of inheritance. Distribution has been sensitive to circumstance rather than choice, so it is unjust. The first problem, then, for luck egalitarianism is that it appears to condemn *all*

Kymlicka claims that Rawls would have endorsed luck egalitarianism had he grasped "the full implications of his own argument" about the moral arbitrariness of fortune (2002: 70–2). Similarly, Susan Hurley argues for "a luck neutralizing view of the deep structure of Rawls's egalitarianism" (2003: 135–6). Such interpretations are rejected by other readers of Rawls, for example Scheffler (2003: esp. 8–12) and Freeman (2007: ch. 4).

[11] I am here suppressing doubts about whether any combination of tax bases can "isolate" brute luck; see Barbara Fried (2000: esp. 394–5). I take it to be implicitly present in Anne Alstott's (2007) account of the lack of continuity between US estate tax law and the basic idea of equality of opportunity.

[12] Though some have noted that receipt of inheritance is a matter of brute luck: see Dworkin (2000: 347); Rakowski (1991: 159).

inheritance no matter its size, so long as it reflects the working of circumstances rather than choices. This is intuitively too strong—nobody really cares about unequal inheritance of beer tankards. There is a way of generalizing the worry here. The choice/circumstance distinction is apparently qualitative. It concerns different *ways* in which distribution can be influenced. But the moral significance of inherited wealth may well be quantitative: with Atkinson, we think there's a moral problem particularly when inherited fortunes become large for some but not for others. The problem is that it is hard to see how qualitative principles can accommodate quantitative claims.

A second concern has to do with another difference between inheritance and other ways in which wealth may move around and affect a distribution. While the *receipt* of inheritance looks like an effect of brute luck, the act of bequest or transfer is not. Intergenerational transfers of wealth are instances of what are sometimes called "gratuitous" or "asymmetric" transfers.[13] A transfer is asymmetric when it involves no real exchange—someone is given something for nothing. Employment contracts involve symmetric transfers because someone pays a recipient in return for some agreed amount of his or her work.[14] Gifts and bequests are asymmetric because the recipient does nothing except receive. Relevant here are Robert Nozick's remarks on distributive justice:

[13] This usage also appears in Murphy & Nagel's discussion of inheritance (2002: ch. 7), also Braun (2010: 702–3). I am going to assume here that characterizing inheritance as asymmetric is correct, but this is a substantive assumption. Economists have for some time considered the possibility that bequests aim to provide one's offspring with an incentive to give care in old age, for which inheritance is promised in exchange. Philosophers sometimes endorse the exchange model, e.g. Hillel Steiner (1992: 83–4). Perhaps significantly, the model may undermine the idea that bequest is a virtuously altruistic act, as libertarians sometimes suggest it is; see White (2008). I shall discuss this claim more fully in 7.3. For an extended discussion of the bequest motive, see Fried (1999). Rakowski (1991: 158–61) is also useful, as is Batchelder (2009: 26–33). Recent empirical studies that aim to understand the motive itself are reviewed in Kopczuk (2009). As some economists point out, the problem is made even more difficult by the need to focus on the motives of very wealthy testators, which might differ from the general (less wealthy) population. On this, see Gale & Slemrod (2001: 22). A concise overview of the major models of the bequest motive is in Edward Wolff (2015: 12–14). Ultimately, the exchange model is not very plausible: plenty of bequests are made to offspring who do nothing to support their parents in old age, while bequests to organizations and charities represent another problematic case for the model.

[14] Note that calling a transfer 'symmetric' does *not* typically mean that it promotes distributive equality, only that something of value (not necessarily equal value) passes in both directions.

Proponents of patterned [e.g. egalitarian] principles of distributive justice focus upon criteria for determining who is to receive holdings.... Whether or not it is better to give than to receive, proponents of patterned principles ignore giving altogether. In considering the distribution of goods, income, and so forth, their theories are theories of recipient justice; they completely ignore any right a person might have to give something to someone.... Thus discussions tend to focus on whether people (should) have a right to inherit, rather than on whether people (should) have a right to bequeath or on whether persons who have a right to hold also have a right to choose that others hold in their place. I lack a good explanation of why the usual theories of justice are so recipient-oriented; ignoring givers and transferrers and their rights is of a piece with ignoring producers and their entitlements. But why is it *all* ignored?[15]

Other libertarian authors have made similar claims.[16] In Nozick's case, the complaint is somewhat rhetorically formulated. It is unclear whether Nozick thinks there is actually some interesting theoretical mistake associated with privileging recipients over donors or merely arousing the suspicion of a mistake's existence by leaving the question unanswered.[17] He cites no actual "discussions" of inheritance. But Nozick is right to say that when distribution is sensitive to one person's circumstance, it is often thereby sensitive, also, to another person's choice. Asymmetric transfers will always maintain a situation in which some persons' distributive position is influenced by their brute luck. The only way to prevent this is to somehow arrange things so that no person benefits from such transfers to a degree greater than anyone else. But there is no plausible way of doing this.[18]

When it comes to inherited wealth, simple luck egalitarianism may be too strong in its implications. First, it apparently requires the abolition of all intergenerational transfers, no matter how tiny they are in monetary terms. Second, it apparently requires the abolition of all *asymmetric* transfers. I am not suggesting that these implications are inescapable. They merely indicate a difficulty for what we might call *naïve* luck

---

[15] Nozick (1974: 168). As mentioned in chapter 1, Nozick's later writings give a different impression; see 7.3. I think they are compatible with what he says in this quoted passage, though probably not with everything else in the 1974 discussion. For exegesis of Nozick's idea of a patterned principle, see Schmidtz (2005).

[16] I list some more of these claims in Halliday (2013a). For more discussion, see 7.2.

[17] Some of Nozick's critics have suggested that this strategy is one he uses often; see Fried (2005).

[18] This point has been stressed at greater length by Hugh Lazenby (2010), though he extends it to a broader set of acts than material transfers (e.g. acts of affection).

egalitarianism. By 'naïve' I do not mean 'false'. Instead I mean something like reliance on the choice/circumstance distinction without elaboration or qualification as to the distinction's precise content or what role it should play in a more complete theory of justice. My suggestion is that the luck egalitarian idea will need to undergo some development before it is able to grapple properly with the matter of inheritance and asymmetric transfers generally. At least, this calls into question any optimism that we might have had about how easy it is for luck egalitarians to handle the problem of inherited wealth. There are two broad ways in which luck egalitarians might proceed. One is to supplement the choice/circumstance distinction with some independently plausible constraints in ways that might protect some freedom of bequest or transfer. Another is to try to refine the precise content or scope of the distinction itself, so that it doesn't imply anything as strong as the total abolition of inheritance. One way or the other, this is what more sophisticated conceptions of luck egalitarianism attempt to do.

## 4.3 Pluralism and Personal Prerogatives

Whenever a principle of justice turns out to have intuitively demanding requirements, there is the option of adopting 'pluralism'. This involves claiming that the requirements in question look demanding only when viewed in isolation from some larger set of requirements in which they are embedded. These other requirements can override or constrain the first set of requirements. This idea has some promise.

G. A. Cohen explicitly adopts pluralism as part of his defence of luck egalitarianism.[19] Specifically, Cohen combines luck egalitarianism with the idea of a 'personal prerogative' that has been developed in ethical theory. Broadly speaking, a personal prerogative is a sort of individual entitlement to exercise partiality, which may be weighed against demanding 'impartial' or 'impersonal' requirements, including any requirement to make a distribution reflect choice but not circumstance.[20] Cohen

---

[19] Here I will work mainly with what Cohen says in the appendix to his (2008). Hugh Lazenby's (2010) discussion of asymmetric transfers also suggests that an endorsement of pluralism may be the best way for luck egalitarians to handle the problem posed by asymmetric transfers.

[20] The prerogative "entitles agents not to be fully constrained by egalitarian demands in their personal choices" (Cohen 2008: 389).

wants to adopt this sort of pluralism so he can permit individuals to make some choices that may create or preserve brute luck inequality, like choosing to work for a high salary. I should say that Cohen doesn't try to defend the right to bequeath wealth, though he does make an attempt to defend the right for wealthy persons to benefit their children in certain circumstances.[21] The prerogative has been proposed not just with self-regarding conduct in mind but also partiality to others. People's personal goals in life usually involve some commitment to improving the well-being of other persons, particularly family members, or beneficiaries of some charitable activity that one finds personally valuable. The personal prerogative might ground a limited right to transfer wealth as a means of acting on such commitments.

The problem is that there must be some point at which a person's 'partiality allowance' gets used up. The personal prerogative has no substance otherwise if it is unlimited, and Cohen concedes as much. This casts doubt on whether any such personal prerogative could protect some individual freedom to bequeath or transfer wealth. Bequests normally occur only after much other partiality has been exercised throughout the donor's life. Other wealth transfers typically occur 'on top of', so to speak, the great many other acts through which parents exercise partiality towards their children.[22] Apart from their number, the more informal acts of partiality, made early in a child's life, may be among the most morally important. One way to measure this is to think of what we would say about parents who fail to act partially in the relevant ways. We think more poorly of a parent who ignores his or her children as they grow up than we do of a parent who provides plenty of loving attention but who openly bequeaths his or her wealth to a charity. This suggests that the most plausible formulation of the personal prerogative might be one that gives priority to acts of partiality other than formal wealth transfers, particularly where partiality towards children is concerned.

I appreciate that there may be certain complexities attached to measuring the limits of what a prerogative permits. Acts of partiality might be measured according to various dimensions at once, for example in terms of the burden they place on the person who exercises the partiality, but

---

[21] See for example the discussion in his (2000: 175–6), though I should note that Cohen defends these claims without reference to the personal prerogative.

[22] See Alstott (2008: 21).

also the amount of good done to the beneficiary, and also the opportunity cost with respect to any forgone pursuit of more impartial goals. The most important observation may be that wealth transfers carry a higher opportunity cost than acts of partiality that do not involve giving tangible things. Acts of love and affection could not have been usefully given to charity instead. But by purchasing my child's house or education, I often forgo an opportunity to do much more for a group of needy strangers. The prerogative might be compatible with special permission to make bequests in the event of premature parental death.[23] There is also the possibility that one could 'accrue' extra permission to exercise partiality as a result of having done a great deal to promote equality throughout society in general, and thus gain a stronger right to bequeath.[24] I take no stance on whether the personal prerogative is more plausible if understood to work in this sort of way. But such possibilities do not undermine the general claim that there may be a significant tendency for intergenerational wealth transfers, especially posthumous ones, to exceed the limits of the personal prerogative.

There are further reasons against grounding the right to bequeath in ideas about the personal prerogative. These become visible when we ask what the moral foundations for such a prerogative might actually be. For Cohen, the basis for the prerogative is little more than moral intuition. He says that the prerogative "grants each person the right to be something other than an engine for the welfare of other people: we are not nothing but slaves to social justice". In a similar vein, he asserts that limited personal prerogative would be denied only by "an extreme moral rigorist".[25] Cohen's claims here are largely rhetorical.[26] To be fair, Cohen is explicit in attributing the prerogative he endorses to Samuel Scheffler's

---

[23] Recall the discussions of Locke and Mill in chapter 2. See also Mason (2006: 146).

[24] See Scheffler's original (1982/1993) way of construing the prerogative, whereby agents are permitted to give greater weight to their pursuit of personal projects, relative to the weight they must give to bringing about states of affairs favoured by an "impersonal ranking" of states of affairs.

[25] Cohen (2008: 10, 61).

[26] The rhetorical use of "slaves to social justice" conflicts with an argumentative move that Cohen famously made, elsewhere, against Nozick's (1974: 169–70) contention that taxation is on a par with forced labour. Cohen's (1995: 230–6) response was (in part) to point out, quite correctly and at some length, that talk of slavery is inappropriate in the absence of some slave-owning agent who possesses significant discretion as to how to utilize their slave. The requirements of social justice are unlike the rights of a slave owner in that they are typically very specific. Thus it is misleading to speak of being a slave to social

relevant work in theoretical ethics. Here, the foundations of the prerogative draw on ideas about an agent-centred prerogative as a way of
accommodating "certain important anti-consequentialist intuitions".[27]
While Scheffler's account has some sophistication, its point is to temper
the moral demands of consequentialist ethical theories, which differ
from the demands of egalitarian justice. This sort of justification may
not count particularly in favour of any *specific* type of partiality rather
than some limited *amount* of partiality more generally. Accordingly,
there is little in what Scheffler says, or in Cohen's adaptation of it, that
indicates any specific support for exercising partiality by way of wealth
transfers.[28]

Other philosophical work on partiality is more helpful. Harry Brighouse and Adam Swift have developed an account of legitimate parental
partiality that is grounded in the goods of an intimate familial relationship, whose distinctive character explains both why the family is justified
in general and why parents might have some specific rights to exercise
partiality in certain ways.[29] Importantly, this view also explains when
some acts of partiality exceed what is permitted. Brighouse and Swift
make it clear that acts of transferring wealth are rarely necessary to
sustain any important goods associated with the parent–child relationship. After all, many children inherit little or no wealth from their
parents, and we rarely take this as evidence of any defect in the relationship. There may be contexts where parent–child relationships can be
corrupted in ways that involve a parent withholding a wealth transfer.[30]
For example, it is wrong to use a threat of disinheritance to coerce a child
into (say) marrying a certain partner or giving up a chosen career in

justice, just like it is misleading for Nozick to talk of taxation (levied in the pursuit of social
justice) as akin to forced labour.

[27] See Scheffler (1982/1993, esp. ch. 1.).

[28] For some further criticism of how Cohen handles the idea of the personal prerogative,
see Thrasher & Hankins (2015: esp. 183–6). Other ways of justifying the prerogative may
exist, but I lack space to explore any here.

[29] See especially Brighouse & Swift (2014: ch. 5) and (2009). Brighouse and Swift (2006)
have also explored the way in which the ethics of parenting should include some attention
to the way parenting is distinctively good for parents, though this doesn't obviously ground
a right to transfer. The pursuit of relationship goods may also ground duties that children
owe to parents. On this, see Keller (2006).

[30] Brighouse and Swift themselves suggest that, in cases where a child expects to receive
great wealth, the parent–child relationship may have been corrupted, as might have the
character of the child (2014: 138).

order to take on the family business, or as a way of sowing conflict among multiple children. But these are cases where a relationship has been impaired by an *abuse* of the power to transfer rather than its absence. There is also something wrong with a parent who chooses to never buy his or her child a birthday or Christmas present, although the specifics of any proper evaluation will depend on the presence of certain background cultural or religious conventions. But while such cases show that gifts plausibly play some important role in maintaining loving relationships, it is not obvious that they ever need to have a very large monetary value to do so. Examination of the parent–child relationship once a child has reached adulthood does not feature prominently in the Brighouse–Swift view.[31] But I would suggest that the role of gifts becomes rather less important after childhood. At least, parents' failure to give any gifts to an adult child does not violate a fiduciary duty. This is not to say that gifts given to adult children can't increase well-being. They may clearly do so quite substantially, as when relatively wealthy parents buy their adult child a house or a car. The financial value of this sort of gift, not to mention the corresponding level of parental sacrifice, is likely to be greater than what was spent on childhood birthday presents. Overall, the main implication of the Brighouse–Swift view is that, to the extent that gifts and bequests have any sort of relationship-maintaining role to play, they can play it even if medium or large intergenerational transfers are highly restricted. So once we actually look at why parental partiality is worth protecting in a variety of cases, we find reasons to doubt whether such protections ought to extend to inheritance flows.

Before concluding this section, I want to suggest an important exception. I've talked mainly about assessing the personal prerogative with respect to the support it provides for intergenerational transfers. But not all bequests instantiate such transfers, because not all bequests select children, or even other people, as their beneficiary. The personal prerogative may well turn out to support bequests made to charities and

---

[31] Brighouse and Swift have been criticized for this omission; see Ferracioli (2015: 209–12). In response, Brighouse and Swift (2015: 238–9) suggest that the value in parent–child relationships after childhood is not relevant to justifying the family as a protected institution because the relationship is by this stage one "among consenting adults". Their acknowledgement that the post-childhood relationship is nevertheless valuable is, however, compatible with its value being relevant to the question of justifying the restriction of inherited wealth.

similar organizations. Charitable bequests might be worthy of protection even if the prerogative is denied, so long as recipient charities pursue justice effectively. There is also the matter of giving to a charity that pursues justice less efficiently than do other charities that one does not favour. Here there is room for some convergence between the pursuit of impartial requirements and the exercise of one's own personal projects: on some views, there is a case for giving persons a degree of latitude when acting on their other-regarding duties. Roughly speaking, testatory freedom for charitable bequests might be compared with what Kantian moral theorists describe as an imperfect duty. Duties of this sort might be demanding when measured purely in terms of how much sacrifice they require, and yet be 'undemanding' in the sense of permitting extensive freedom about where to direct one's efforts. Such views may explain why it is permissible to be partial towards less efficient charities when one simply cares more about the cause.[32] But it is hard to accept similar claims about bequests to adult offspring. This is just because bequests to offspring will almost never qualify as ways of discharging imperfect duties in ways that bequests to charities sometimes could. I won't develop this line of thought in detail, but these points should remind us that a defence of bequest that appeals to a right to be partial and independent when deciding what to do with one's wealth can be accommodated without thereby conceding any right to confer advantage specifically on members of one's own family.

To summarize: It looks like a personal prerogative, of a sort that permits departures from distributive equality, can be granted as a means of protecting the right to bequeath or transfer wealth, in the face of any egalitarian demand against being allowed to do so. But there are two ways in which the appeal to personal prerogatives gets into trouble. First, we can observe that restricting the right to transfer is compatible with literally a lifetime of other acts of partiality, which is probably already more than a plausible prerogative can plausibly protect. It is unclear why the prerogative would select the power to transfer as a particular sort of act to which it grants special protection. Second, the foundations of a personal prerogative might discount the significance of intergenerational transfers compared to other familiar acts of partiality.

---

[32] This may be intuitive but is not actually straightforward. See Pummer (2016).

This is because transfers (especially large ones) play little or no role in promoting the goals that justify permission to act partially in the first place, principally the goal of pursuing the goods of an intimate relationship. A personal prerogative may still succeed in providing support for transfers aimed at nonheirs, such as charities. But luck egalitarians seeking to defend the right to transfer wealth to heirs will have to find another way.

## 4.4 The Institutional Approach

I'll now examine how the choice/circumstance distinction might be refined rather than supplemented. One plausible version of this approach is the "institutional luck egalitarianism" developed recently by Kok-Chor Tan. Broadly speaking, Tan's project is an attempt to better integrate luck egalitarianism with elements of liberalism, such as privacy and neutrality about the good life, in ways that address some influential objections to other versions of luck egalitarianism. A core foundational element of the project is Tan's endorsement of the traditional liberal principle that justice ultimately regulates institutions and not personal conduct.[33] To see how this modifies the naïve luck-egalitarian endorsement of an unmodified choice/circumstance distinction, it is worth quoting some of Tan's own claims:

Luck egalitarianism ought not to be in the business of mitigating all natural contingencies (due to luck) that people face. As an aspect of social justice, luck egalitarianism is only concerned with how institutions deal with such natural contingencies. Its goal is to ensure that institutions are not arranged so as to convert a natural trait (a matter of luck) into actual social advantages or disadvantages for persons. So, only those natural contingencies that have an institutional consequence in this way fall within the scope of egalitarianism.[34]

Tan's idea, then, is to narrow the scope of the choice/circumstance distinction, making it applicable only to types of brute luck disadvantage attributable to institutional design.

---

[33] The sort of liberal principle that Tan endorses draws on Rawls (1993: ch. 7; 1999: 7–9, 47–52; 2001: 10–12) and Thomas Nagel (1991: esp. chs. 1, 6). Tan's own use of the distinction differs somewhat from the usage of both Rawls and Nagel, neither of whom aimed to integrate it with luck egalitarianism.

[34] Tan (2012: 103). Similar formulations occur at (141).

A review of some simple examples shows what difference this can make: Hiring practices very often discriminate against women of child-bearing age because employers fear having to grant maternity leave. In Tan's terminology, such disadvantage here is "post-institutional". It is the labour market (an institution) that generates the disadvantage, which could therefore be removed by bringing about the right institutional reforms. In this particular case, employers could be provided with substantial compensation for workers who take maternity leave, so that they lack the incentive to discriminate against female applicants of relevant age. On Tan's view, the fact that the disadvantage can be blamed on the contingent design of a relevant institution is crucial to its qualifying as an injustice. Many familiar cases of brute luck disadvantage are similarly "post-institutional". Physical disabilities leave their bearers at a disadvantage largely because of how we've designed infrastructure, vehicles, and jobs. The institutional approach allows these cases to be plausibly separated from other instances of brute luck disadvantage that cannot be blamed on institutions. People who have involuntary tastes for expensive fine wines, people whose faces are not 'beautiful' enough to attract the desired number of romantic partners, and people who want to become professional athletes but aren't talented enough, might all count as victims of bad brute luck. But the disadvantage that occurs in these examples cannot be blamed on the institutional background. Instead, it comes directly from the "pre-institutional" natural traits of the persons concerned. Accordingly, institutional luck egalitarianism does not treat such cases as involving any distributive injustice. In this way it differs substantially from naïve luck egalitarianism.

Tan's approach has a number of genuine theoretical advantages, including some force against popular criticisms of the luck egalitarian project.[35] The important question for this book concerns what the institutional approach implies about the regulation of intergenerational wealth transfers. Tan doesn't identify any implications himself or mention the problem of inheritance anywhere in the development of his project. But it is clear that the crucial matter is whether the institution of wealth transfer is one that can "convert" persons' "natural traits" into

---

[35] I have raised some views about Tan's approach in Halliday (2013b). For a response see Tan (2013). Other general discussions of Tan's approach are Sanyal (2012) and Schemmel (2012a).

advantage or disadvantage. If it can, then inheritance is postinstitutional and there's a case for some restriction of inherited wealth, probably with some flexibility. If not, then inheritance is pre-institutional and hence irrelevant to egalitarian justice. This would mean that *no* regulation of inheritance were required as a matter of justice, which would be hard to believe.

Much hangs on the idea of a "natural trait". This can be understood broadly or narrowly. One rather narrow reading is that a natural trait is just any intrinsic property of a person on which institutional design could potentially operate. Formulations of Tan's such as "natural and arbitrary facts *about persons*" are at least compatible with this reading.[36] Properties such as having a talent or a certain physiological feature can all count as intrinsic to their bearer.[37] Although coherent, such a narrow understanding of a natural trait must be rejected if institutional luck egalitarianism is to say anything interesting about inheritance. This is because there is no intrinsic natural feature that plausibly gets operated on by an institution when someone inherits wealth or property. On any view, receiving an inheritance depends at least partly on one's standing in certain relations with other persons, not on one's narrowly intrinsic properties. So if the scope of institutional luck egalitarianism is supposed to be restricted to disadvantage resulting from how institutions operate on a person's intrinsic features, then the institutional approach will treat inheritance as pre-institutional, and it will be impossible for inherited wealth to cause any unjust inequalities.

There is no compelling reason, however, to insist on quite such a narrow reading of "natural trait".[38] Natural traits might instead be identified in ways that include relations between their bearer and other persons. So in order to apply institutional luck egalitarianism to inheritance, we might identify the relevant natural trait as that of standing in whatever interpersonal relationship partly motivates the bequest or transfer. A candidate for the mediating institution, then, would simply be whatever apparatus facilitates the legal transfer of wealth between

---

[36] Tan (2012: 15, italics added; also 144).

[37] The *market value* of a talent is not intrinsic. But talents themselves could still be among a person's intrinsic properties.

[38] The idea of institutions as things that operate on "natural" facts is an idea that Tan takes from Rawls's writings. A relevant passage is Rawls (1999: 86–93). Here, Rawls seems to vacillate between wider and narrower readings of "natural fact".

persons standing in any such relationship. The fact that some people inherit while others do not is, therefore, a postinstitutional inequality.

What is problematic this time is not the *division* between institution and natural trait. Instead it is the attribution of *causal priority* to the institution *over* the natural trait. Disadvantage cannot be postinstitutional, on Tan's account, unless it is really the institution that makes the decisive difference to whether some natural trait turns out to put its bearer at a disadvantage. But the causal priority here lies with family relationships, to which institutions merely respond when facilitating bequests. There is a sense in which one's inheritance is channelled into one's possession 'from' some institution like a bank account, because that is where cash is held, but the real source of the inheritance is the individual benefactor: we inherit *from* our parents or other people. Importantly, this requirement of causal priority cannot be relaxed by classifying disadvantage as postinstitutional whenever institutions play at least *some* prior causal role. Relaxing the requirement in this way would qualify all sorts of disadvantage that institutional luck egalitarianism is designed to exclude from the scope of justice. Having an ugly appearance, for example, brings disadvantage (let's say) only if one participates in some group activity in which norms of appearance exist and where members of this group might shun or reward people in accordance with their conformity to these norms. Here, institutions are having *some* causal role. But part of the distinctiveness of the institutional approach is that it avoids the proliferation of entitlements that has given rise to counterexamples invoked by the various critics of luck egalitarian views. So relaxing its requirement about when causal priority can be attributed to institutions would bring inheritance into its scope only at the cost of sacrificing much of its main appeal.[39]

There may yet be ways of adapting the institutional approach so that it can be brought to bear on the problem of inherited wealth; I emphasize that this is a new theory of egalitarian justice whose potential may not have been fully realized.[40] My sense, for what it is worth, is that Tan's

---

[39] A similar, generalized version of this point has been suggested by some of Tan's other critics; see Forcehimes & Talisse (2015).

[40] In personal communication, Tan has suggested to me that some sort of counterfactual test, invoking a state of nature, may qualify large inequalities due to inheritance as postinstitutional but not qualify small ones. This is because family ties and some practice of partiality would exist in a state of nature, but that large amounts of transferable wealth, and

approach relies on its being relatively easy to distinguish institutions from persons within them, in ways that keep it similarly easy to separate their causal roles. Unfortunately, there are cases in which it is difficult to establish a fact of the matter as to whether an inequality can be blamed wholly or primarily on one or the other. Inequalities due to inherited wealth present one such case.

## 4.5  Reciprocity and Idleness

One objection to large inheritances is that they make recipients unjustly idle. This worry surfaced many times in the writings or the early liberals discussed in chapter 2, though in such writings it typically resubmerged without being developed in a very sophisticated way. Contemporary political philosophy has gone further. Such work shows that a case for restricting inheritance based on an objection to idleness need not rely on the choice/circumstance distinction. Rather, it owes more to the concept of reciprocity.

Rawlsian egalitarianism is founded on various ideas about society being a cooperative venture for mutual advantage and about justice being a matter of rules under which such cooperation is fair. Crudely put, the idea of reciprocity is that nobody should be able to benefit from such cooperation without also making a contribution to it, at least when able to do so. It should be noted that reciprocity is not the only concept that Rawls used to derive requirements of justice, and that he did not actually invoke the concept of reciprocity when alluding to why justice might require restrictions on inherited wealth.[41] Nevertheless, the concept of reciprocity can still be used to develop a more direct objection to unrestricted inherited wealth.

According to Stuart White, the point of reciprocity is that citizens carry what he calls a "contributive obligation" to participate in the maintenance of society. Violation of this obligation is incompatible with what White calls an "ethos of democratic mutual regard".[42] What

---

the institutions enabling it, would not. This idea has some promise, though I suspect it may be vulnerable to counterexample. Consider the much-discussed example of brute luck inequalities that are due to expensive tastes. Since the state of nature would not contain an industry for producing wine (fine or otherwise), relevant inequalities would get qualified as postinstitutional.

[41]  See the opening section of chapter 1.      [42]  See White (2003: ch. 3).

does this view about reciprocity imply about inheritance? Inheritors who can opt out of the labour market will continue to benefit from the labour-market participation of other people. This is because the continued labour of others is necessary to provide all sorts of goods that lucky inheritors will continue to consume, such as law enforcement, electricity, and food. Some of these goods are nonexcludable, meaning that wealthy persons cannot opt out of consuming what the state has provided. Inheritance may therefore enable conditions in which its beneficiaries violate reciprocity by evading their contributive obligation to society. White defends inheritance taxes precisely as a means of preventing such conditions from occurring.[43]

This sort of argument bears a resemblance to one that has been widely discussed, by White himself and by others, in relation to proposals about universal basic income.[44] Such proposals favour the provision of a regular cash grant to all citizens or residents, large enough to make it economically feasible for recipients to avoid paid work altogether, should they wish. Basic income grants will almost certainly not be large enough to support the kind of lifestyle enabled by a large inheritance. But grant-holders who exit the labour market resemble inheritors by retaining a dependence on the many goods whose production requires other persons' labour and which are often provided for free with the help of taxing the earnings of those who remain in the labour market. Now, it is not obvious whether any objection gains or loses force when applied to freeriding by inheritors rather than to freeriding by recipients of basic income. This is because these are two different kinds of freeriding. On the one hand, the sort of freeriding enabled by basic income involves a cross-subsidy: those who work don't just produce the goods that idle grant-holders consume; they also fund the grants themselves through the income taxes they pay. Freeriding inheritors get their wealth from a person who has chosen to make them wealthy, so the extent of their freeriding is narrowed somewhat. If lucky inheritors are consuming only public goods rather than direct subsidies, then their consumption may

[43] White (2003: 179–86). White's more specific view is in favour of a progressive receipts tax. (Recall here the taxonomic points made in section 3.3.) I discuss the distinction between estates and receipts in chapter 8.

[44] White develops this objection first in (2002), and then as part of the larger framework constructed around the reciprocity principle in (2003). Other relevant discussions of reciprocity and basic income include Galston (2001) and Birnbaum (2012: ch. 3).

not require any extra work from the workers on whom they are freerid-ing, making it less objectionable.[45]

On the other hand, there are ways in which the freeriding of inheritors may be more objectionable than that associated with basic income. Basic income is supposed to be universal—everyone qualifies for it. This means that there is a sense in which anyone who stays in the labour market has *chosen* to be freeridden on by those who prefer to live off their basic income grant alone. Even if this sense of 'choice' is nonstandard, the point is that it separates freeriding in the basic income case from that due to inheritance. Any individual worker could join the freeriders and live off their grant alone, but workers who support the lives of idle inheritors cannot make the same choice.[46] Nobody can choose to live off an inheritance that they never get. In this respect, then, the freeriding of wealthy inheritors might be more objectionable.

More needs to be said about what is meant by 'idleness'. We can recall here the claims made by some of the early liberals. Godwin's view was that a life of complete idleness was a life less well lived than one that contained at least a significant amount of work, or at least mentally engaging work. One might point out that, while great wealth might make an inheritor idle in terms of his or her own behaviour, his or her wealth itself may yet be put to social use. For example, someone who inherits a large amount of real estate can rent it out to tenants, and financial capital will still be invested in all sorts of places. These points help separate wealthy inheritors from their counterparts in the eight-eenth century, whose idleness bothered classical liberals like Smith because it reduced the agricultural potential of inherited land. As I suggested in chapter 2, these older concerns about idleness may by now be superseded owing to the fact that inheritors are less likely to be involved in directly managing the assets they've inherited.

The nature of capital has changed since the eighteenth century, but the freeriding objection is really about what persons do or do not do rather than about how productive their assets can be made to be. Sending one's inherited capital to a financier so that it can be put to some socially

---

[45] Relevant here would be the fact that public goods are nonrival, in the sense that one person's consumption doesn't diminish its supply for others.

[46] A common criticism of basic income is that this strategy is collectively self-defeating, but that does not change the choices available to a given individual.

beneficial use is not really a way of making one's own contribution to some reciprocal system of cooperation, even if the capital still works hard (thanks largely to the work of those employed by the institutions that control it). This reveals that we might distinguish between 'idleness' in a broad sense and the more specific idea of 'absence from the labour market'. The narrower sense suffices to class inheritors as idle even when their assets work hard for the rest of us. But as a criterion of idleness it may have some false positives. This is because there are ways that one can contribute to society without participating in the labour market. Perhaps the most obvious example is domestic labour, which society greatly needs but which goes almost entirely unpaid. Indeed, the injustice may be that such activities go unpaid in the first place, rather than that it is unjust when people perform them instead of getting paid work. There are also workers who sell their labour in the informal economy and who cannot be made subject to income tax by the state. Again, there is a sense in which such workers are not contributing in the way that taxed formal employment makes possible, but this may not be their fault (informal employment is usually not preferable to the formal sort, but is hard to avoid especially in developing countries). Finally there is the possibility that refusal to sell one's labour may be a legitimate form of protest against status quo injustices.[47] Such considerations suggest that it may be difficult to specify exactly what is meant by 'idleness'.

Philippe van Parijs has spoken of a sort of 'work fetishism' motivating the idea that everyone ought to be in paid work.[48] Domestic labour aside, there are plenty of things that wealthy inheritors can do to make themselves socially useful. Historically, much important scholarship and exploration was carried out by the rich and privileged. Of course, this was partly because the less privileged simply couldn't compete. Indeed, most views in political philosophy will imply that an injustice is done when the wealthy have a monopoly on access to opportunities to flourish. But to express the objection to idleness in this way is really to turn it into something else, possibly a complaint more about segregation with respect to social roles, which does not need to presuppose anything about the moral importance of reciprocity (though getting people to engage in

---

[47] For an illuminating discussion of this possibility, see Shelby (2012), also White (2003: 86–94).

[48] See van Parijs (2001: 19).

localized reciprocal exchanges may be conducive to getting them to form desirable sorts of relationships, increasing social integration). Indeed, the view that everyone should experience at least *some* labour market participation is most persuasive when expressed as the view that everyone with privilege should learn about what it is like to have to earn money and be bossed around, possibly in boring or nasty jobs, simply for the sake of learning what life is like for less fortunate people. Again this view is compelling enough as a claim in favour of integration rather than as the view that laziness per se is a bad thing.

So I don't think idleness needs to be considered especially problematic. Objections to it often turn out to be grounded in a more fundamental concern about something else. It is worth adding that even if idleness were unjust, taxing inheritance would not be the only way of removing it. The state could, for example, coerce the idle rich into a variety of social roles that, for one reason or another, need not or should not be filled through market supply. Coerced military service might be one. Alternatively, wealthy inheritors could be made to supply organs for transplant or to be guinea pigs for the testing of new medicines or to clean the sewers. I am not trying to be facetious here, as there is a genuine issue about the way in which certain tasks need to be performed and might be left to the poor and vulnerable (meaning such work may remain stigmatized) if we rely on the labour market to sort out who gets the job done. Moreover, any coercion here would be of a rather weak sort, because an idle inheritor could avoid the threatened outcome simply by getting a job like everybody else (while keeping his or her inherited wealth). Coercion is generally more morally objectionable when imposed in ways that seriously degrade an individual's choice set, as when military service can be avoided only by incurring a prison sentence, which it still is in some countries. I don't really wish to defend these proposals: the point is merely that opposition to the freeriding of the most wealthy inheritors may not lead unavoidably to an argument for inheritance taxes.

In any case a tax on inheritance, unless it is quite dramatic, will not remove the freeriding altogether; it will only make the free ride less comfortable. Those who pay tax on an inheritance may still be viewed as performing less of a contribution than those who have no option but to work for a living. One might say that a moderate inheritance tax turns freeriding into 'cheapriding'. But this is not enough if reciprocity is really an egalitarian requirement. In order to bring about complete reciprocity, an inheritance tax will have to be so high that it reduces all inheritance to the extent that inheritors must still go out and find paid work to support themselves. This is not quite abolition, and maybe it is not so counter-intuitive. But this is unlikely to provide a foundation for much less than a very aggressive tax on wealth transfers.

## 4.6 Hypothetical Insurance

I'll conclude with a view that is closest to those defended in the next two chapters.[49] For Dworkin, the broad goal of egalitarian justice is to make the distribution of resources sensitive to persons' ambitions rather than to their prior endowments. This distinction departs slightly, but cru-cially, from the one between choice and circumstance.[50] One difference is that brute luck disadvantage might be the sort of thing that its bearer regards as part of who they are—essential to their personality or sense of self. This can happen when someone has an ambition that is very hard to achieve or a taste that is expensive to satisfy. I might struggle to achieve my life plan of visiting all the countries in the world. I might view those who have cheap life plans as more fortunate than me in some sense. But I might think that I'd be a changed person if I didn't have such a plan, and the cost of pursuing my goals wouldn't dispose me to change places with someone whose goals were cheaper to pursue but are ones I regard as less worthy. Dworkin wants to acknowledge such cases by making justice "ambition-sensitive" but not "endowment-sensitive". If I plan to visit all the world's countries only because this is necessary to access some very complex set of treatments for some unwanted disease, then things are different. Generalizing, Dworkin's idea is that entitlements depend on which sorts of brute luck persons would *choose to seek protection against hypothetically* and how *much* protection they would have purchased. Importantly, this hypothetical insurance disqualifies some forms of brute luck disadvantage (those that reflect genuine ambi-tions). Just as importantly, hypothetical insurance also qualifies some cases of option luck disadvantage.

---

[49] The discussion in this section overlaps with a longer evaluation of Dworkin's position on inheritance that I've provided elsewhere; see Halliday (2016a).

[50] On this point, see the exchange between Cohen (2004) and Dworkin (2004). For some further discussion of Cohen's criticisms of Dworkin, see Williams (2013).

Everything depends on what would be chosen by "the average person, acting prudently", when ignorant of how easy it will be to pursue his or her ambitions in actual society.[51] Plausibly, hypothetical insurance would be taken out against disadvantage due to physical disability and the inability to find employment. Hence, justice requires some degree of redistributive compensation by way of institutions such as universal healthcare and the welfare state, as well as certain adjustments to the social environment. (Wheelchair ramps in public places may also be justified on grounds of hypothetical insurance choices.) At the same time, free healthcare provision does not necessarily extend to injuries sustained as a result of wildly imprudent behaviour, and unemployment benefits will not be provided for people who can't bear to accept paid work outside of a very narrow set of professions for which there is little market demand or stiff competition. The average prudent person simply wouldn't purchase insurance against the difficulty of making a living from playing the bassoon.

This makes for a very complex and rich view of egalitarian justice that the above summary only partly captures. The hypothetical insurance approach is, among other things, an attempt to show how the ideas of equality, liberty, and individual responsibility can be theoretically integrated.[52] Justice is about arranging a society in which people are free to pursue their goals in ways that accommodate the needs and preferences of each other.[53] Brute and option luck act as important organizing ideas within this theory, but not as fundamental determinants of entitlements.[54] Much can be said about the application of these ideas to such topics as welfare state capitalism, education, and healthcare. What matters here are the implications for inheritance.

According to Dworkin, "bad inheritance luck" is just another hazard against which the average prudent individual would hypothetically

---

[51] Dworkin (2002: 111).

[52] Accordingly, Dworkin would hesitate to accept the idea that the demands of egalitarian justice can conflict with intuitive personal prerogatives as per the way this conflict was framed in 4.3.

[53] Dworkin is at greatest pains to distance himself from the luck-egalitarian project in his exchange with Samuel Scheffler. See Dworkin (2003) and Scheffler (2003, 2004).

[54] Dworkin (2003) stresses that his ideas about equal concern, the envy test, and hypothetical insurance do the fundamental theoretical work in *equality of resources*. He denies the "much more extreme" claim that egalitarian justice aims at eliminating inequalities deriving from differential brute luck.

purchase protection. A progressive inheritance tax, he suggests, might represent the premium that people would be willing to pay, so as to fund payouts to those whose inheritance luck has been bad.[55] Quite plausibly, Dworkin claims that the chief concern with unrestricted flows of inherited wealth is that they give rise to a system of social stratification, or class hierarchy. Hypothetical insurers are supposed to be motivated by this concern in particular:

> We should begin by asking why people would want [inheritance] insurance and what considerations would affect how much they would be willing to pay for it. The harm such insurance protects against is, we might say, relative rather than absolute. . . . Inheritance insurance would make sense, therefore, to guarantee not a higher standard of living in absolute terms, but against the different and distinct harm of occupying a lower tier in a class system—against that is, life in a community where others have much more money, and consequently more status and power, than they do and their children will.[56]

So Dworkin thinks that an inheritance tax models the hypothetical desire to insure against "class harm". This move gives Dworkin's approach to inheritance an added element of sophistication. But it creates problems for his commitment to hypothetical insurance. In effect, the quoted passage treats inheritance luck and 'class luck' as identical. But Dworkin's remarks in the surrounding text highlight the bad brute luck of simply having ungenerous, imprudent, or stingy parents. Such possibilities represent bad inheritance luck but not really bad *class* luck: it goes without saying that parental generosity needn't vary straightforwardly with class position, setting aside the question of what class position even amounts to (which Dworkin does not explain). Indeed, some of Dworkin's readers have formulated the problem of insuring against inheritance simply as a trade-off between seeking to benefit one's own children while seeking protection against one's own parents lacking ambition or ability to bequeath.[57] This interpretation shows how an inheritance tax might be

---

[55] This might suggest that, strictly speaking, Dworkin's approach requires a receipts tax rather than an estates tax. See Dworkin (2006: 117–18).

[56] Dworkin (2000: 348).

[57] This appears to be the reading adopted by Matthew Clayton, who writes, "Individuals will come to the choice they face with different views concerning the importance for them of giving to particular individuals who are close to them and of ensuring that they or their children receive monetary resources, and it is their view of the relative importance of these ambitions that will guide their insurance decisions" (2012: 109). Clayton recognizes Dworkin's preoccupation with class harm later in his discussion; my point here is merely to highlight

grounded in hypothetical insurance choices without relying on ideas about class hierarchy at all.

Dworkin's failure to properly separate inheritance luck from class luck remains a weakness in his short discussion. A second doubt emerges once it is asked whether, when applied to inheritance and bequest, the hypothetical insurance approach retains all the motivations behind its application to other contexts in which bad brute luck operates. Insurance is typically understood as a device of mitigation or compensation rather than prevention.[58] There might be nothing wrong with regarding inheritance tax as a device for removing or preventing class hierarchy, as Dworkin favours.[59] But there is something strange about treating inheritance tax as a model of insurance purchases.

I do not want to rely on the idea that insurance, hypothetical or otherwise, must be understood as providing protection in an ex post fashion. Protection in an ex ante form, such as a vaccination, might be justified by appealing to hypothetical choices made by people acting prudently in selecting which risks they would seek to protect themselves against. But the point of insurance, in any form, is to provide protection against the hazards imposed by some activity or investment that is, on balance, worth preserving. In the real world, we have travel insurance because we want to go travelling and car insurance because we want to drive cars. This general truth is even emphasized in Dworkin's original motivations for the hypothetical insurance approach, which draw on his views about the role of the market in the pursuit of liberal equality. The case for invoking hypothetical insurance relies partly on the claim that markets have some valuable features but also some undesirable ones that

the way in which protection against bad inheritance luck comes apart from protection against class harm.

[58] The idea that the hypothetical insurance approach mitigates rather than removes or neutralizes the effects of brute luck features in some other general interpretations of Dworkin's position. See for example Mason (2006: 150–2). My points in this paragraph also resemble a criticism that Colin Macleod (1998: ch. 4) has made about Dworkin's position on disability. As I read him, Macleod's point is roughly that many injustices suffered by persons with disabilities are features of their social environment rather than the resource distribution, including patterns of stereotyping and stigma. Macleod uses this point to suggest that the hypothetical insurance approach misconstrues certain types of disadvantage, partly by seeking to mitigate or compensate disadvantage rather than directly address underlying factors.

[59] Dworkin: "I must now say something about why equality of resources *would not generate* class distinctions" (2000: 346, emphasis added).

call for regulation. For example, some brute luck disadvantage is unavoidable given that some persons lack the sort of talents that can command job security, let alone decent income, in the labour market. One view is to regard the market as, therefore, a source of injustice. A pillar of Dworkin's liberal egalitarianism is his unwillingness to accept anything like this. He claims that "the idea of an economic market, as a device for setting prices for a vast variety of goods and services, must be at the center of any attractive development of equality of resources".[60] Among other things, markets promote a form of fairness by requiring people to spend more of their resources if they want to acquire something that other people want as well. The fact that some people lose out as a result of an unplanned market economy is part of the price we pay for the advantages (moral as well as economic) of markets as a mechanism of allocation.

So the hypothetical insurance approach draws much of its appeal from the idea that it addresses some inegalitarian side effects of the market processes that a liberal theory of justice requires.[61] The problem with applying the hypothetical insurance to the problem of inheritance is that class hierarchy is not like the market in having this very specific status of being a device that is necessary to the pursuit of justice while prone to create unjust side effects. As noted earlier in this chapter, inheritance is a system of asymmetric or gratuitous transfers rather than a system of *exchanges*. As such, it is not structurally part of any overall market order but something external to it.[62] The right response to class hierarchy is just to do what we can to get rid of it.[63] Because of this, it becomes less obvious why the defence of a substantial tax on inheritance should be grounded on hypothetical insurance choices, even granting that whether persons gain any inheritance is largely a matter of brute luck. The point of car insurance is that we want to keep driving while reducing the harms that might occur due to various risks. Seeking protection against such

---

[60] Dworkin (2000: 66).

[61] Hypothetical insurance has other theoretical advantages, not least the avoidance of having to find a purely 'metaphysical' way of separating brute luck from option luck. There may be ways of responding to this metaphysical problem without invoking hypothetical insurance; see Tan (2012: 93–4).

[62] This observation has been more fully developed against Dworkin by Michael Otsuka (2002, 2004); compare Williams (2004).

[63] I admit that this claim may be easier to accept on the view that class injustice involves oppression as well as low mobility, but I think it is correct on either view.

harms is better than just forgoing driving altogether. But class hierarchy is something we could presumably just do without.

More can be said about Dworkin's egalitarianism than I have offered here. His wider views on the regulation of property rights include a variety of other principles that operate separately from the hypothetical insurance approach. As I have argued elsewhere, these other elements of Dworkin's theory may have more promise than hypothetical insurance in specifying the foundations of an inheritance tax, even though Dworkin himself did not see this.[64] Although I have developed some opposition to Dworkin's actual position here, I should say that his diagnostic position on inheritance's role in creating a more hierarchical society has influenced the way I draw on ideas about segregation in the next two chapters. To that extent, the views I develop in this book are indebted to his relatively brief but well-motivated discussion of the problem.

---

[64] See Halliday (2016a: esp. 110–13).

# 5

# Inequality and Economic Segregation

## 5.1 Segregation and Equality

This chapter unpacks the idea of economic segregation, emphasizes its connection to egalitarian justice, and then applies it to the problem of inherited wealth. I will aim to focus on the way in which certain groups are able to monopolize superior life prospects for their members, thanks to their ability to retain wealth over time. This lays a foundation for later claims that diagnose the injustice of (unrestricted) inheritance in terms of the role it plays in enabling this sort of structural feature to endure. This view contrasts with the less plausible position that inheritance is unjust simply because its receipt is a matter of brute luck, thereby lumping together all inheritances irrespective of their size and regardless of what sort of social structures might be being maintained by the most large and enduring inheritance flows. This chapter is really a precursor to the next one: it works through some important concepts and claims so that the arguments of the next chapter, more directly concerned with the role of intergenerational wealth transfers, can be given a smoother presentation.

In the most abstract and formal sense, 'social segregation' occurs when social groups are cut off from each other. Colloquial uses of 'segregation' often encourage a geographical or spatial understanding. They bring to mind such things as ghettos and separate public bathrooms. The concept of segregation is sometimes associated with legislation that deliberately sought to keep groups apart in a hierarchical manner, as in the case of apartheid-era South Africa and the southern United States prior to the Civil Rights Act. Philosophers currently use the term in ways that include these geographic and legalized senses of segregation. But philosophers now use the term in ways that include more subtle instances of segregation, some of which are less visible and often not the product of legal design. Social segregation often has to do with institutional environments being largely closed off to certain groups, for example, the underrepresentation of women or nonwhites in particular professions. Economic segregation is a *type* of social segregation that occurs when groups have their boundaries defined by economic difference rather than by (e.g.) racial or religious difference. I emphasized in section 1.2 that it is an open question whether the concept of segregation, economic or otherwise, is normative. In other words, it is not immediately obvious whether social segregation constitutes some kind of injustice all by itself or might merely help to cause or maintain some injustice that can be independently condemned and might be capable of being caused by factors other than segregation. This chapter will develop the concept of economic segregation such that neither possibility is ruled out, but let me make a few remarks about the normative status of economic segregation in particular.

Economic segregation is very close to the more familiar ideas of social class hierarchy and social immobility. But it is distinct from both. In short, it is logically weaker than both of these ideas. Some prominent ideas associated with class, but not with economic segregation as I understand it, include the connection between class and the performance of certain sorts of work, the idea of identifying with one's class (and being proud of it) as partly constitutive of class as such, and the idea of an ongoing class struggle. Claims about economic segregation presuppose nothing like this. Therefore, while eliminating social class would entail the elimination of economic segregation, the reverse may not be true, given the potential for an analysis of social class to contain rather more than the mere idea of segregation. Saying anything more precise than this is made impossible by the sheer variety of meanings attaching to social class. The idea of social mobility is sometimes used interchangeably with claims about social class. Roughly speaking, social mobility is what increases with people's chances of moving between different economic levels over the course of their lifetimes. Strong conceptions of social mobility as a goal of social justice may amount to some sort of view about equality of opportunity. This is hard to say, since political philosophers do not use the term 'social mobility' nearly as often as social scientists do, making it harder to know which conception of egalitarian justice it should be most closely associated with. Again, I will not try to say anything precise about how social mobility could or should be understood. It is worth noting that mobility is typically understood in scalar terms, such that people are located at different income levels but are not otherwise subject to qualitative differences that give some added content to ideas of segregation or class. I suspect its relation to economic integration is something like the following: Generally speaking, an increase in economic integration should be correlated with an increase in social mobility. This is partly due to the fact that economic integration will reduce the extent to which certain groups are able to hoard opportunities and will make the most valuable social capital more evenly spread around different groups.[1] At the same time, a requirement to pursue economic integration is likely to prove less demanding than a requirement to pursue social mobility. While integration is likely to increase mobility, it is likely that something like maximal integration would be reached before maximal mobility would be reached. Nevertheless, the concepts are sufficiently similar that an argument for restricting inheritance on grounds of integration is probably compatible with a similar argument invoking social mobility. But again, a requirement to pursue economic integration is probably a less demanding requirement (if only slightly) than one of pursuing social mobility.

I think economic segregation becomes normative when it is understood in connection with luck egalitarian claims about choice and circumstance. Economic segregation can occur when wealthier groups are able to retain wealth and privilege over time. Being born into one of these groups, as might happen by being born to parents who have inherited, and with some expectation of inheriting oneself, provides one with brute luck advantage. When construed in this way, economic segregation is an injustice in itself because it is a subset of the ways in which distribution is dependent on personal circumstance rather than personal choices. This leaves it open as to which conception of egalitarian justice is ultimately fundamental, i.e. whether it is distribution's sensitivity to circumstance over choice that explains the injustice of economic segregation, or the other way round. The position I develop will be easier to accept if there is

---

[1] I allow, but am not troubled by, the fact that trying to spread valuable social capital more widely may destroy some of it. This is because, as noted above, some social capital is valuable only because it comprises knowledge known only to a few.

some possibility of viewing social and luck egalitarian views as somewhat complementary.[2]

Even if economic segregation is not unjust in itself, it may be a source of injustice, causally speaking. This claim might be defended by focusing on possible or expected social consequences of a situation in which members of different economic groups live lives cut off from each other. For example, it might be that the mutual isolation of economic groups has a detrimental effect on the way members perceive and treat nonmembers. Development of this concern draws further on ideas about social equality in which the idea of group difference is of much importance. This approach has some diagnostic promise. It has probably been powerful against patterns that inherited wealth has taken at certain points in history, and could do so again under certain conditions in the future. I will seek to develop it as far as I think it can be done, particularly in section 6.6.

I shall argue that the prospects for using economic segregation as a normative concept, staying close to ideas associated with luck egalitarianism, may prove more defensible than relying on causal claims about its role in triggering independent injustices. The former approach, though, may turn out to owe much to philosophical ideas about the value of equality more commonly associated with the latter type of approach.

## 5.2 Contemporary Social Egalitarianism: A Brief Sketch

To a first approximation, social egalitarians typically make two claims about the negative and positive goals of egalitarian justice.[3] The negative claim is that equality requires the elimination of oppressive social

---

[2] I am encouraged by recent work such as Lippert-Rasmussen (2015) and Vallentyne (2015). An earlier account of the disagreement between luck egalitarian and social egalitarian views is Anderson (2010b), to which these articles respond. Other attempts to explain how luck egalitarian views can accommodate social egalitarian concerns are Nicholas Barry (2006) and Anca Gheaus (forthcoming).

[3] I take this from Anderson (1999), which has been influential. Another important foundational statement of social egalitarianism is Miller (1998). Barry (2005: ch. 13) makes useful points pertinent to the place of social egalitarianism in this book. For a very up-to-date overview of the main ideas and key publications, see Lippert-Rasmussen (2016: ch. 7).

hierarchies. The positive claim is that such hierarchies need to be replaced by social arrangements that improve the quality of interpersonal relationships between citizens so as to create a genuine society of equals. Pursuit of the positive goal is thought to require a range of policy reforms relating to education, political participation, commerce, and so on.[4]

For social egalitarians, injustice either consists in or depends on relevant hierarchical relations between social groups.[5] This focus on group difference has considerable attraction, as it allows certain concepts to be brought into the diagnosis that might otherwise be hard to include. Much oppressive phenomena, such as stereotyping, stigmatization, and targeted violence, are hard to understand as isolated interactions between small numbers of persons, even though they are objectionable ultimately because of their impact on individuals' lives. For example, a person cannot be stereotyped without being identified as a member of a relatively large group, such as a gender, ethnicity, or religion. Stigmatization typically occurs in ways that depend on whole groups being seen as possessing some kind of vice or moral failing. Violence, though sometimes aimed arbitrarily at individuals, is also very often targeted at people because of their group membership. Injustices like genocide can, like other forms of persecution, be identified only with reference to some victimized group. Many of these cases are easy to see, but some are quite subtle. Sometimes groups may be made worse off by an enduring practice that appears not to harm anyone when viewed as a set of isolated actions. This is sometimes said of private schooling: nobody is made worse off when some specific set of parents select a school for their child, but, over time, the segregation of children in schools might contribute to an "accumulative harm" of whatever group is excluded or left behind.[6]

Social egalitarians typically deny that achieving equality involves the absolute equalization of any distributed thing. This owes much to a complaint made by Iris Marion Young, who thought preoccupation with material distribution "focuses largely on aspects of persons and

---

[4] A classic statement of social egalitarian ideas about democratic participation is Joshua Cohen (1997). White (2003) is an important defence of social egalitarian ideas about citizenship, including their implications for taxation and other areas of economic policy.

[5] On this point, social egalitarians have been much influenced by Iris Marion Young (1990: esp. ch. 2).

[6] See Mason (2015: 136–8) for discussion of this example.

ignores or rejects a theoretical place for bringing social structures into view".[7] Christian Schemmel claims that social egalitarianism avoids being "recipient oriented" because it focuses on how institutions treat people rather than what people have or haven't got.[8] In Samuel Scheffler's words, social equality is "a form of practice rather than a normative pattern of distribution".[9] Social egalitarians allow that the material distribution has important *indirect* significance. It may do much to cause and maintain oppression, even if complete distributive equalization is not necessary to stop this.[10] Social egalitarians have every reason to be interested in things like taxation as ways of addressing these causal relations, even if distribution is not what is of final importance.[11] Although social egalitarians have often been vehement in stressing opposition to luck egalitarianism, it is not obvious why the focus on groups, and relations between them, cannot be combined with a view that grants some importance to how luck operates on people's life prospects.

The social egalitarian project remains very much a work in progress and is subject to some unresolved internal disagreements. Much of this has to do with distinguishing oppressive from nonoppressive social hierarchies. A hierarchy of positions that can be sustained without group difference might be perfectly compatible with justice. Elizabeth Anderson claims that "some hierarchy of *office* is necessary for efficient production of goods and services".[12] An important question for social egalitarians is whether hierarchies of esteem might always mean there is some underclass that lacks self-respect.[13] These questions aside, the idea of equality as a relational rather than (purely) distributive ideal, as something essentially about group difference, is clear enough to work with.

[7]   Young (2011: 30).        [8]   See Schemmel (2012b).
[9]   Scheffler (2015: 31; see also the remarks at 37–8).
[10]   Anderson (1999) argues that social egalitarians should be concerned with the distribution of what Amartya Sen has called 'capabilities', and that justice requires that each person's shares reach a certain 'sufficiency' threshold. Anderson (2007) applies this view to the distribution of educational resources.
[11]   See Schemmel (2011) for more on how social egalitarians should care about distribution.
[12]   Anderson (2007: fn. 3). See also the similar remarks in Anderson (2010a: 108).
[13]   The distinction between esteem and respect was first raised in a philosophically egalitarian context by Runciman (1967). Also important is Darwall (1977). For a useful discussion of esteem hierarchies, see Fourie (2015). See also Lippert-Rasmussen (2015: 180–3) on the difficulty of distinguishing unjust from more benign social hierarchies.

## 5.3  Segregation and Nonfinancial Capital

Of central importance to *economic* segregation is the concept of nonfinancial capital.[14] Two types of such capital are most relevant. First, there is *social* capital. This consists in valuable knowledge and opportunities. Second there is *cultural* capital, which consists in certain behavioural norms or dispositions. Both forms of capital become concentrated within social groups that share them internally while withholding them from nonmembers. A group can, for example, use its social capital to 'hoard opportunities' for itself and to maintain networks of information from which nonmembers are excluded.[15] Displays of cultural capital help group members to identify each other and often shape the default modes of interaction between members and nonmembers. There is very good evidence that the sort of nonfinancial capital that a group can accumulate is strongly influenced by the wealth of that group: a group's financial capital (wealth and property) is a significant factor in shaping that group's nonfinancial capital.

When economic segregation occurs, one's group membership strongly affects what nonfinancial capital one can access. This includes such things as one's accent and dress sense, which may trigger positive and negative stereotyping. It also includes less obvious elements of nonfinancial capital, such as the ability to deal effectively with institutions. Importantly, the distribution of nonfinancial capital is subject to the strong prior influence of the distribution of *financial* capital such as wealth and property. In short, the most valuable nonfinancial capital clusters around wealth, but not always quickly. Much of the time, it cannot be directly redistributed by state institutions or anyone else. The speed (often slow) with which wealth attracts valuable nonfinancial capital provides a clue as to how inherited wealth may prove important. In particular, the significance of inheritance owes much to the way in which intergenerational transfers help groups maintain their accumulated nonfinancial capital, even if nonfinancial capital is not transferred

---

[14] These terms originate in the work of Pierre Bourdieu, which I won't make any extended comment on. In this section I rely on Anderson's (2010a: 31–8) discussion of nonfinancial capital, which she applies to the problem of racial segregation in the United States. See also Lareau (2011: 361–4). Both authors acknowledge Bourdieu's influence.

[15] For an influential sociological discussion of this idea, see Tilly (1998: esp. ch. 5).

down the generations simply as an automatic consequence of the transfer of wealth.

Segregation of any sort typically makes members of different groups increasingly ignorant about the realities of each other's experiences and situations. Such ignorance leads people to form alternative (i.e., inaccurate) explanations for each other's conduct and experiences. People's reliance on these misleading or bogus explanations is what often leads to stereotyping, stigma, and other oppressive relations between groups. Unemployed members of low-income groups often perform poorly in the labour market because they lack certain connections or access to information. This may lead them to be stereotyped as lazy or stupid by members of other groups, who possess superior social capital. This happens at least partly because wealthier individuals are prepared to discount the role of their nonfinancial capital in their labour market success, attributing it instead to effort and talent.[16] It bears emphasizing how powerful such stereotyping can be. For example, there is evidence that popular opposition to the welfare state in countries such as the United States is not, despite appearances, traceable to widespread moral opposition to the concept of state-provided assistance. Instead, sociologists report that most Americans support a welfare state in principle (i.e. support the idea of state assistance for people eager to find employment), but simply believe, as a matter of fact, that persons who actually receive welfare are too lazy to work.[17]

Cultural capital also plays an important role with respect to how members of segregated groups interact with each other. Again this is true of various forms of segregation besides the economic sort. An African American may adopt an appearance of looking 'tough' as part of a wholly defensive strategy against the threat of violent crime in the poorly policed district where he or she lives.[18] Members of other groups, who aren't in a position to appreciate the reasons for such strategies, interpret this behaviour as evidence of a threatening or violent disposition. This effect is most severe in societies where racial

---

[16] See Lareau (2011: 285–6).

[17] For a comprehensive discussion, see Gilens (1999). In this book, Gilens makes it clear that American attitudes towards the poor are partly reinforced by racial stereotyping. The demonization of the poor in Great Britain may be more 'purely' about economic position.

[18] I'm borrowing this example from Anderson (2010a: 35–6).

segregation is high, and more moderate in societies with high racial diversity but where different racial groups are well integrated. But similar stereotyping can occur when segregation is economic. A well-dressed man drinking wine at a picnic may be an alcoholic who subjects his spouse to domestic abuse. But a shabbily dressed man drinking extra-strong beer on a nearby park bench is the more likely to be stereotyped as the violent addict even if he is neither of these things. These examples show how the possession of relatively low-value non-financial capital, both social and cultural, plays a role in disadvantaging badly off groups.

The significance of nonfinancial capital, and its variable value, can be seen in many other cases. Some of these pertain to the distribution of certain scarce and often 'positional' goods. Places at an elite university and coveted internships are goods whose supply cannot be increased to meet demand, partly because their value depends on their being scarce in the first place.[19] One way of seeing off the competition for access to these goods lies in knowing how to distinguish oneself when applying to university or in having some personal connection with whoever makes decisions about hiring interns at the relevant organization. Here, wealth plays an important role. The most expensive secondary schools often have teaching staff who are alumni of elite universities.[20] They can advise students on how to sell themselves effectively when applying to top undergraduate programmes, including how to write a good personal statement or behave during an interview. Schools that can charge high fees also tend to be the best placed to provide extracurricular activities that 'distinguish' applicants (this is on top of the fact that the best secondary schools will also maximize a student's chance of gaining the best exam results or SAT scores). Wealth can attract valuable cultural capital, too. Being able to speak and dress in the right way is often crucial in getting taken seriously or being able to benefit from forms of positive stereotyping. How one speaks is partly a matter of dispositions formed as a result of one's group membership.

---

[19] The term 'positional good' was coined by Hirsch (1977). Despite its age, Hirsch's discussion of such goods remains relevant and somewhat underutilized by political philosophers.

[20] See Lareau (2011: 287–8).

In highlighting these cases, I do not mean to give the impression that there is a perfect correlation between long-term concentrations of wealth and concentrations of valuable nonfinancial capital. There are 'pockets' of valuable capital in some low socio-economic groups. These help explain why certain groups tend to be overrepresented in some professions due to opportunity hoarding, such as the existence of immigrant 'niches' in particular industries.[21] On the whole, groups with the most valuable nonfinancial capital tend to be groups possessing the most financial capital.

Social integration, in the sense relevant here, requires breaking up, or rendering inert, differential concentrations of nonfinancial capital.[22] This makes life prospects less dictated by group membership and goes some way to undermine whatever social hierarchy might be driven by group difference. But nonfinancial capital cannot be broken up directly. As I have said, it cannot be redistributed or confiscated. The state cannot tax accents, let alone spread them around, as it often can financial capital like money and property. An attempt to reduce the concentration of valuable nonfinancial capital into certain groups is more likely to be indirect. It might involve use of taxation to break up the wealth inequalities that enable it to be so concentrated. Another possibility, which might be more intuitively attractive, is to pursue institutional reform that strips some nonfinancial capital of its value (see 5.6).

## 5.4 Segregation and Luck: Some Theoretical Advantages

I argued in chapter 4 that it is hard to deliver a satisfactory egalitarian evaluation of inherited wealth while relying solely on some version of the choice/circumstance distinction. But a more plausible view may be reached if the focus is restricted to ways in which luck operates through group membership. If we take this approach, then we may be led to say that inherited wealth is unjust when it helps sustain the sort of group

---

[21] See Tilly (1998: ch. 5).

[22] Anderson claims that nonfinancial capital "designates assets that *constitute* one's socioeconomic status *or enable one* to achieve higher socioeconomic status" (2010a: 31, emphasis mine). These remarks suggest that differential concentrations of nonfinancial capital can be constitutive of unequal opportunity.

differences that make it a matter of luck which group one is born into. In terms of its implications, this is equivalent to a certain kind of restricted (i.e. logically weakened) luck egalitarianism. But it assigns essential explanatory work to a central organizing idea of social egalitarianism: economic group membership is a matter of brute luck but group differences are best understood in terms of wealth inequalities bringing about differential concentrations of nonfinancial capital in such a way as to have segregating effects on the population.

There are several advantages of integrating the basic luck egalitarian concern about choice and circumstance with the social egalitarian concern that injustice is about group difference. One is that this approach provides a principled justification for discounting the moral significance of very small inheritances. I noted earlier that a serious challenge to luck egalitarianism is in getting a qualitative principle of justice to diagnose injustices that are essentially sensitive to quantitative considerations, i.e. that big inheritance flows matter in ways that small transfers do not. If choice and circumstance are understood as forces that operate on an individual's life prospects, in abstraction from any sort of social structure to which they are reducible, then *all* inheritances will be treated alike. Hence, naïve luck egalitarians will struggle to escape the conclusion that all inheritance is unjust. The view I have advanced here is that inheritance is unjust when the flow of intergenerational transfers does enough to help maintain economic segregation. But not all inheritance does this. Very small inheritances are simply not significant enough at attracting nonfinancial capital to contribute to any significant degree of economic segregation. This is true even if small inheritances count as instances where the material distribution is influenced by individuals' brute luck. I want to stress that the focus is being shifted here from the brute luck of receiving any sort of inheritance at all to the brute luck of being born into an economic group whose nonfinancial capital is maintained partly by relatively large flows of inherited wealth. This is what makes it possible to ward off counterexamples that involve isolated cases of small inheritances that are disconnected from the larger forces working to maintain segregation and group differences. It is notable that many of the alleged counterexamples to luck egalitarianism seek to expose implications that may not exist if luck egalitarianism were restricted so that it attached significance only to inequalities that depend on the brute luck of group membership.

Another influential criticism of luck egalitarianism is that it has the wrong focus. The objection here is that the preoccupation with the choice/circumstance distinction makes for a theory of justice that is focused on individuals too much in abstraction from the social structures through which they interact with each other. This is partly what is conveyed by the earlier quote from Young about the importance of social structures, which luck egalitarians allegedly ignore. Recent growth in the popularity of social egalitarianism owes much to dissatisfaction with this supposed shortcoming of the luck egalitarian project.[23] In the words of Scheffler, a luck egalitarian theory suffers from being an "administrative" conception of justice, as if all that matters is an assessment of each individual's separate holdings, with redistributive adjustments made when appropriate to the individual under examination.[24] These criteria are atomistic in the sense that they are applied to persons in isolation from each other and without consideration of their institutional background. This criticism has force largely because the effects of brute luck have not normally been articulated in terms of group membership. There is no reason, however, why group membership cannot count as an instance of brute luck. This undermines the accusation that a concern about luck is atomistic, individualistic, or asocial.

There may be some further advantages in restricting luck egalitarianism in ways associated with group difference. In particular, it may help efforts to show that the choice/circumstance distinction is not metaphysically obscure, since there is nothing particularly obscure about the existence of group membership or the existence and possession of non-financial capital such as accents, hobbies, or useful social connections.[25] I will not push these points, partly because they do not have much to do with my main agenda of applying luck egalitarianism to the problem of inherited wealth.

---

[23] See especially the discussions in Anderson (1999) and Scheffler (2003), both of which defend social egalitarianism somewhat indirectly, in part based on objections to luck egalitarianism and in part as a more plausible way of building on the Rawlsian concerns about moral arbitrariness presented earlier. Wolff (1998) has had similar influence, but compare Wolff (2010).

[24] See the remarks at Scheffler (2003: 37). These claims occur as part of a general criticism of luck egalitarianism as Scheffler understands it, though the "administrative" objection is aimed at Dworkin's egalitarianism.

[25] For more discussion of the metaphysical objection, see Tan (2012: 136–41).

# 5.5 Economic Segregation and Unjust Consequences

I have so far emphasized the way in which social segregation, and economic segregation in particular, can be regarded as *constituting* a certain sort of injustice. But the more familiar social egalitarian diagnosis of what is unjust about segregation emphasizes its objectionable social consequences. Most relevant here are the psychological effects that segregation has on individuals. These bear heavily on how members of segregated groups perceive and interact with each other. I have already mentioned the concern that economic segregation makes people ignorant about the situation faced by persons at other economic levels. When people live segregated lives, they will become more ignorant of important details concerning each other's circumstances. This is unjust because of its consequences for how people treat each other and how institutions and political narratives begin to internalize these norms of treatment. This is a different way of motivating a concern about segregation and is worthy of separate comment.

Clearly, the claim that social segregation causes certain independent injustices is an empirical hypothesis rather than a conceptual truth. That said, it is supported by good evidence where certain sorts of social segregation are concerned. Some of this evidence appears to involve cases of economic segregation. There is some evidence that wealthy individuals exhibit higher levels of narcissism and lower levels of compassion than less wealthy individuals.[26] To use one more specific example, a recent study of attitudes among high-paid lawyers and bankers in London revealed a startling combination of ignorance about the financial and social circumstances of the poor, accompanied by forthright views about why the poor have only themselves to blame and why the economic status quo remains easy to justify and in any case impossible to change.[27] The demonization of poor and unemployed people is a core symptom of economic segregation.[28] By 'demonization' I have in mind extreme forms of stereotyping whereby poor people are variously

---

[26] See for example Piff (2014) and Stellar et al. (2012).

[27] See Toynbee & Walker (2008: ch. 1). Dorling (2015) provides a more lengthy account of this phenomenon and a range of closely related symptoms of inequality in the UK.

[28] For example, the phenomenon of 'chavs' in Great Britain. On this see Jones (2012).

portrayed as stupid, lazy, or otherwise immoral. These attributions are often used to justify harsh socio-economic reforms, such as cuts to welfare programmes and other policies that generally disempower poor people in the labour market while undermining their privacy and sense of dignity.[29] Demonization is compounded by related ways in which segregation undermines democracy, or even effective governance. Persons from wealthier families are always going to have better chances of gaining access to coveted careers. These include, among other things, jobs with substantial levels of influence, such as senior roles in business, politics, the media, and government bureaucracy. The general point to be made here is that, when these roles become disproportionately occupied by members of a segregated elite, they will be occupied by persons whose competence, including their capacity to empathize with fellow citizens, is importantly limited.[30]

Demonization narratives usually overlook the facts about the situations in which people actually find themselves. The London lawyers and bankers mentioned above greatly overestimated the salaries attached to low-income jobs. They also overestimated the degree of material support provided by the welfare state. Such beliefs make it much easier to interpret long-term unemployment and financial misfortune as attributable to personal failings rather than the influence of uncontrollable external factors.[31] There is evidence the poor are often more rational than the financially better off when it comes to financial management. For one thing, they usually have a better sense of the opportunity cost attached to small purchases.[32] A poor person may rationally decline paid employment even though it pays better than what he or she will receive by remaining on state welfare: the job might be temporary and, when it ends, inefficient state bureaucracy may take weeks to start providing welfare payments again, meaning that taking the job is a net loss. The supposedly immoral behaviour of poor people is often not relevantly

---

[29] For more on the significance of this, see Wolff (1998).

[30] Such considerations have influenced social egalitarian perspectives on education. Anderson (2007) makes explicit the idea of educating elites in ways that make them properly suited to social roles in which they will need to serve less privileged members of society. Satz (2007) defends a similar view.

[31] The same group displayed evidence of negative stereotyping of the poor; see Toynbee & Walker (2008: ch. 1).

[32] See the excellent discussions of the evidence in Mullainathan & Shafir (2013: esp. 88–90).

different from the conduct of wealthier people. Instead it is just interpreted differently. To pick one example, poor parents who stay at home
to raise children are often classed as 'work shy'. Wealthier parents who
do the same are often lauded, or at least tolerated, on grounds that they
are trying to give their children a better upbringing. And yet the only
difference may be that the costs are met by the paid labour of the other
partner rather than (partly) by the state. Even if this difference is morally
significant, it does not justify the discrepant attribution of vice and
virtue. Here we have an instance of what psychologists call 'attribution
bias', where praise or blame is attributed according to whether the person
being evaluated is a member of the evaluator's own group or a group
from which he or she is segregated. The important point is that all of
these findings cannot simply be blamed on the statistical presence of
economic inequality, set apart from the facts about group difference and
segregation.

So long as economic segregation remains, demonization narratives
will occur more readily. Nonpoor members of the electorate will be
unlikely to vote for policies that seek to support rather than 'punish'
poorer members of society. Politicians will seek to exploit demonization
narratives in order to win votes for policies that suit them and will often
be subject to the same epistemic failings as everyone else (perhaps worse,
given that political careers are becoming increasingly difficult to embark
on for anyone who is not relatively wealthy and endowed with excellent
social capital). Bureaucrats who design policies relating to employment,
education, and healthcare will continue to draw up plans influenced by
the conception of poor people as lazy, stupid, and immoral. The consequences are often extremely severe, particularly with respect to institutions that have the power to confer substantial burdens, such as the
criminal justice system. Crimes that tend to be committed mainly by
poor people are often subject to much harsher sentencing than crimes
committed mainly by members of higher income groups.[33]

Reflection on any of these cases helps make it clear that social integration is typically a positive-sum game.[34] Clearly the poor would be
better off if they weren't demonized. But wealthier persons would benefit,

---

[33] For a comprehensive discussion, see Reiman & Leighton (2010).
[34] Anderson stresses the way in which integration increases everyone's prospects for a
wider set of rewarding relations with others (2012: 2).

too, if they were less prone to negatively stereotype their fellow citizens. Economic integration might in some cases address oppression that falls on people at higher income levels. Women from higher income levels might become less reluctant to report domestic violence if not for prevailing attitudes that associate these harms with uneducated couples living in relative poverty. Revealing oneself as a victim of domestic abuse undermines the life narrative of the ideal middle-class woman as someone whose education and professional success should prevent the 'mistake' of choosing a violent partner. This can make it difficult for abused women to reveal their situation to friends and family as well as the authorities.[35]

I have spent most of this section reproducing what other scholars have discovered about the sad character of ways in which people at different economic levels relate to each other, and how this is correlated with high levels of intergroup ignorance. It might be noted that the sorts of policies and attitudes highlighted here are not *always* the result of epistemic differences and nothing more. Consequently, integration, assuming some account can be given of what it requires, may not be a quick fix. Disagreement about whether to cut the welfare state is partly a matter of normative disagreement and partly about empirical beliefs about economic systems that may be based on considerations that would persist in an integrated society. It is also important to note that epistemic position and political conviction still interact: segregation might enable confirmation bias if it helps insulate individuals from certain data that put pressure on their political convictions. Individuals in the Toynbee and Walker study simply didn't realize how high their own incomes were above the average and how low welfare payments actually were in absolute terms. Revision of this belief may have affected their willingness to support welfare cuts without actually changing their political principles. This shows that the possession of empirical knowledge will often work to constrain one's political principles, helping to indicate when they recommend exceptions on their own terms.

And of course it remains a very open question whether these possible consequences of economic segregation could be mitigated or pre-empted by taxing inherited wealth, and whether they can really be blamed on

---

[35] For a detailed and revealing discussion of some of these cases, see Weitzman (2000).

inheritance flows in the first place. Before grappling with this, I'll try to clarify the significance of economic segregation further by commenting on how hard it might be to address economic segregation through other sorts of institutional reform.

## 5.6  The Robustness of Economic Segregation: Taxation versus Alternative Types of Institutional Reform

Much injustice has to do with the difficulties of gaining access to certain opportunities and institutions without possessing wealth. Rather than attack the wealth distribution, or any way in which it replicates itself through intergenerational transfers, something could be done to make institutional access less dependent in the first place on wealth possession. Taxation, after all, is not the only instrument possessed by the state.

What is more, some experts on taxation call into question its potential as a device through which greater equality might be pursued. Here, for example, is the economist Frank William Taussig:

> Progressive taxation, so far as it aims to correct unjustified inequalities, evidently deals with results, not causes. It is obviously better to go to the root of the matter, and to deal with the causes. Much the more effective and promising way of reform is to promote the mitigation of inequality in other ways—by equalization of opportunity through widespread facilities for rational education, by the control of monopoly industries, by the removal of the conditions which make possible illegitimate profits. Progressive taxation, which deals with income (or property) solely according to size...is less discriminating and also less effective in reaching the ultimate goal than the various other ways of spreading material welfare.[36]

Taussig is considering the causal relation between taxation and economic or 'distributive' inequality. He doubts that taxation is the best way to tackle economic inequality and may not have been disposed to say

---

[36] Taussig (1921: 514). This quotation is taken from a long and detailed discussion of taxation and inequality. Taussig did regard inherited wealth as a major cause of inequality's replication, as is clear from earlier passages (265–76). Later passages show that he regarded the case for progressive inheritance tax as morally stronger than for progressive income tax (536). Nevertheless, his claim about the post hoc character of taxation has been influential; see for example the approval it receives in Blum and Kalven's discussion of how taxation "deals with effects and not causes" (1952: 497).

similar things about its impact on social inequality or group difference. But it is tempting to agree with a generalized version of Taussig's claim, namely, that it would be better to try to prevent social *or* distributive inequality than to cure it, through tax reform, after some damage has already been done. I shall aim to defend the causal power of tax reform, at least inheritance tax reform, in the next chapter. In the meantime, I shall attempt to show that the effectiveness of alternative institutional reforms in combatting economic segregation is something that can also be called into question.

It is true that regulating institutions such as schools, universities, and major employers could do much to integrate people at different economic levels, perhaps through policies such as affirmative action and free access to higher education and forms of training. Done well, changes like these might integrate otherwise segregated groups even if they do not target the wealth distribution. Strategies of institutional reform have been well defended, sometimes drawing heavily on social egalitarian foundations, as ways of combatting the serious racial segregation that currently endures in the United States.[37]

There is good sociological evidence that, even when institutions are made open to people from different and even segregated economic levels, internal economic segregation still persists. Universities are a particularly well-studied case.[38] Looking at US campuses that admit students across a wide range of economic levels, studies report very strong patterns of segregation that develop as students progress through their university careers. On many campuses, student housing is differentially priced. Consequently, students from different economic levels will tend to cluster in different accommodation buildings. In terms of academic course selection, poorer students are driven towards degree programmes whose career prospects do not depend on social capital and the ability to take unpaid internships. These are clear ways in which inequality of opportunity persists in spite of what is supposed to be equality of access to an institution. Profound variation in the ability to afford social

---

[37] Here again I have in mind Anderson (2012). Fabian Schuppert (2015: 118–20) has summarized this general idea with respect to the role of wealth inequalities in undermining civic equality.

[38] See especially the lengthy recent treatments in Armstrong & Hamilton (2013) and Stuber (2011).

participation segregates further, as poorer students are often left socially isolated. Generalizing, the evidence suggests that wealth has a strong sorting effect within institutions whose members come from different income groups. Of course, institutional reform can be pursued with the aim of reducing this effect. The authors of the university study recommend, for example, that universities cease trying to instrumentalize the revenue potential in offering expensive housing options.

In the case of higher education, patterns of segregation are already in place prior to university enrolment. Some students are already anxious that, by entering university, they are dabbling in a role that is 'above their station'.[39] In addition, the ability of wealthier students to take on things like unpaid internships is not something that could even be addressed by regulating universities directly. This leaves room for proposals about labour market regulation, such as banning unpaid internships so that poorer students are not left behind in the race for work experience. While this may make a difference, wealth will still find ways to have an impact. For example, there is evidence that success in gaining selection to various graduate professions is linked to being able to purchase expensive business attire to wear in an interview—an arms race in suits.[40] Again, this might motivate legislation about hiring practices (e.g. prohibitions on face-to-face interviews). Such proposals, however, risk magnifying other distortions known to influence hiring decisions, such as stereotyping people based on their names, which can indicate membership of an ethnic group or nationality.[41] As legislation piles up, other problems begin to accumulate, such as the burdens imposed on the courts.

Let me provide one other example. Attempts to promote geographical integration in cities with large distributive inequalities involve the formation of planning laws that require developers of luxury apartment buildings to include some number of affordable housing units. Developers have managed to comply with this law by creating separate entrance lobbies for wealthier and poorer residents. Occupants of the expensive units enter and leave through a luxurious lobby at the front of the building, while tenants in affordable units are required to use an entrance

---

[39] See Crompton (2008: 130). See also Lareau (2011: 291–4).
[40] I owe this example to Frank (2008).
[41] See for example King et al. (2006).

down a side or back alley, often where the building's rubbish gets dumped. This is a very recent practice and I don't believe social scientists have yet written on it.[42] But further studies are not needed for the significance of the case to be clear. Apart from the fact that the integration doesn't really occur (residents at different economic levels simply do not share the same space), there are clearly oppressive effects of requiring one group of residents to literally leave the building through the same exit as the garbage. Apart from being stigmatizing, a requirement to use a dimly lit alley may expose poorer residents to physical dangers in many cities. Apart from anything else, the practice is disrespectful. Publicly, developers defend it on grounds that the wealthier tenants pay fees for the superior facilities in their lobby, like a concierge. But whatever the intentions, the case exemplifies the way in which an attempt to achieve economic integration through focused legislation can severely backfire.

To be clear, I am not saying that institutional reform is always a waste of time. The examples I have selected may represent exceptional cases. Institutional reform may be a much better way than taxation when there is an opportunity to target a relatively specific injustice, such as finding ways to help higher-income women report domestic abuse. This might be hard to do, but economic segregation is not the root cause of domestic violence in any case, rather something that compounds the seriousness of this problem. It would certainly be implausible to think that domestic violence could ever be adequately addressed through taxation. But this leaves room for the possibility that segregation in general might yet be addressed by taxing the movement of wealth that enables segregation through the replication of economic inequality over time. Similar remarks might apply to problems like campaign expenditure in electoral politics and access to legal representation in criminal justice systems. Both are examples wherein wealth inequalities threaten to exercise undue influence on an important institution, but much may be achieved by reforming the institution (caps on campaign spending and legal aid for poor defendants) even if the wealth inequalities are left untouched.

To summarize: It is at least *often* true that wealth has a way of getting around attempts to make it less crucial in determining the life

---

[42] There has, however, been some detailed media coverage: H. Osborne, "Poor Doors: The Segregation of London's Inner City Flat Dwellers," *The Guardian*, accessed 25 July 2014.

prospects of those who do and do not possess much of it. This is enough to support continued effort to target the wealth distribution more directly, principally through taxation. Again, I concede the hazards of generalizing from a small number of examples. But my main claim here is not very radical. It should not be surprising that economic segregation is hard to avoid, once inequality of wealth becomes good at replicating itself down the generations. The ways in which wealth can impact on institutions, social conventions, and other practices is simply so broad. This is quite apart from more general objections that a focus on institutional reform risks idealizing institutions and idealizing governments in their abilities to regulate them (e.g. to create legislation with no loopholes). Trying to regulate institutions in such a fine-grained way will be massively labour-intensive and may often be unintentionally intrusive both to individuals and to institutions' own agendas. Ultimately, there is no reason why the problems being discussed here must be solved wholly through taxation or wholly through alternatives. The fact that there are reasons to doubt that alternatives can work by themselves is enough to motivate paying attention to taxation, even if there will be similar doubt as to whether it can solve the same problems all by itself.

# 6

# Inheritance and the Intergenerational Replication of Inequality

## 6.1 Some Doubts

This chapter defends the claim that intergenerational wealth transfers help group inequality to replicate itself from one generation to the next. More specifically, it defends the claim that inheritance flows have a cumulative impact on the ability of wealthy groups to retain valuable nonfinancial capital over time in ways that enable economic segregation to endure. This supports the conclusion that justice requires restricting the set of intergenerational wealth transfers to such an extent that this impact will be reduced.

The main task is to get clear on what sort of causal claims need to be made plausible. Two claims are particularly important: (1) Flows of inherited wealth help make group membership (in particular, being born into a wealthy family or class) an important determinant of one's life prospects, and (2) flows of inherited wealth account for unjustly oppressive consequences of such group differences. Claim (1) asserts that inheritance maintains conditions of economic segregation, with such conditions being constitutive of injustice. Claim (2) asserts that inheritance maintains group segregation in perhaps a less specific sense, but which is robustly correlated with certain specific injustices. In this way, claims (1) and (2) parallel the claims about the unjustness of segregation laid out more fully at the beginning of chapter 5. It is not the case that both claims need to be true. A case for taxing inherited wealth depends on at least one of them being true.

Evidence for the intergenerational *replication* of economic inequality is quite strong. This is just to say that inequality *actually* replicates itself down family lines, regardless of whether this is being caused by wealth transfers or anything else. Inequality's replication extends over multiple generations rather than just from parents to children. Sociologists have begun to talk of the 'grandparent effect' when observing that a person's lifetime income and wealth can be better predicted by his or her family's wealth two generations before than by the wealth of his or her parents.[1] This suggests that while the wealth of one generation will influence that of later ones, it may do so only slowly. More recently, data on the frequency of surnames at different social levels has indicated that families with high status tend to keep it for many generations.[2] But again, it needs to be emphasized that however strong this evidence is, it is only evidence that inequality's replication *actually* occurs and that economic segregation is durable over time. The evidence is not decisive in showing that the primary causal work is being done by wealth transfers.

Offhand, it may sound strange to warn against blaming inequality's replication on inherited wealth. It may seem natural, even obvious, to say that distributive inequality gets replicated down the generations because actual wealth and property are being *passed* down the generations. But here there is a danger of making a straightforward fallacy: inequality's intergenerational replication, and the presence of intergenerational wealth transfers within the better-off family lines, may simply be joint effects of some prior set of mechanisms that are simply less visible. Perhaps the biggest mistake one could make about inherited wealth is to decide that, just because it *occurs*, we can infer that it is also doing the primary causal work with respect to the segregating consequences of inequality's replication. The work might, instead, be being done by a range of other factors, principally the practices of parents that can occur without wealth transfer to children, and the impact of institutions, such as schools. Unfortunately, contemporary social science has produced relatively little work aimed at directly *comparing* the effect of wealth transfers with the effect of other factors. Sociologists have described inherited wealth as "a sociological lacuna"[3] and have asserted that "the sociology of inheritance is only in its infancy".[4] Fortunately, however, considerable sociological scholarship has looked at the other factors by

---

[1]  See for example Chan & Boliver (2013); Pfeffer (2014).    [2]  Clark (2014).
[3]  McNamee & Miller (1989).    [4]  Beckert (2008: vii).

themselves and drawn some important conclusions. It is possible to use this work to draw some plausible conclusions about the role being played by inherited wealth alongside such other mechanisms.

There are also independent reasons to doubt the causal power of inherited wealth in maintaining economic segregation down the generations. The simple fact here is that inheritance typically shows up too late in the life of its beneficiary to make a great difference to his or her social position.[5] In the feudal era critiqued by the early liberals of chapter 2, inheritance of good quality land may have been necessary and sufficient to gain access to high social status. But things have changed.[6] Whatever social hierarchy is around nowadays lacks the binary character of society's pre-industrial division into aristocrats and landless peasants or artisans. Such practices are typically enacted *before* parents bequeath any wealth and perhaps before any large *inter vivos* transfers. Windfalls of cash and property usually improve a recipient's quality of life and may have some effect on his or her social status thereafter. But inheritance or gifts received during adulthood rarely change one's education or other elements of social and cultural capital. These days, parents have many ways of conferring distributive advantage and social position onto their offspring. Given the presence of these other practices, inheritance may prove to be sociologically inert.

One shortcoming of moralized discussions of inheritance and social inequality in the early twentieth century was a failure to grapple with precisely this sort of doubt. One example worth mentioning is the work of R. H. Tawney, who had a vehemently egalitarian complaint about inheritance in Great Britain. Tawney regarded long-running inheritance flows as a principal element of the economic conditions driving class hierarchies, although he also attached causal significance to other factors, such as private education. He described inheritance as an "overwhelming" cause of "hereditary" inequality of status. In this way he follows some of his predecessors in Britain during the eighteenth and nineteenth centuries. Tawney favoured aggressive levels of inheritance tax, including Rignano-type schemes, which Tawney thought powerful enough to ensure that "the social poison of inheritance would largely

---

[5] The increasingly late arrival of inheritance, given trends towards greater longevity, is pointed out by Ackerman & Alstott (1999: 36).

[6] See Langbein (1988).

be neutralized".[7] All of this makes it clear that Tawney believed that class hierarchy remained entrenched due to the ability of economic or distributive inequality to reproduce itself from one generation to the next. Tawney's work is an important milestone in the early development of social egalitarian theorizing. Indeed, a patient reader can find some endorsement of almost all the current tenets of social egalitarianism at some point in Tawney's writings.[8] Although I am highlighting one weakness here, I would like to register a more general appreciation of what his work has to offer, though I lack space to discuss it at length.[9]

Tawney's references to inheritance merely seem to assume that, because inheritance moves *wealth* from one generation to the next, it must also account for the transmission of status down the generations, as if the replication of social hierarchy is not already being caused by something else. Contemporary philosophers sometimes say similar things.[10] While Tawney did explicitly identify the *presence* of other mechanisms, such as differential access to education, he didn't venture any inquiry into the relative priorities of these mechanisms. Most charitably, since Tawney was not a professional philosopher, he perhaps regarded these complexities about causation as too subtle for the polemic and accessible prose style he wanted for his political writings. But similar points apply to the perspective taken on inheritance in more scholarly work of this period. Here, again, is Frank William Taussig:

Environment and opportunity have already been considered. . . . More important, however, is the direct inheritance of property. Its influence is enormous. . . . It

---

[7] All quotes in this paragraph occur at Tawney (1931: 149–50).

[8] These include Tawney's claims that social hierarchies involve relations between groups rather than individuals (1931: 58; compare Anderson [2012]); that status hierarchies militate against participatory democracy (1931: 90, 196–7; compare Anderson [1999]); that education should aim at the integration of different socio-economic groups (1931: 144; compare Anderson [2007] and Satz [2007]); that making wealth the basis of esteem can crowd out a spirit of public service (1921: 33–6; compare Anderson [2012]); that the injustice of certain group hierarchies is compatible with hierarchical divisions of labour (1931: 71, 112–13, 150; compare Anderson [2007: fn. 3] but note the disagreement with Young [1990: ch. 7]). At other points, Tawney drifts into what sounds like the language of contemporary luck egalitarianism; see for example his remarks on private education at (1931: 145).

[9] Tawney is rarely discussed by contemporary political philosophers, but see White (2003: 180) and, for a lengthier appraisal, Jonathan Wolff (2015).

[10] Consider, for example, Thomas Nagel's remarks on the need for inheritance taxes to prevent class hierarchy enabled by dynastic wealth (2009: 117). I offer some reaction to Nagel's claims below.

serves also to strengthen all the lines of social stratification, and to reinforce the influences of custom and habit. Persons who inherit property also inherit opportunity. They have a better start, a more stimulating environment, a higher ambition. They are likely to secure higher incomes, and to preserve a higher standard of living by late marriage and fewer offspring. The institution of inheritance promotes social stratification thru its indirect effects not less than thru its direct.[11]

These remarks suggest that social egalitarian thinking was present in influential American work on taxation and inequality and that Tawney's complaints about the class system were not just a British concern. Unfortunately, though, Taussig shares Tawney's failure to ask whether the intergenerational transfers are really doing the causal work, or whether they are a symptom of whatever other mechanism is keeping the relevant social stratification alive. He speaks of inheritance as determining one's "start" in life, which misrepresents the fact that inheritance typically comes years later than life's actual start. Taussig gives no argument for why inheritance is "more important" than other elements of a person's "environment" early in life.

Similar failures to get clear on the causation show up in more recent work, too. Charles Tilly's important work on segregation connects inheritance with the practice of "opportunity hoarding". This occurs when social capital becomes highly concentrated in groups that are then able to exclude nonmembers from accessing certain social roles that they keep for their own members. Tilly has advanced our understanding of how social capital concentrates within groups. But he falls short when he suggests that inherited wealth is "central" to the ability of wealthy groups to hoard opportunities for their children.[12] Once again, this is because he does not explain how inheritance manages to enable such hoarding given that children will often receive it much later in life than their enjoyment of opportunities that have *already* been hoarded for them through other practices. Indeed, much of Tilly's work illuminates the way in which economically poor migrant populations hoard opportunities as part of an economic niche, such as restaurants. This strongly suggests that the ability of a group to internalize large intergenerational wealth transfers is not a necessary condition for the accumulation or 'hoarding' of that group's nonfinancial capital over time.

---

[11] Taussig (1921: 266).      [12] See Tilly (1998: 155–6).

Political philosophers, too, often take it for granted that when a society becomes subject to hereditary class distinctions, it is wealth transfers that do the causal work. Thomas Nagel, for example, claims that "if the class of those who are very rich by inheritance becomes significantly larger and richer, it will make the society much more inegalitarian in atmosphere". He adds that "the modification of inherited wealth is one place where [society] can exert some influence" and that an inheritance tax "would put a significant break on the runaway accumulation of hereditary fortunes".[13] Nagel's added claims may be true, but he does not explain why the existence of wealth transfers accounts for the truth of his first claim. It could be that intergenerational wealth transfers cause the endurance of class hierarchy and its unjust impact on "atmosphere". But it could be that the transfers and the hierarchy are the joint effect of something else.

These doubts are serious, and it is unfortunate that they have been suppressed, over the years, by naïve claims about the causal power of inheritance in influential work on wealth inequalities and taxation. The good news is that something can be done to address these doubts. In chapter 1, I observed that much work in political philosophy works with a simplified 'snapshot' conception of material distributions, as if the persons in them are causally isolated from the persons up and down their family lines. The reality is that earlier distributions tend to affect later ones as generations of members come and go. Taking the diachronic nature of the wealth distribution seriously is to introduce a complexity that the snapshot approach sets aside. But it also introduces a resource: it allows us to take seriously the more delayed effects of wealth transfers.

I will develop two more focused arguments in this chapter that exploit this strategy. Both of these arguments *rely* on the way in which inheritance is very often received too late in life to make a difference to the social position of its immediate beneficiary. The most crucial claim that enables the assignment of causal priority to inheritance flows is that they have important cumulative effects. The two arguments deal with two different categories of cumulative effect. The first is centred around the claim that inherited wealth provides recipients with the financial

---

[13] Nagel (2009: 117–18).

resources to confer the most valuable competitive advantages on their own children. In other words, whatever mechanisms appear to pre-empt inheritance are themselves enabled or modified by inheritance further up the family tree. The second argument is centred around the distinct claim that receipt of inheritance can, in the long run, attract its own sort of valuable social and cultural capital. This is the sort of status associated with 'good breeding' or having come from old money. In both cases, inheritance stands to advance the social position of its beneficiaries' offspring more than that of the beneficiaries themselves. The first argument retains a commitment to the choice/circumstance distinction, whereas the second is an attempt to explore a more purely social egalitarian evaluation of inheritance.

Setting up these arguments requires careful attention to the various mechanisms, besides wealth transfer, with which parents confer advantage on their children. Therefore, I am going to comment on the parental conferral of advantage at some length, even though I will not be making any really new observations about it. Thankfully, there is much excellent work, both in political philosophy and in the social sciences, on which I can draw.

## 6.2 Parental Conferral of Advantage

One straightforward way in which parents can benefit their children is by transferring wealth and property to them. This includes bequests (i.e. posthumous wealth transfers), but also gifts, trusts, loans with generous conditions, and so on.[14] But parents routinely benefit their children in ways not involving any sort of formal wealth transfer. These include familiar practices, such as reading to one's children, helping them with

---

[14] I have said nothing at all about trusts in this book. This is regrettable, since trusts play an important role in allowing very rich families to preserve wealth with their passing of generations. They also raise certain questions about the kind of posthumous control they grant to those who set them up, compared to standard wealth transfers, where a donor has little say as to what the recipient does with what he or she is given. In jurisdictions that permit them, the law surrounding trusts is rather complex. For more discussion of US law, see Lawrence Friedman (2009: chs. 6 & 7) and also Goodwin (2010) on how trusts are essentially a device for preserving family wealth. From a moral point of view, I am inclined to say that trusts are quite objectionable, at least when they are set up to benefit individual adult heirs rather than (say) support a charitable organization or orphaned children. But I have not been able to properly develop any such claim in this book.

schoolwork, exposing them to forms of learning and culture, giving specific and sometimes expert advice, and enhancing their social and intellectual confidence through various forms of encouragement, love, and affection. I will speak of such practices as 'informal' so as to distinguish them from wealth transfers. As I shall later emphasize, many informal conferrals of advantage depend on, or become most effective when, parents also purchase some accompanying good or service, even if no money is actually transferred to a child. One notable feature of informal conferral of advantage is that it tends to occur mainly, or has its greatest impact, during the years before a child reaches adulthood. Informal practices such as those listed above are deeply embedded in the internal workings of family life. As Anne Alstott has noted, "the family *itself* forms part of the structures of inheritance that determine what children receive from their elders".[15] Certainly these informal and familiar practices have great importance. They may even act as enabling conditions for the benefits gained by formal wealth transfers later on. For example, a child that has been neglected in early life may be less well placed to benefit from formal transfers of property later on, such as a loan to pay for university fees, because he or she lacks the intellectual confidence to flourish in a university environment. Cases of this sort may suggest that informal practices are often the ones that ultimately make the greatest difference to a child's prospects.

Much of what I'm calling 'informal' parental advantage-conferral occurs either unintentionally or as a consequence of acts that aim at something different. Very often, parents confer advantage on their children simply by pursuing and maintaining a valuable relationship with them. As Brighouse and Swift note, much shaping of children "will arise as an unintended by-product simply of parents being themselves in their relationships with their children".[16] For example, a parent may take his or her child to a museum, national park, or sporting event because it makes for a fun day out. But in addition to being enjoyable, such activities provide a way for parents to pass on their own interests to a

---

[15]  Alstott (2009: 124).

[16]  Brighouse & Swift (2014: 154). Joseph Fishkin makes precisely the same claim (2014: 50). The role of parents in shaping a child's personality is an influential way of grounding the value, and importance, of parent–child relationships. Although I will use Brighouse and Swift's version as a model, others have developed similar accounts. See for example Macleod (2010) and Overall (2012: esp. ch. 10).

child, so that parent and child can come to have more in common. Sometimes this 'passing on' requires a good deal of parental guidance and assistance. For example, a child might struggle to appreciate the plot of *Richard III* without some explanation of its historical background. Pursuit of these shared, relationship-building activities seem to be morally permissible even when they confer competitive advantage as a side effect. Such practices may be limited in *some* cases by requirements of social justice. Parents who wish to make their child exempt from state education on religious grounds represent a problematic case if exclusively religious schools turn out to restrict social integration.[17] More generally, most of us would agree that there is something wrong with parents who see their child as a 'project', as may happen when parents try especially hard to shape their child's life according to some premeditated plan and in ways that might ruin his or her childhood. On the whole, though, these cases are exceptions to what seems to be a wide range of permissible advantage-conferring actions.

Some of the advantages conferred by parent–child interactions are absolute—they simply help children to live better lives. The benefits conferred in these cases obtain independently of whether the same benefits are also conferred by other parents on other children. Many parent–child activities, however, also confer *competitive* advantage over other children. This happens most obviously when such activities endow the children with knowledge that will help them academically, such as when knowledge of Shakespeare proves helpful in an exam. Somewhat separately, much parent–child interaction will do much to develop the child's confidence as a person, including his or her ability to communicate easily and effectively with others. While confidence and communication skills usually have some absolute value, they very often provide some sort of competitive edge in academic and professional contexts that children will eventually have to navigate. Many other activities will endow a child with social and cultural capital. For example, helping one's child gain competency and enjoyment in horse riding or sailing will often have an impact on what sort of social circles he or she might enter in later in life, or even help the child gain access to a top university.

---

[17] On this, see Brighouse (2005: ch. 5).

Importantly, some parents confer different and better advantages than others. Parenting practices have been found to vary quite markedly across different economic levels. Middle-income and wealthy parents raise their children in ways that exhibit what sociologist Annette Lareau has called "concerted cultivation".[18] Broadly speaking, wealthier parents do more to plan their children's activities in ways that promote academic success, individuality, and a greater competence at navigating institutional environments. Parents at lower income levels raise their children in rather different ways, with much less structure. These differences in practice are not spread evenly across a spectrum. They do not vary gradually, in proportion with gradual changes in parental wealth and education. Instead, they correlate strongly with what Lareau regards as robust class differences that mark out segregated groups rather than differences of degree.[19] For short, I will say that parental advantage is conferred *differentially* across families.

These patterns begin to explain the way in which parent–child interactions may replicate distributive inequality and perpetuate economic segregation. There is the sad fact, easily forgotten, that many children miss out on parental advantage-conferral altogether just because they don't have parents or have been taken away from their parents due to abuse or neglect. Many such children grow up in institutions that are very poor substitutes for an intimate and nurturing family environment. Among the larger set of children who are raised in families, typically by at least one parent, there is much variation as to how, and to what extent, relationship goods are pursued through parent–child interactions. Parents will often choose to introduce their children to the sorts of activities that they find interesting and are competent at and which they think most worth sharing with a child. Here, there may be little or no variation in terms of the absolute benefits being conferred; taking a child skiing might not be any more be enjoyable (for the child) than taking him or her to watch the football. But there is room for much variation concerning how much *competitive* advantage is received. Although the conferral of advantage is often a side effect to the pursuit of relationship goods, there is good sociological evidence that parents are aware of it and will

---

[18] See especially the studies described throughout Lareau (2011). I make more specific references below and in the last chapter.

[19] As emphasized in Lareau (2011: 233–45, 310–11).

often tailor their activities with children in ways that partly aim to confer advantage. But there is evidence that such awareness, and consequent tailoring, is much lower among relatively poor parents, who are often intimidated by institutions, particularly when it comes to their children's education.[20] Wealthier parents will often work hard to encourage their children to (say) read a novel or watch Shakespeare when they would rather concentrate on less intellectual pursuits. Crudely speaking, many parents want their child to grow up to be 'the right sort of person', and this works alongside their desire to ensure their offspring has a valuable childhood.[21] In short, the value of a child's social and cultural capital, along with his or her prospects for getting more of it, is highly dependent on what sort of activities he or she engages in while growing up.

The design of higher education admissions shows how the 'hobbies' of a child can matter as he or she enters adulthood. Leading universities in the United States offer admission to students based partly on a demonstration of involvement or excellence in extracurricular activities. Such offers often include scholarships or substantial financial support. What counts as an extracurricular activity in these admissions contexts is interestingly constrained. Stanford University, one of America's wealthiest and among its most committed to a wide range of student athletics, offers scholarships in sports as obscure as fencing, water polo, and synchronized swimming.[22] No scholarships are offered, however, for darts, boxing, or tenpin bowling, even though each of these sports is popular enough to have an international professional league. The most prestigious universities in other countries make admissions officially a matter of academic merit. However, many of these countries, such as Britain and Australia, are ones in which extracurricular potential features in admission to the most academically successful high schools, who are in turn disproportionately represented (statistically speaking) at the level of the undergraduate university population.

[20] Lareau points out (2011: 198–9).

[21] This starts as early as choosing one's child's name. See Savage (2015: ch. 11). Such cases represent Fred Hirsch's (1977) suggestion that economies eventually become dependent on selling competitive consumption once basic necessities have been made affordable.

[22] See Stanford, 'Cardinal Athletics', http://facts.stanford.edu/campuslife/athletics (accessed 1 May 2015).

Generally speaking, the sorts of informal conferral of advantage that do most to enhance a child's prospects *are the ones that are expensive.*[23] This is increasingly the case in societies with advanced economies, where industries target parents with products that promise to give one's child an edge. Nursery schools sometimes advertise their services as including an early opportunity for a child to start learning French, rather than as places to simply learn through playing.[24] Nevertheless, their presence emphasizes the competitive potential when it comes to ways in which parents raise their children. Regardless of how far such markets have managed to advance, the variable cost of advantage conferring helps account for its being differential across economic groups. The connection between a child's extracurricular activities and the economic position of his or her family has been well documented by sociologists.[25] There is a well-known 'summer learning loss', manifest in the decline of academic skills, particularly among poorer children, during the school holidays. The existence of concerted cultivation in middle- and upper-income groups is not wholly a matter of conferring benefits without cost. Parents' purchase of goods and services designed to advance their child often comes at the expense of *shared activity* between parents and their children and is increasingly including things that parents simply *buy* for their children. A lot more could be said about these trends and their impact on the goods of parenting and of childhood.[26] I rely, however, only on their status as evidence of the way in which parental wealth is likely to make a difference to parental ability to confer advantage in ways that still fall short of formal wealth transfers to children.

These facts begin to show how flows of inherited wealth have a significant sociological impact. The cost of conferring advantage means that it is often dependent on parents' earlier receipt of formal transfers from (typically) their own parents, or on the expectation of receiving such transfers in the relatively near future. Receiving an inheritance may

---

[23] As Lareau (2011: 58–60, 248–50).

[24] See Vincent & Ball (2007). Pamela Paul (2008) provides a more extensive discussion of the industry surrounding parenting, with reference to many products that (purportedly) help with concerted cultivation.

[25] See for example Vincent & Ball (2006).

[26] Lareau calls for more research on "the drawbacks of middle-class family life" (2011: 307), particularly in view of the "rationalization of child-rearing" (246–8) and the frenetic lifestyle and common exhaustion exhibited by both parents and children in families that practice concerted cultivation.

happen too late to make a difference to one's own social position, but it can come early enough to help raise the status of one's child. Pre-existing flows of inherited wealth, which some parents enjoy and others do not, help enable and increase the degree to which parental conferral of advantage is differential in the sense I have identified. As parental conferral of advantage becomes more differentiated across economic groups, children in these groups become more economically segregated from each other and take this into adulthood. This problem is likely to compound itself with successive generations.

Before moving on and defending these claims in more detail, a few brief qualifications are in order. First, the points above are merely supposed to report what *quantity* of variation exists with respect to how parents can advantage their children through different sorts of interaction associated with different economic levels. This is not meant to imply anything about the intrinsic value of different activities when evaluated in isolation. So far as a conception of the good life is concerned, there is nothing superior about weekends spent watching Shakespeare and playing cello compared to weekends spent watching Millwall FC and playing darts. The point is just that being a seasoned cellist will open more (and different) doors for a child than being skilled at darts. This entails nothing about richer or poorer parents having better or worse relationships with their children based solely on the activities they can afford to engage in.[27] Following others, I have suggested that parents who purchase services designed to advance their child may often sacrifice valuable time spent with their child engaging in relationship-building activities. But I do not think this claim is very controversial. A related qualification is that parental conferral of advantage is rather fallible. The sheer number of children that a parent has will affect his or her ability to give them the attention necessary to confer advantage. Sometimes 'external forces' may hold back a child's development. When a child becomes a victim of violent crime, this may alter his or her prospects for development in ways that parents can do something to mitigate, but where their wealth may not make much difference.[28] In addition, children may simply fail to uptake the advantages that parents attempt to confer on them. Being taken along to performances of Shakespeare on a frequent

---

[27] Lareau makes a similar point (2011: 173).
[28] I owe this example to Fishkin (2014: 108–9).

basis may simply make the child sick of theatre and less disposed towards such art as an adult. Purchasing an expensive education for a child may increase his or her chances of getting an academic edge, but the child may still have to endure burdensome hours of study.[29]

Egalitarianism is going to have to come to terms, in some way, with the role of the family in replicating distributive inequality across generations and (thereby) in stimulating or exacerbating forms of segregation. This is not going to be easy. But it is a natural consequence of recognizing that distributions are, at any given time, cumulative effects of prior distributions and not isolated entities that might merely be evaluated according to their internal structure. It is far from obvious whether restricting the right to bequeath would be the most defensible strategy for combatting economic segregation. Even granting that inheritance has a significant sociological impact, it may be that other proposals are better (either more effective or less morally costly) for breaking up economic segregation. I have already argued against proposals of institutional reform in chapter 5. But this did not include any discussion of the family as an institution that could be reformed.

## 6.3  The Problem of Regulating the Family

For egalitarians committed to reducing social hierarchies and group segregation along economic lines, the existence of differential parental practices might seem to present am embarrassing problem. To many, there is something intuitively offensive about seeing injustice in the ways that parents form valuable relationships with their children. This may make it hard to accept further claims favouring state interference with these activities for the sake of pursuing egalitarian justice through integration. Interfering with the family for other sorts of moral reasons, for example when preventing domestic abuse or neglect, is less controversial, though subject to difficult questions about exactly when and how such interventions should occur. It is quite another matter to interfere with activities that, by and large, all members of the family will benefit from, consent to, value, and enjoy. Admittedly, when parents pay for their children to undergo enrichment activities provided by third parties,

---

[29] This has significance for how we should think about the moral problem of private education. I discuss this point more fully, along with some related ones, in Halliday (2016b).

they're less obviously pursuing relationship goods.[30] Certainly there are *some* kinds of advantage-conferring behaviour that parents can be legitimately prevented from doing for their children. Nobody believes that parents should be permitted to, say, bribe a judge to help their child avoid a criminal conviction.[31] But this case is made easier because bribery is typically a wrongful act on prior, independent grounds.

Overall, then, when the pursuit of parental partiality lacks any independent and obvious wrong-making features, it is hard to justify any state interference aimed at limiting it. Structurally speaking, the value of pre-empting or reducing high levels of economic segregation might be outweighed or defeated by independent moral requirements associated with the protection of the family. Many political philosophers accept that the family remains an essential part of any functioning society and that there should be a very strong presumption against imposing intrusive forms of regulation on it.[32] This is likely to make it hard for egalitarians to accept much intrusion into the family as a means of breaking up practices that nevertheless allow inequality to persist down the generations.

One can, of course, question whether intuitive opposition to interfering with family life is well founded. Plenty of families fall short of the ideal that political philosophy often attributes to them. Some families are horrible, or at least might not be made internally worse by certain interventions from outside that aimed to regulate parent–child interactions. I take these considerations seriously, and I do suspect that intuitive opposition to interfering with families derives partly from an overly idealized conception of family life, and not just from considerations of the fallibility and other shortcomings of whatever state powers might do the intervening. Rather than get sidetracked by questions of how sacrosanct the family should be in political philosophy, it is perhaps worth emphasizing that regulating parental conferral of advantage, in

[30] Giving gifts is, however, one way of pursuing an intimate and valuable relationship. Membership of the pony club could, after all, be a nice birthday present for a child.

[31] There is more to be said about the significance of such cases and their implications for the ethics of parental partiality more generally, but I will set this aside. For more discussion see Bou-Habib (2014).

[32] For further defence, see Munoz-Darde (1999). Tax theorists sometimes express a similar outlook, e.g. Blum & Kalven (1952: 505).

ways that would address how it is differential across different economic groups, is extremely difficult.

First, there is the fact, mentioned earlier, that cultural and social capital cannot actually be redistributed or taxed in the manner of physical or financial capital. Parents couldn't easily reduce advantage conferral even if they wanted to. A parent who consciously attempted to "monitor" his or her behaviour in ways aimed at reducing the conferral of competitive advantage might jeopardize his or her ability to secure a valuable relationship with his or her child.[33] Interference from outside is hardly likely to overcome such hazards. As Joseph Fishkin has recently claimed, "unless we are willing to destroy the family...life chances will never be completely independent of circumstances of birth".[34] It is tempting to conclude that the direct regulation of the family can never completely address its role in replicating distributive inequality, to the extent required to really combat economic segregation. This point can be upheld without overly idealizing what the family is actually like in practice. I shall later suggest that the taxation of intergenerational wealth transfers is rather less intrusive than anything that might "destroy the family", but Fishkin's point also reflects a plausible sort of scepticism about the efficacy of attempts to regulate the many informal practices of advantage conferral that may operate apart from intergenerational wealth transfers.[35]

It might be suggested that families need not be coercively interfered with at all in order to change. Talk of government 'interfering' with the family by 'restricting' practices that lead to unequal conferral of advantage on children may strike some readers as misleadingly one-sided. The state could, for example, pursue policies that make some parents better at advancing their children's competitive edge rather than holding back the effectiveness of parents who are especially good at it or better placed to pay someone else to do it. There need be nothing objectionable about policies that aim to pursue such ends, and to do so may confer various

---

[33] This point is suggested by Brighouse & Swift (2014: 142). Others have suggested that parents may yet have a reason to mitigate the extent to which they confer advantage when pursuing relationship goods as per the Brighouse–Swift view; on this see Segall (2013: ch. 7).

[34] Fishkin (2014: 53).

[35] One objection to Fishkin, and others who talk broadly of "the family", is that he obscures the important differences that separate different things that families do. Consider Alstott's observation that the provision of financial support is not an essential part of what the family is really *for*, even if families can and do provide such support when it is not provided from alternative sources, such as state services (2008: 19).

absolute benefits on the children of poorer parents. Such proposals also avoid idealizing the family to any great extent. But it is important to keep in mind the roughly 'zero-sum' nature of positional competition. The relative ease with which middle-income parents are led to spend increasingly large sums on advancing their children's position is a natural, and perhaps rational, response to other parents doing the same. Positional goods are those for which the distinction between 'levelling down' and 'levelling up' inequalities becomes blurred. It is not possible to decrease the position of the better off without raising the position of the worst off, and vice versa. This means that, when it comes to designing policies that seek to address the differential (unequal) patterns of parental conferral of advantage, it is all but impossible to bring about an outcome in which every child is made better off in any competitive or positional sense.

## 6.4 The Cumulative Effects of Inheritance (1): Effects on Differential Parental Conferral of Advantage

It is now helpful to look more closely at some claims made by Brighouse and Swift about wealth transfer within families. On this matter, Brighouse and Swift express the now mainstream view that the social impact of inheritance is pre-empted by mechanisms whose effects on a person's social position occur early in life:

Some strands in the egalitarian tradition have tended to assume... that something close enough to fair equality of opportunity can be achieved through a combination of public education policies intended to marginalize the impact of expensive private schooling and tax transfer policies designed to mitigate the effects of unequal parental wealth on life prospects. Things would be easier if the reason why inequality persisted across generations was that well-off parents bequeathed property to their children, or used their money to buy superior access to such advantage for their children. However, recent research in economics and sociology casts doubt on this assumption, suggesting that in fact parenting styles, culture, personality, and other factors... have as much if not more impact on prospects for income and wealth than transfers from parents to children.[36]

---

[36] Brighouse & Swift (2014: 125–6). Swift makes some similar claims when reviewing some of the social science literature in his (2005). I am also in agreement with Brighouse and Swift's remark about the limited power of public education policies, which fits with the

In making these remarks, Brighouse and Swift make an implicit but important assumption. They write as if the only inheritance that shapes a child's life prospects is whatever inheritance is received by *that* child. This claim is correct when understood in a restricted way, as a claim only about a wealth transfer's immediate effects on its actual beneficiary. The problem is that the claim is often understood in the wrong way, as a claim about inheritance in general. This happens when it is assumed that intergenerational transfers of wealth are isolated transactions rather than, as is very often the case, iterations within longer inheritance *flows*—chains of transfers that extend along successive generations. In either case, the causal impact of an intergenerational transfer may be delayed. Overlooking this is an important mistake. It means obscuring the distinction between immediate and cumulative effects of any particular wealth transfer, along with the related distinction between first- and second-generation inheritance.

Here is a similar quote, this time from some of the social scientists whose work I mentioned in section 1.3 when offering a brief review of empirical data on inherited wealth:

Very few individuals receive inheritances of significant magnitude.... [I]t seems unlikely that for most of the population a substantial degree of economic status is transmitted *directly* by the intergenerational transfer of property or financial wealth. It thus seems likely that the intergenerational persistence of wealth reflects ... parent-offspring similarities in traits influencing wealth accumulation, such as orientation toward the future, sense of personal efficacy, work ethic, schooling attainment, and risk taking.[37]

This is an important set of remarks. Much hangs on what is being conceded by the claim that the influence of wealth transfer is simply not *direct*. In mentioning "parent-offspring similarities", the passage alludes to the various informal practices discussed above and by Brighouse and Swift. But this does not leave out the possibility that wealth transfers can have a powerful, perhaps delayed, indirect effect.

Overlooking the possibility of any long-run effects of extended inheritance flows has led others, over the years, to discount the effectiveness of

---

claims I defended at the end of chapter 5. Like Brighouse and Swift, however, I believe that education policies still make enough of a difference that certain policies may be necessary from the point of view of social justice.

[37] Bowles, Gintis, & Groves (2005: 19, italics added).

inheritance tax. Representative here is Walter Blum and Harry Kalven's seminal discussion of taxation from the mid-twentieth century:

Looking only at the inequality involved in some children inheriting wealth at the death of kin and other children inheriting no wealth ignores the more far-reaching instances of economic discriminations among children. These can most easily be pointed up where the parents survive until the children have reached adulthood. In such situations the critical economic inheritance occurs prior to the death of the parents and need not be related to the wealth, if any, which they pass on directly at death or by way of *inter-vivos* gifts of wealth. The critical economic inheritance consists of the day to day expenditures on the children... [which are] in our society gravely disparate. No progressive inheritance tax, or combination of gift and inheritance taxes, can touch this source of economic inequalities among children.[38]

These claims are made in spite of Blum and Kalven's explicit acceptance, as the passage makes clear, that the differential conferral of parental advantage may be an injustice.[39] But the whole passage is expressed as if the causal power of inheritance is somehow confined to the parties (parent and child) involved in any single, isolated intergenerational transfer of wealth. Again, the mistake being made is one of construing inheritance as isolated transfers rather than links in longer chains of transfers, and thereby overlooking its cumulative effects.

I have been building up to a point that I now hope will be easy to see. The crucial matter is that inheritance can have a delayed sociological impact. This impact is just as real, and just as morally significant, even if it falls on people who are the offspring of the direct recipient of an intergenerational transfer rather than the recipient himself or herself. The *cumulative* effects of inherited wealth become more easily recognized once it is conceded that a person's accumulation of nonfinancial capital can be a long-run consequence of the history of inheritance flow higher up in the family tree. I should say that, while this point is somewhat suppressed in the passage from Brighouse and Swift that I have quoted above, it is one that they effectively make later in the same book:

---

[38]   Blum & Kalven (1952: 503).
[39]   Blum & Kalven (1952) ground this concern in fairness or equality of opportunity, not as a concern about social hierarchy or economic segregation. But this does not matter so far as the distinction between immediate and cumulative effects is concerned.

In the real world, many of those children who in fact enjoy unfairly superior prospects have parents who are themselves beneficiaries of an unjust distribution of resources. Perhaps their parents also had parents who were able to tilt the playing field in their favour.... In that case the question of their rights to confer advantage on their children looks rather different.[40]

Like in the famous passage from Rawls that appeared in section 4.1, Brighouse and Swift are recognizing that the actual distribution of resources, opportunities, and talents is not an isolated, 'intragenerational' sort of thing. They do not, however, spend any further time working out the significance of this fact. The quoted passage does not actually mention inheritance, only that the effects of parental partiality can compound or accumulate over successive generations. Their lack of attention to the deeper cumulative complexities here is not grounds for special criticism. Brighouse and Swift are interested in parental partiality and the value of the family as a topic in its own right. This project is largely about questions to do with the parent–child relationship unrelated to inherited wealth, and not especially related to anything about family lines extended beyond any single pair of generations.[41] Again, though, the cumulative significance of inheritance risks being obscured.

The cumulative effects of inheritance begin with the way it affects an inheritor's ability to confer parental advantage onto the next generation. Generally speaking, parents become better able to confer advantage on their children, especially *competitive* advantage, the wealthier they are. This is particularly so during the formative years of their child's life. This was noticed in the 1920s by Josiah Wedgwood, whose views were discussed in chapter 2:

It is obvious that... the well-to-do parent can procure for his children a more healthy environment and a better education than the poor, and can thus equip them for the more highly-paid and attractive employments.[42]

---

[40] Brighouse & Swift (2014: 145–6).
[41] Thomas Douglas (2015) has recently argued that the compounding effects of parental partiality may force Brighouse and Swift's account to place greater restrictions on when such partiality is limited. This is because, as Douglas points out, the effects of partiality on subsequent generations have a very limited capacity to secure relationship goods in the way that Brighouse and Swift take to be supportive of limited partiality of parents towards their immediate offspring. This point is plausible, although not one that establishes anything about economic segregation.
[42] Wedgwood (1929: 80).

While he did well to draw attention to this fact, Wedgwood didn't process it very effectively. He immediately suggests that these practices would remain even if inheritance were abolished. Wedgwood is partly right. *Motivation* for parental conferral of advantage does not depend generally on the presence of wealth transfer in the family line. But to claim that this type of practice would simply "remain" suppresses the way in which the ability of parents to confer advantage on their children may in practice be highly differential across economic groups. Indeed, Wedgwood later claimed that inheritance "perpetuates and may intensify inequalities arising originally from other causes".[43] Taken together, these claims make an important point: parents may well be equally motivated when it comes to the pursuit of actions that confer advantage on their children, but parents who inherit (or expect to inherit) are much better placed to enact such strategies, especially during the earlier years of their child's life.

The cumulative effects of inheritance make it a mechanism that *enables* and *enhances* other mechanisms causing the concentration of valuable nonfinancial capital in groups at higher levels of the wealth distribution, and the replication of this pattern from one generation to the next. This is the principal claim I will defend regarding the causal priority of inheritance in terms of segregating effects of replicating economic inequalities. But it is also a bit of a mouthful. To fill it out a bit, I think there are at least three sub-mechanisms that can be identified, each of which shows how parents who inherit are in a better position to enhance the social position of their offspring, even if they have inherited too late to make a comparable difference to their own position.

First, there is sheer *time*: parents who inherit, or expect to soon inherit, can reduce the time they spend competing in the labour market, and perhaps drop out of it altogether. This will greatly enhance their capacity to confer advantage onto their children, especially if *both* parents can restrict their labour market time. A theoretical advantage of this obser-vation is that it will endure irrespective of what variation there might be in which forms of nonfinancial capital happen to be the most valuable. Parents with spare time will generally be better placed to introduce their child to activities that help him or her accumulate nonfinancial capital,

---

[43]  Wedgwood (1929: 84).

irrespective of what these activities might be. Again, spending time with children is particularly important during the early years of their life, especially before the onset of formal schooling. It doesn't really matter which childhood activities put one at a competitive or absolute advantage later on. It will almost always be the case that, for some large set of activities, a child will have greater opportunities to engage in them if he or she has a parent who is not distracted by the demands of the labour market. Such parents will always be in a better position to join in with, supervise, or otherwise facilitate the child's engagement in the activities in question.[44]

Second, there is *positional purchasing power*: conferring advantage on children, especially competitive advantage, is usually expensive. It costs much more money for one's children to take fencing or cello lessons than to help them take up darts. Inheriting wealth makes it more likely that parents will become wealthy *early enough* to make these purchases. Generally speaking, children will do better in the race for competitive advantage if they get an early start. A parent who is in a position, perhaps due to hard-earned pay rises over the years, to purchase music lessons or other such advantage-conferring activities when his or her child is a teenager, will often be less able to confer advantage than a parent who can afford to help his or her child earlier on, with the help of inheritance from the previous generation. Many skills are simply easier to learn when one starts young, including musical instruments, foreign languages, and sports. As I have said, parents can overdo things. Children who are constantly being packed off to expensive extracurricular activities are often getting a worse childhood than children who get time to simply relax, often with their parents. Still, the point remains that parents who are wealthy from the *beginning* of their child's life will be in the best position to purchase whatever balance of expensive activities is optimal for their child's relative advantage.

Third, there is *proximity to a reference point*. This is a more subtle matter. Social scientists have recently illuminated the phenomenon of

---

[44] Granted, historically gendered divisions of labour mean that it will typically be a female parent who reduces her time in the labour market. I am not trying to obscure the significance of this, but it is not strictly relevant to the point I am trying to make, which would continue to hold even if there were no gendered divisions of labour.

'expenditure cascades' with respect to markets in positional goods.[45] These occur when extremely wealthy people engage in certain kinds of purchasing behaviour, of sorts visible to members of lower-income groups. The conduct of wealthy consumers serves as a reference point against which less wealthy consumers fix their consumption targets. Most study of expenditure cascades focuses on especially conspicuous consumption, such as the purchase of designer clothes, cars, and big houses. But there is an important parallel with parental conferral of advantage, which involve purchases of things like educational services. What the two cases have in common is that they involve arms race competition for a positional good. Louis Vuitton handbags are coveted because (perhaps only because!) their cost makes them an exclusive item, thereby distinguishing the people who can be seen owning them. Education is valuable insofar as it endows one with knowledge and qualifications that put one ahead of competitors. There is good sociological evidence that parents seek to spend money on their child's education because they believe that wealthier parents are already doing this.[46] Like people coveting Louis Vuitton items, they worry about being left behind in a sort of arms race for positional advantage.[47]

There is one important theoretical advantage of this observation about reference points: it has force even if most people in the arms race are not actually inheriting any wealth whatsoever.[48] The presence of large inheritance flows concentrated into wealthy families may do enough to push up the reference point for parents who may not be inheritors. It is very hard indeed to make arms races go away through institutional reform. Possibly, the best, or most feasible, way of dampening an arms race is to cut off the relevant expenditure cascades at their source by lowering the reference point. For example, social scientists interested in conspicuous

---

[45] This term was coined by Robert Frank; see for example his (2011: 61–2). An important account of reference points and their role in setting positional consumption goals is Schor (1998).

[46] See for example Vincent & Ball (2007).

[47] Arms races are an interesting problem in their own right. Arms races in education are different in some important ways from arms races in conspicuous luxury goods. I have discussed the philosophical significance of this phenomenon, albeit in ways that do not highlight their connection with inherited wealth, in Halliday (2016b).

[48] Some sociologists suggest that inheritance plays a limited role in the replication of inequality just because relatively few individuals inherit large sums, e.g. Bowles & Gintis (2002: 18). Here I am disputing this claim somewhat.

consumption often support consumption taxes on luxury items, so that the very wealthy are forced to become less extravagant, pre-empting the sort of mimicry among lower-income consumers. Taxing inheritance could have a similar effect. Indeed, inheritance taxes may be somewhat more effective than consumption taxes as a means of tackling arms races: taxing specific forms of consumption is an ex post method through which to dampen the purchase of positional advantage. Unless consumption taxes are applied equally to all forms of consumption (which raises various problems), any consumption tax that attached to acts of arms race participation may trigger a shift towards using some other sort of activity as a way of sorting people. If the taxing of (say) piano lessons were successful as way of reducing competitive consumption, some other untaxed form of consumption might just take its place. Taxing inheritance, on the other hand, may be more effective because of its ex ante status: the flow of wealth is what is targeted rather than particular ways of using it.

I don't wish to press any strong claim about the relative prominence or potency of any of these sub-mechanisms relative to each other. Quite likely this is a context-sensitive matter in any case, such that different mechanisms are more prominent in different societies where economic segregation occurs. What matters is just that some combination of these mechanisms is usually present in societies with significant freedom of gift and bequest. This is what reveals inheritance's long-term role in allowing social inequality to replicate itself as an effect of the replication of distributive inequality through intergenerational transfers of wealth and property. The effect is 'long term' at least in the sense that it may not obtain within a single generation and will remain harder to appreciate so long as inheritance is understood as something that connects only the two generations of parent and child, and not subsequent generations of successive offspring. These considerations form the basis of a sound egalitarian case for restricting the right to bequeath property and wealth to individual descendants.

## 6.5 Compounding

So far, I have argued that inheritance is sufficiently important, causally speaking, for taxing it to make a difference. I have also argued that the moral costs of doing so compare favourably with the moral costs of regulating other relevant mechanisms, such as practices integral to the pursuit of valuable relationships within families. But this doesn't establish anything detailed about *how* to tax inheritance, that is, about what should serve as inputs into a calculation of tax liability. Something might now be said, therefore, about whether the argument so far is one that supports the Rignano scheme in particular, as opposed to standardly progressive taxation.

One possibility is that the parental conferral of advantage compounds over successive generations. While parents who have inherited are better placed to advantage their children than parents who have not, parents who have inherited *and* whose own parents inherited are in a still better position. This provides one justification for attaching greater restrictions to second-generation inheritance than to first-generation inheritance.

Let me first develop this point with respect to the attraction of social capital. Recall that this kind of nonfinancial capital is basically epistemic: it concerns access to certain sorts of useful information, through membership of networks to which such information is largely confined. One way to purchase access to such networks for one's child is by paying for expensive school fees or purchasing a home near an elite school with a local intake. Parents can purchase this sort of access for their child even if their own social capital is relatively poor. But children who grow up with good social capital and are already placed within relevant social networks will often be able to bring their child into the same network without having to purchase access. There is evidence that access to unpaid internships is becoming increasingly important in enabling young people to compete for certain sorts of graduate employment. But such internships are particularly difficult to secure without knowing someone in the relevant organization.[49] This often comes through parental contacts or contacts at an elite school or university. The latter will cost money to obtain, but the former can already be possessed by a parent who had such access bought for him or her. This represents one way in which transfer of wealth in the first generation can enable a second-generation transfer of social capital that relies less heavily on the transfer of wealth. Should the wealth be transferred a second time, it can be expected to augment,

---

[49] See for example Savage (2015: 204–8).

rather than merely maintain, the advantage gained from the first-generation transfer. This affects its just liability to being taxed.

A parallel point can be made about the attraction of cultural capital, particularly that gained through the "concerted cultivation" associated with child raising in middle- and upper-income families. The clue here is that concerted cultivation doesn't just benefit a child. In addition, it is often a sort of training for a child's eventual role as a parent later in life. Consequently, parental experience and competency can displace money, at least to some extent, as a driving force behind concerted cultivation. Consider a variety of activities that contribute to successful cultivation of a child's talents, such as learning musical instruments and languages and participating in organized team activities such as sports and acting. All of these activities can run up quite expensive bills. But if parents engaged in them as part of their own childhood, they will often be in a position to reduce their child's dependency on purchased services with what he or she can do for free. A parent who learned cello can help a child practice cello; a parent who studied Shakespeare can help explain the plot of a Shakespeare play in which a child has been given a tough acting role; a parent who learned French can help a child practice speaking French. More generally, children often become more confident in approaching an activity when a parent can do it with them. As with the transmission of social capital, cultural capital may be bought with the help of first-generation inheritance but then transmitted for free (or with less expense) to the second generation. The fact that child raising resembles training for later parenthood helps explain the much documented tendency for poorer parents, or parents who had a poor childhood, to forgo practices that are not beyond their financial reach. The more significant fact is that such parents did not enjoy being at the receiving end of such practices during their own childhood.

Of course, social and cultural capital do not come apart as cleanly as the above remarks suggest. Social scientists generally accept that they "intersect and reinforce each other".[50] One might need good social capital to acquire an internship but rely on good cultural capital to 'fit in' at a workplace where the conversations are about skiing and opera. But the evidence suggests that once wealth attracts valuable nonfinancial

---

[50]  Savage (2015: 204).

capital through expenditure, further expenditure may not be needed to maintain such capital, though the capital attracted may 'pay for itself' through such things as increased labour market advantage. Further wealth transfers may then equip the subsequent generation to attract yet more nonfinancial capital, giving rise to yet more economic segregation.

I am not suggesting that the compounding effect of iterated inheritance is massive. It is important to remember that we are considering the choice between the Rignano scheme and progressive taxation. Here, the task is to justify the sort of difference that would warrant granting "complete control" by exempting first-generation inheritance altogether, while taxing older inheritance at rates approaching 100 per cent, as in Rignano's "rough draft". Nor am I suggesting that the compounding effect continues, in anything like a linear fashion, beyond the second generation. It is not obvious how much added effect can come from third-generation inheritance. There could even be an opposite effect later on, as children without a self-made parent or grandparent to set an example grow lazy or complacent.[51] But as long as there is *some* compounding, there will be a corresponding case for attaching *some* greater liability to older fortunes than to similarly sized fortunes that are being bequeathed for the first time. Accordingly, any degree of compounding counts in favour of a Rignano scheme over traditionally progressive inheritance taxes. Exactly how much compounding occurs is, however, rather hard to establish. It is possible that it makes only a rather small (albeit real) contribution to any comparative case for the Rignano scheme over the main alternative.

## 6.6  The Cumulative Effects of Inheritance (2): Effects as an Attractor of Nonfinancial Capital

I have argued that inherited wealth plays a substantial role in shaping an inheritor's ability to subsequently confer valuable nonfinancial capital on his or her children. In making this argument, I have granted that

---

[51] Such judgement was sometimes passed by the early liberals, for example Mill's remark that "the heir of entail...has much more than the ordinary chances of growing up idle, dissipated, and profligate" (2004: V.9.11).

inheritance does not, itself, transfer any status or nonfinancial capital. Inheritance merely provides the sort of wealth that helps beneficiaries of enduring inheritance flows to engage in the less formal activities that ultimately confer such benefits, through activities associated with family life. In this sense, inheritance is not itself an attractor of social and cultural capital but an enabling condition for the operation of other attractors. This section's argument seeks to develop the point that, in certain circumstances, inheritance may nevertheless attract social and cultural capital more directly. The crude way of putting this is that, in certain societies, status comes simply from old money.

A more ambitious argument for restricting bequest can be formulated using this further hypothesis that wealth confers additional status on its bearer just because it is old, i.e. has been passed down some sufficiently large number of times as inheritance. The lagged attraction of nonfinancial capital is structurally distinct from the sort of compounding that was described in section 6.5. This is just because, although superficially similar, temporal lagging and temporal compounding are different ways in which cumulative effects can come about. They may of course obtain side by side and reinforce each other, which might make it harder to notice the difference. Less abstractly, the point is that compounding advantage involves the steady growth of more valuable nonfinancial capital within a family line over time. The lagged accumulation of nonfinancial capital can be understood, differently, in terms of a fortune's age being valuable in itself.

Very likely this is the sort of role that Tawney took inheritance to have. Broadly egalitarian British authors of his generation have taken a similar or at least complementary view about social hierarchy. The common notion of *nouveau riche* reflects the fact that sudden cash windfalls often do not immediately attract the valuable nonfinancial capital that wealth can attract in the longer term. In *The Road to Wigan Pier*, George Orwell provides an apt description of the way this process can be symmetrical: *loss* of nonfinancial capital lags loss of wealth. Members of the upper and middle classes in Orwell's Britain would, on occasion, suffer a decline in their economic position. But Orwell reports them as being extremely good at retaining their accents, ways of dressing, networks of contacts, and other ways of 'keeping up appearances'. This might suggest that the ability to signal that one has wealth up one's family tree, so to speak, may be valuable even if one cannot signal current possession of wealth through, for example, forms of conspicuous consumption, which may even have a less valuable signalling effect. Orwell's observation, though hard to test, indicates another important matter: this is the possibility of family lines in which wealth is transferred downwards without interruption, and the weaker idea of family lines in which some *level* of wealth is more or less consistently maintained, allowing for temporary periods in which wealth diminishes and then recovers. This distinction may prove important when working out a fuller defence of what it means for inheritance taxes to be progressive over time. Indeed, the distinction is already implicit in Wedgwood's observations about Rignano's failure to accommodate such cases of inherited fortunes that might be lost and subsequently recovered.

More could perhaps be said concerning the more specific effects of very old money. For example, some sociologists believe that long-running inheritance flows help create dynasties of political influence, as each generation of a wealthy family builds on the social capital, in the political world, accumulated by the generations before.[52] Political dynasties may subvert relational egalitarian ideals about democratic participation, although this might depend on how widely such participation occurs beyond the occupancy of political office. Such concerns are present in Rawls's claims about background justice that were mentioned in chapter 1. It is not obvious, however, whether inheritance taxes would be the only or best way of breaking up political dynasties, as opposed to other measures that make it easier for people to enter politics without growing up in a relevantly well-connected family. For one thing, money in politics doesn't always come from wealthy individuals but from large corporations, which do not inherit.

Any claim about inheritance having this capacity as a direct attractor stands a greater chance of being true in societies that have long histories of status inequality based around economic distinctions. These might include various countries in Europe and possibly other societies that have a feudal history and were not colonized, such as Japan. It is harder to know what to say about countries whose histories lack a feudal era but in which wealth has long been esteemed, such as the United States. The argument may be even less forceful in the

---

[52]  See McNamee & Miller (2009: ch. 3).

case of young countries, such as Australia and New Zealand (though such countries may be in the process of developing relatively large flows of inherited wealth that may make them subject to greater levels of economic segregation in future). Suffice it to say that the distinction between inherited wealth as an enabler of status-attracting mechanisms versus its potential as a status attracter in its own right may prove important and could be used to frame further empirical research that could aid attempts to further illuminate the moral significance of inherited wealth.

To summarize: Once the cumulative power of inherited wealth is appreciated, it becomes possible to address initial doubts that inheritance flows are an effect rather than a cause of the persistence of group inequality and economic segregation over time. The case for the Rignano scheme becomes stronger the more these effects compound with successive iterations of inheritance flow down the same family lines. I do not claim that the causal priority of inheritance is absolute with respect to the other mechanisms at work. Rather, I claim that its cumulative effects show that its causal role is substantial enough to motivate the claim that regulation would make a difference. I have tried to emphasize this by describing inheritance flows as an enabler and enhancer of the other mechanisms through which parental conferral of advantage takes place. Overall, the relation between inheritance and other mechanisms is rather complex, and I have tried to draw attention to this fact rather than suppress it. Consequently, the argument of this chapter draws on several claims that are highly contingent and may not obtain very strongly in all societies at all times. But this is not a problem. Indeed, there should be nothing wrong with acknowledging that inheritance may be more detrimental to social equality in some countries than it currently is in others. Nevertheless, I would like to close by repeating a consideration that I think is fairly robust across social contexts, which is that parental conferral of advantage has strong tendencies to be differential once families are located at different economic levels, and will have segregating effects if it is just left to do its natural work. Egalitarians need not be embarrassed about recognizing this as a problem. One way to become less embarrassed is to pursue responses that avoid the unpalatable option of directly interfering with the more valuable aspects of family life. Taxing the flow of inherited wealth offers a promising balance.

## 6.7  The Egalitarian Complaint about Inherited Wealth: A Summary

Since the arguments in the previous three chapters comprise what is perhaps the main point of this book, I will summarize their conclusions here.

Why exactly should egalitarians believe that justice requires some restriction on inherited wealth? The answer I prefer goes as follows: Society is unjust when certain groups possess an arbitrary enjoyment of privileges and status that places them hierarchically above other groups. To the extent that inherited wealth enables such group difference to endure, thereby making the fortune of receiving inheritance a condition of group membership in this sort of segregated hierarchy, justice requires that some restriction be placed on it.

This view draws on two important philosophical ideas about equality as a moral ideal: the influence of luck on distribution and the nature of relationships between different social groups. In one way, the position I've defended embodies an endorsement of both positions. This is true insofar as I've endorsed the idea that luck cannot be eliminated from an egalitarian diagnosis of what is objectionable about unrestricted inheritance, while also endorsing the idea that injustice is most plausibly construed in terms of group difference rather than differences that obtain between isolated individuals. The complaint I have developed essentially uses social egalitarian ideas to constrain the application of a luck egalitarian principle: Inheritance is unjust when it allows some people to enjoy brute luck advantage, but the specific kind of brute luck advantage is understood in terms of group membership. This results in a narrower complaint than one aimed against any sort of inherited wealth, since inheritances can be discounted when they are not connected with group membership. In principle, some inheritance could exist in a society without any troubling segregation of social groups. This would be more likely if inheritance flows remained small and/or equally distributed.

The egalitarian complaint developed here is distinct from two 'purer' complaints that draw on either egalitarian idea to the exclusion of the other. First, there is the pure luck egalitarian complaint that inheritance is unjust simply because it confers brute luck advantage on whoever receives it. I argued in chapter 4 that we should reject this complaint in this general form. Various attempts to make it more plausible, without embedding it in a concern about group difference, turn out to be unsatisfying. Of these attempts, the most promising (Ronald Dworkin's) happened to include some allusion to group difference, or class hierarchy, as a source of its inspiration.

Second, there is the pure social egalitarian complaint that inherited wealth will in some way cause (e.g. enable, maintain, exacerbate, entrench) intergroup relationships that have an oppressive or otherwise objectionable character. This complaint is supposed to make sense without any reliance on the idea that justice is about eliminating (unjust) effects of brute luck. I've argued (in chapters 5 and 6) that this complaint may have force in some contexts but not others. This reflects its status as a contingent empirical hypothesis that may or may not be true. Most importantly, I want to emphasize that any version of the pure social egalitarian complaint could easily supplement the complaint isolated above, should it turn out to be accurate.

The case for actually restricting inherited wealth relies on the claim that inheritance plays *some* causal role among the mechanisms enabling intergenerational replication of inequality to take place *and* that intergenerational wealth transfers are unlike other mechanisms in enjoying some special moral status. Even if wealth transfers are not the most efficacious mechanism, they are one whose restriction by the state is among those least disruptive to family life. It is precisely because justice does not permit disrupting much parental conferral of advantage directly that makes it more defensible to disrupt factors aiding and abetting such practices. Any justification for taxing older inheritances at a higher rate than younger inheritances relies on the extent to which wealth transfers have a compounding effect over the generations as described above. It may prove that, so far as the pursuit of equality is concerned, there is not much reason to be more concerned about the inheritance of old money than of big money, whatever its age. That said, the case for a Rignano scheme also draws on certain non-egalitarian considerations, which will arise at various points in the closing chapters of this book. This reflects the fact that worries about inheritance have never been wholly about a concern to promote equality of some kind, even if one of the strongest cases for restricting inheritance flow in *some* way remains thoroughly egalitarian.

Finally, it is worth registering a point about the positive aspect of intergenerational wealth transfers. This book seeks to develop a treatment of inherited wealth based on its role in maintaining conditions of economic segregation. But inheritance need not always segregate, and wealth transfers may sometimes help integrate. Broadly speaking, attempts to mitigate economic segregation should avoid strategies of levelling down in favour of levelling up. First-generation inheritance may be a valuable means of promoting upward mobility. It may allow some parents to introduce their children to ways of life not available to them while they were children, while their own parents did not possess the wealth they later were able to bequeath. Generalizing, there is nothing wrong with wealth attracting valuable nonfinancial capital if this is what enables people to get out of poverty and into an expanding middle class. There is a sense in which second-generation inheritance may do more to create hierarchies within a middle class rather than expand it. There is something valuable about creating a larger middle class and allowing family lines to retain some amount of private wealth over the generations. But there is much to be said against allowing further segregation within the middle class as some are able to hold onto wealth for longer. It is hard to say precisely what the consequences of long-run inheritance might be. But if the goal is to reduce segregation in ways that aim at an enlarged middle class that is free from its own internal segregation, then permitting first-generation inheritance while restricting second-generation inheritance may be a plausible strategy for the advancement of greater social equality.

# 7

# Libertarianisms

## 7.1 Preliminary Remarks on the Libertarian Tradition

This chapter addresses various perspectives on inherited wealth that can be found in libertarian writings. I said in this book's opening pages that the problem of inheritance should be approached as an open question. This goes for libertarians as much as anyone else. As this chapter will demonstrate, many different positions on the regulation of intergenerational wealth transfers can be given some sort of libertarian defence, though some of these defences are more persuasive than others.

Libertarianism has a certain reputation in contemporary political philosophy, one that suggests little potential for openness on questions of taxation and property. Libertarianism is often associated with the idea that property rights have some sort of primitive importance. By and large, libertarians see the burden of justification as falling more on the restriction of such rights than on their protection. Many people have this sort of intuition about bequest in particular. Indeed, it is sometimes said that the very idea of owning something includes some power to transfer it to someone else: it is mine, so it is mine to give. Indeed, John Stuart Mill once wrote that "the ownership of a thing cannot be looked upon as complete without the power of bestowing it, at death or during life, at the owner's pleasure".[1] This concession didn't dissuade Mill from providing a host of reasons, in the same book, for restricting the right to bequeath or transfer property. As a utilitarian, Mill was prepared to concede that the 'completeness' of property rights was not morally significant enough to rule out certain limits on what a person could do with his or her property. Anyone can make this point so long as he or she is prepared to

[1] See Mill (2004: II.2.iv).

say that some moral values are more fundamental than private property rights. In order to resist such a move, one has to make a case for the fundamental importance of private property. And even then one might find reasons to doubt Mill's claim that the power to bequeath or transfer is an essential part of what it means to own something.

One might also try to discount our everyday intuitions about property and taxation. According to Liam Murphy and Thomas Nagel, such intuitions are likely to be infected by a misplaced belief that one's pretax income is something that comes into existence prior to the system of taxation that might reduce it.[2] The reality, though, is that pretax income is largely a consequence of the tax system and the various institutions and other practices upheld by or otherwise working alongside it. According to Murphy and Nagel, we should evaluate the legitimacy of taxes by the legitimacy of the system overall, not with reference to any free-standing initial entitlement people have to what we *call* their pretax income. What an owner can and cannot do by way of exercising his or her property rights has to start with an appraisal of the system overall, not with the fact that persons own particular things within and because of that system.[3]

These observations could be used to raise the question of exactly what property is supposed to be in the first place. This has always been an enormously fraught question, and I won't try to make progress with it here.[4] It is more useful, I think, to emphasize that the libertarian tradition

---

[2]  See especially Murphy & Nagel (2002: 8, 31). A very similar set of remarks can be found in Tawney (1931: 154), which emphasized that the state and its institutions were typically a "partner" in any successful commercial enterprise.

[3]  This is a point about method, not about substance; it could be that some other sort of libertarianism could be true even if everyday libertarianism is false. Even if property rights are consequences of state-designed laws, it hardly follows that the state can infringe property rights whenever it wants, or that the state has the authority to impose any sort of regulation of property that it chooses. Others have criticized Murphy & Nagel for being too dismissive of the idea of pretax income. See for example Geoffrey Brennan (2005).

[4]  At least in part, the question is of whether property is anything more than a hetero-geneous bundle of subsidiary rights. These may have little unity apart from whatever more fundamental principle justifies both their existence and any restrictions placed on them. Nowadays, this question seems to be more extensively discussed by legal theorists than philosophers. Some theorists have sought to ground a power to transfer in the idea that property rights can be unified according to the idea that ownership consists in a right to exclusive use. According to James Penner (1997: esp. 88–9), this approach makes property inclusive of powers to bequeath and transfer, so long as transferring something is a way of treating the recipient's use as one's own use. In a different vein, Thomas Merrill

is not a one-eyed obsession about the importance of private ownership, along the lines of 'property rights good, coercion bad'. Broadly speaking, libertarians will tend to attach substantial and primary importance to economic freedoms (property and contract), whereas other traditions see a broader set of rights, or a different set of moral values, as having primacy alongside, or perhaps over, economic liberty. But interesting libertarian arguments do not simply presuppose that property and contract are absolute or near-absolute rights. Instead, libertarians worth discussing argue from premises about the fallibility of governments, the efficacy of markets, the independent moral cost of limiting personal freedoms, and so on. In this way, the importance of property is argued for, not presupposed. This makes for a wide variety of arguments, and hence the wide variety of conclusions about inherited wealth.

First I will offer a quick survey of the various brands of libertarianism. Much of the heterogeneity in the libertarian tradition can be traced to disagreement on what makes economic rights so important. Some libertarians seek to adapt Lockean claims about a fundamental individual right of self-ownership. Roughly, self-ownership includes a property right in one's body and its powers.[5] Here are the famous remarks made by Locke himself in the *Second Treatise of Government*:

Every man has a property in his own person: this no body has any right to but himself. The labour of his body, and the work of his hands, we may say, are properly his. Whatsoever then he removes out of the state that nature hath

---

(1998: 740–3) argues that transferring property is a way of exercising the right of exclusive use against oneself. I have some doubts about both views but cannot do justice to Penner's or Merrill's ideas here. A classic modern discussion of the 'bundle' view is Grey (1980). See also Attas (2006) and Glackin (2014). More focused criticisms of property as exclusive use can be found in Dorfman (2010) and Katz (2008).

[5] It is not obvious whether owning oneself includes owning one's *talents* as well as one's body. Some Lockean libertarians explicitly include ownership of one's talents as part of ownership of one's self, e.g. Mack (1995: 186). Referring to a person's 'talents' is ambiguous in that it is unclear whether this includes referring to the market value of that person's powers or just to the powers alone. Talents in the sense inclusive of their market value exist dependent on what other people do—the value of an athletic ability is greatly dependent on the invention of televisions. Egalitarians have sought to ground an obligation to surrender part of what one's talents can attract by way of income, given the way in which wider schemes of social cooperation are really what decide what one's talents are worth. The best-known example of this approach may be the egalitarian appeals to reciprocity highlighted towards the end of chapter 4.

provided, and left it in, he hath mixed his labour with, and joined to it something that is his own, and thereby makes it his property.[6]

A right of self-ownership can ground a right in external things: If I own myself, I own what I produce as a result of having put myself to good use. Adapting Locke's views, one might suggest that any restriction on how I use my external property runs a risk of infringing my right of self-ownership.[7] This represents the sort of 'Lockean libertarianism' that has been defended by various philosophers, Robert Nozick being the best known.[8] Lockean libertarianism, as represented by Nozick and others, probably comes closer than any other libertarian view to treating property and contract as morally absolute freedoms. This raises a question of whether it is *ever* possible to justify coercive interference with individual people, in which case Lockean libertarians may end up having to endorse anarchism.[9]

Some Lockeans do succumb to the view that property is sacrosanct and taxation a gross injustice. Murray Rothbard, for example, claims that taxation "is indistinguishable from theft".[10] If it is to be of any interest, Rothbard's claim must add some moral force to the rather trivial observation that taxation is *coercive*. Plenty of legal coercion restricts what I can do with my property, such as a law requiring me to stop my car when I reach a red light. But it would be strange to suggest that such laws 'infringe' my property right in my car. Unless one is really prepared to

---

[6] Locke, *Second Treatise of Government* V.27, 2009: 287–8.

[7] This point is somewhat delicate. See for example Mack (1995: 190–1).

[8] See Nozick (1974). Important other Lockean libertarian discussions of self-ownership include Mack (1995), Narveson (1988: esp. ch. 7), and Rothbard (2006: esp. ch. 2).

[9] See for example Fried (2011), who makes the point that the minimal state's remit of protecting property rights may prove arbitrary. Eric Mack (2006) has argued that while libertarians have often been evasive on the matter of whether they really believe that property rights are absolute, conceding their nonabsoluteness does not entail the justness of any particular infringement of property rights, particularly redistributive taxation.

[10] Rothbard's claim appears at (1998: 166). To be fair, I should say that Rothbard's claim is the conclusion of an argument rather than a mere assertion. He is trying to reject the claim that at least some taxation can be justified on grounds that it is necessary for the provision of "unanimously desired projects", e.g. public goods whose taxpayer-funded production is often endorsed by libertarians other than Rothbard, who is an anarcho-capitalist. Rothbard's claim is that there is no way to establish exactly how much people are willing to pay, and therefore coercive taxation is nonvoluntary. He appears to equate nonvoluntary coercion with theft, which adds rhetorical force but merely begs the question: if taxation is just the nonvoluntary extraction of a *possessed* asset, then it can be nonvoluntary without this entailing theft.

treat all state coercion as illegitimate and embrace anarchism, one requires an explanation of what makes taxation theft as opposed to something potentially quite defensible, albeit coercive. The prospects for this are not good. Anarchism (of a certain sort) was indeed what Rothbard believed. But it is hard to avoid the impression that his remarks about taxation simply parrot the naïve intuition that whatever I own is mine to give, and that anyone who takes part of it (e.g. through taxation) is engaging in stealing.

Apart from the threat of anarchism, there is a more moderate question of why self-ownership is so important that it cannot sometimes give way to the pursuit of other moral goals, as Locke probably allowed—in part due to his theistic commitments.[11] There are some contemporary, secular Lockeans who think that a fundamental right of self-ownership is ultimately compatible with redistributive taxation and associated regulation of property rights. Here I have in mind the 'left-libertarian' school, which contrasts with the Lockeanism defended by Nozick and others. In addition to the inspiration they take from Locke, left libertarians draw on Thomas Paine's insistence that everyone has some sort of equal claim on worldly resources.[12] Left libertarianism is supposed to retain the importance that all libertarians attach to property rights. But, as is clear from Paine's own work, any concession that the world is in some sense 'jointly owned' has implications for how much an individual can acquire by mixing his or her labour with external objects, and further implications for the regulation of distributive inequality.

Lockean libertarianism of any sort is supposed to take seriously the fact that much possession of wealth has come about due to unjust historical events. These include fraud, theft, and other ways in which people came to gain possession of things unjustly. Such injustices need to be corrected according to some distinctive principle of rectification.[13]

[11] Criticisms of the libertarian handling of self-ownership include Arneson (1991), Cohen (1995: esp. chs. 9–10), Nagel (1975), and Sobel (2012).

[12] Representative here are Otsuka (2003) and Steiner (1994). A useful resource on the evolution of left libertarianism since Paine and other historical figures is Vallentyne & Steiner (2000a).

[13] See for example Nozick's remarks on rectification at (1974: 152–3). Some more recent discussions that build on Nozick are Narveson (2009) and Tebble (2001). Historical injustice, and what to do about it now, isn't just an internal problem for a Lockean theory of property rights. For a much broader discussion, see the papers collected in Miller & Kumar (2007).

Much inheritance flow in Great Britain is traceable to state-funded 'compensation' granted to wealthy slave owners in the early nineteenth century after emancipation had deprived them of their slaves. Provision of such compensation may have been unjust. At any rate no compensation was paid to the enslaved, or to their descendants. There have been calls for this inheritance to be redistributed.[14] This may provide an indirect justification for taxing older fortunes more than younger ones, if indeed a fortune's age increases the probability of its being gained due to a particularly heinous injustice. On the other hand, if rectification of past injustice requires the surrendering of some contemporary wealth, it is unclear why things should wait until the next time it is transferred.

Libertarianism does not need to begin from any Lockean idea about self-ownership. The major alternative option is represented by what might be called 'classical liberalism'. On this view, economic rights owe their importance to the (alleged) fallibility of state coercion. One might say that while Lockean libertarians provide a positive justification for economic rights due to self-ownership, classical liberals provide a negative justification grounded in the hazards of relying on state coercion. The point here is that centralized government power is enormously fallible, whereas 'decentralized' power, of the sort enabled by leaving people free from coercion, will have better results. Here the intellectual heritage lies more with Adam Smith than with Locke.[15] An important twentieth-century representative is F. A. Hayek, as is perhaps Milton Friedman.[16] Like the different versions of the Lockean view, ideas descended from classical liberalism have their representatives in contemporary literature.[17]

---

[14]    As happened when the then British prime minister, who has slave owners in his family tree, made a state visit to Jamaica in 2015: "Britain Has Duty to Clean Up Monumental Mess of Empire, Sir Hilary Tells Cameron", *Jamaica Observer*, 28 Sept. 2015, http://www.jamaicaobserver.com/news/Britain-has-duty-to-clean-up-monumental-mess-of-Empire–Sir-Hilary-tells-Cameron_19230957. For a detailed account of the history concerning emancipation and the compensation paid to slave owners, see Draper (2010).

[15]    For a helpful discussion of the role of decentralization in Smith's thinking, see Otteson (2016).

[16]    Passages that generally affirm the market's power while downplaying government's ability as a planner are Friedman (1962: chs. 1–2), Hayek (1960: ch. 2).

[17]    See in particular Brennan (2012) and Tomasi (2012), who defend versions of what they call neoclassical liberalism. This is a young project that has not yet developed any elaborate stance on inherited wealth. But see Reich (2014) on what Tomasi's views might imply about restricting large bequests.

The classical liberal approach is somewhat harder to summarize than the Lockean one, with its singular focus on self-ownership. I won't expand on the various ways of defending the important claim that markets, as 'spontaneous orders', tend to be better at securing desirable ends than the pursuit of such ends through the 'planned order' of state coercion.[18] But it is worth simply emphasizing that the classical liberal view need not rely on a moral objection to legal coercion as a rights violator. The value of economic freedoms may be more instrumental for classical liberals than for Lockeans.[19] But the classical liberal approach certainly leaves things somewhat open as to which sorts of taxation, under which sorts of conditions, represent the sort of centralized government planning to which they are opposed.

These different versions of libertarianism can, and have, gone in different directions with respect to what implications might be identified regarding the regulation of inheritance and bequest. Some left libertarians stand out quite starkly as having argued for the total abolition of inherited wealth. Some 'right libertarians' tend to have been much more in favour of low inheritance taxes, though this tendency may not reflect any deep commitment in classical liberalism. James Buchanan, a prominent economist associated with classical liberalism in its twentieth-century guise, explicitly condemned inheritance as a source of injustice.[20] All libertarians (left and right) are strongly in favour of political rights, namely, those associated with free association, voting, and other forms of political participation. If inherited wealth plays any role in bringing about conditions of plutocracy, then libertarians might have reason to favour wealth transfer taxes in the name of political rights alone.[21] Overall, though, contemporary libertarians resemble members of other traditions in having given the topic of inheritance less prominence than they might have done in recent decades. Libertarian discussions of

[18] Passages that generally affirm the market's power while downplaying government's ability as a planner are Friedman (1962: chs. 1–2), Hayek (1960: ch. 2). Hayek's (1945) is a seminal account of the fundamental importance of price signals.

[19] Consider Hayek's remark that the "chief aim of freedom" is to bring about situations in which people are most encouraged to use their talents and knowledge in ways "useful to others" (1960: 80–1). Brennan & Tomasi (2012) give a fuller discussion of how libertarianism and other forms of classical liberalism come apart, and how they contrast with the 'high liberalism' of Rawls-influenced egalitarians.

[20] This is perhaps most explicit at Buchanan (1986: 133–4).

[21] For defence of this position, see Braun (2016).

bequest tend to occur somewhat fleetingly within texts in which other themes are more prominent. This chapter focuses on the more extended pieces of reasoning that have appeared in libertarian writings since the late twentieth century.

I will argue that there are two types of mistake that libertarians have made when arguing against the restriction of bequest. First, libertarian opposition against inheritance tax has often been insufficiently comparative with respect to alternative forms of taxation. The moral costs of inheritance taxation should be measured in comparison with the moral costs of other sorts of taxation, at least on the assumption that legitimate government is possible and therefore that some taxation will be necessary and justified. Sections 7.2 and 7.3 seek to respond to libertarian objections that make this first mistake. The second mistake is that libertarians have, like many other political philosophers, typically assumed that inheritance taxes will be imposed along traditionally progressive lines. Accordingly, libertarian objections to the taxation of intergenerational transfers may, ultimately, make sense only against the *progressive* taxation of such transfers. Sections 7.4 and 7.5 both deal with arguments making this sort of mistake. Here I will suggest that libertarian views may ultimately provide some support for a Rignano scheme.

Too often, libertarianism is identified in opposition to other views about justice. Although the main arguments in this book have relied on commitment to certain egalitarian views, I am not going to approach libertarianism as a view that I am committed to rebutting. So far as the problem of inherited wealth is concerned, there is more to be gained from using libertarian insights to develop the views that I have already defended, rather than being drawn into the broader fight between egalitarians and libertarians that already accounts for a large amount of published work.

## 7.2 Indistinctiveness Arguments

A general libertarian strategy over the years has been to deny that there is anything special about transferring one's wealth to heirs, compared to other ways of using it. If this is right, then restriction of bequests and gifts might be morally arbitrary. It may be impossible to sustain a case for taxing wealth transfers without being committed to less plausible restrictions on other uses of private property or voluntary behaviour that happens to benefit others.

I call instances of this sort of reasoning 'indistinctiveness arguments'. Such arguments are prominent in libertarian writings from the second half of the twentieth century. I'll focus, first, on the argument conveyed by this fairly lengthy passage from Milton and Rose Friedman:

> Much of the moral fervor behind the drive for equality of outcome comes from the widespread belief that it is not fair that some children should have a great advantage over others simply because they happen to have wealthy parents. Of course it is not fair. However, unfairness can take many forms. It can take the form of the inheritance of property—bonds and stocks, houses, factories; it can also take the form of inheritance of talent—musical ability, strength, mathematical genius. The inheritance of property can be interfered with more readily than the inheritance of talent. But from an ethical point of view, is there any difference between the two? Yet many people resent the inheritance of property but not the inheritance of talent.
>
> Look at the same issue from the point of view of the parent. If you want to assure your child a higher income in life, you can do so in various ways. You can buy him (or her) an education that will equip him to pursue an occupation yielding a higher income...or you can leave him property....[I]s there any ethical difference among these ways of using your property? Or again, if the state leaves you money to spend over and above taxes, should the state permit you to spend it on riotous living but not to leave it to your children?[22]

Although the passage begins by targeting strongly distributive versions of egalitarianism, this is incidental to what is going on in the rest of it. The main claim is that no interesting distinction can be sustained between inherited wealth and inherited genes, or between transfers of wealth and other uses of private property. The passage also makes a methodological point: inheritance should not be evaluated in ways that are overly recipient-oriented at the expense of being donor-oriented.[23]

Why should we accept that there is no moral distinction between inherited wealth and inherited genetic traits? People very often identify with their talents and other physiological attributes even if they recognize them as inherited. In short, my inherited physiology is part of who I am.

---

[22] Friedman & Friedman (1980: 136). The second paragraph in the quote repeats claims earlier made in Friedman (1962: 164).

[23] Much the same point is made by Nozick (1974: 167) and Rothbard (2006: 49–50). As with the Friedmans, Nozick's conception of egalitarianism may be overly narrow, but the methodological point is not less plausible for that.

It is harder to make the same claim about the inheritance of wealth and property—the wealth that comes to me down my family's line is not really part of *me* in the way that my hair colour might seem to be. Egalitarian liberals have even defended this view. Ronald Dworkin distinguishes between personal and external resources, which separates things like genetic endowments from things like received wealth.[24] According to Dworkin, inequalities due to differences in personal resources may be permissible when one's use of one's talents is typically more integral to one's identity than the contents of one's bank account. In addition to this, there is the wholly separate point that genetic talents may take work to cultivate and put to work, whereas large inherited fortunes may generate annual returns without much effort from their owners. I'm not suggesting that these claims are not open to counter-arguments. The point is just that the Friedmans wrote as if the absence of any distinction between wealth and genetic traits was wholly self-evident, as if there is no burden of proof on claims of this sort.

I also want to comment on the Friedmans' concession that the taxation of inheritance can occur "more readily" than interference with genetic sorts of inheritance. This fact is treated in the passage as if it is incidental. But it may well be morally significant, at least if claims defended earlier in this book are along the right lines. The Friedmans talk as if all forms of parental conferral of advantage are morally on a par. This fails to anticipate the sorts of arguments discussed earlier in this book about the way in which many parent–child interactions realize important relationship goods while others, particularly large bequests, do not. As I argued in chapter 6, taxing inherited wealth is considerably less intrusive than trying to regulate the ways in which families confer advantage. It is certainly less intrusive than any attempt to regulate the flow of genes. As Jeremy Waldron has pointed out, taxation typically does not involve any great invasion of personal affairs requiring merely "forbearance".[25] Individuals who have to pay inheritance tax often just see a smaller amount of cash transferred into their bank account, as

---

[24] See for example the remarks in Dworkin (2000: 79–80). Dworkin in part makes the distinction in order to stress the impossibility of redistributing personal resources. He also suggests that personal resources may sometimes be constitutive of a person's identity, something that might also be a moral reason not to *desire* their redistribution.

[25] See Waldron (1986).

happens with income tax withholdings. After all, interference might occur "more readily" partly because it imposes relatively little disruption to the party on whom it is imposed.[26]

This still doesn't settle the question of whether transferring wealth is, after all, simply "another way of using what one has produced". I have argued elsewhere that bequests tend to carry a lower opportunity cost than the various ways in which one might use property during life.[27] As the common slogan goes, 'You can't take it with you'. This is really just one way of saying that individuals have little to lose by bequeathing wealth *compared* to what they stand to lose by giving that wealth away earlier in life. Transferring one's property to someone else while alive means forgoing the use of that property during one's remaining days. Such costs typically go beyond the opportunity costs of bequeathing. If I bequeath a house, for example, then I have to forgo selling it or destroying it, but not retaining property rights over it until I die. Such considerations might count in favour of a moral distinction between bequests and *inter vivos* gifts. If bequests tend to require less sacrifice than other uses of property, then there is a sense that taxing bequests is less burdensome than taxing other uses, like gifts. There may also be a sense in which bequests are not very generous after all. To treat bequests as "another way of using" some property obscures the ways in which the use carries certain costs and benefits compared to other uses. Again, the Friedmans simply write as if bequests and gifts cannot ever be distinguished from each other in this way.

Hayek makes a different sort of indistinctiveness argument. Granting that inheritance is a cause of material inequality, his response is apparently to encourage the view that permitting inheritance is a lesser evil than any attempt to remove it. Hayek suggests that inheritance is the "cheapest" means through which parents may seek to gain power and influence for their offspring. This leads him to claim that abolishing inheritance will simply lead parents to find other ways to confer privilege on their children. Taking communist societies as an example, Hayek

---

[26] The moral disvalue of interference may have something to do with the potential difference between imposing difficulty or disruption as opposed to mere financial cost. This distinction is invoked by G. A. Cohen in a discussion of redistributive taxation (2000: 171–4). Cohen's point is similar to Waldron's about forbearance being a minor evil of taxation; see preceding footnote.

[27] Halliday (2013a).

claims that any such alternative would create "an injustice much greater than the inheritance of property".[28] In making these claims, he remains unclear as to where he stands on any sort of moderate restriction lying between bequest's total abolition and a freedom of bequest great enough to cause "substantial inequality". As such, his view may yet be compatible with some nontrivial amount of inheritance tax.

There are two problems with Hayek's position, which is even more fleetingly stated than the Friedmans'. First, his claim that parents will simply find other ways to confer advantage may not have much substance. It may be uncontroversial that parents will always find some way to confer advantage on offspring, but it is not enough to simply stipulate, as Hayek does, that these other mechanisms will somehow be worse for society. (The claim that such changes in behaviour will actually occur is something I come back to in chapter 8, when discussing substitution effects of transfer taxes.) Second, it is unclear why this should have anything to do with communism. It's true that communism might well be terrible, but taxing inheritance simply isn't tantamount to communism, but rather one way of resolving internal questions about capitalism. (Recall the remarks in 1.6.) In conclusion, arguments for the indistinctiveness of inheritance were never made in a particularly careful way, in spite of appearing in work from some of the most venerated twentieth-century proponents of libertarian views. Libertarians have since offered better arguments about inheritance and bequest.

## 7.3 Virtue, Cruelty, and Family Farms

Loren Lomasky claims that inheritance tax is "equivalent to the violation of a deathbed promise". Expanding on this claim, he writes:

[Inheritance tax] is an especially cruel injury because it deprives the dead of one of their last opportunities for securing the goods that they value. The dead can no longer offer loved ones their advice, their encouragement, sympathy in times of hardship, and joy when things go well; all they can do is pass on worldly goods to intended beneficiaries.[29]

---

[28] This paragraph reconstructs claims made in Hayek (1960: 79–81).
[29] Lomasky (1987: 270).

I think we should start by asking in what way a bequest might count as an act of love in the first place. With Lomasky, Nozick saw bequest as a loving act but was prepared to weigh this against considerations of fairness. Interestingly, Nozick suggested that second-generation inheritance is harder to see as an act of love because the recipient is not properly connected with the party who created the wealth. This is what led him to conceive of a Rignano-type scheme in some of his late-career reflections on distributive justice.[30] Nozick's point is made fleetingly and apparently without any awareness of the earlier work by figures such as Rignano and Wedgwood.[31] It is grounded in the value of the parent–child relationship, combined with an appeal to an intuition about fairness. Nozick's main claim is that inheritance, once rolled over, is "no expression or outgrowth of [the first donor's] intimate bonds". He adds that "the resulting inequalities seem unfair". It is unclear whether Nozick thinks unfairness occurs simply as soon as enough iterations put the next bequest beyond the 'range' of the initial testator's love, or whether all inequalities resulting from bequest are unfair but have a disvalue outweighed by the loving content of first-generation bequests. The claim that "resulting inequalities" are unfair hardly *follows* from the claim that second-generation bequests are not expressions of love. In short, it is unclear what positive work is done by drawing attention to the way in which bequest can be a loving act.

Something seems to bother Lomasky about the *timing* of an inheritance tax. Presumably, this could apply only to bequests and not to gifts made when death is not expected or imminent. Here, it might be instructive to compare inheritance tax with the common practice of imposing sales taxes on coffins and other funeral expenses. I've never heard a libertarian (or anyone else) offer any protest about such taxes, which in practice are timed much closer to the event of death. The processing of estates typically gets completed some months later, and its payment could in principle be deferred in ways not normally possible for sales taxes. Overall, granting that inheritance tax can be

---

[30]  Nozick (1989: ch. 3). Recall also the discussion in chapter 4.
[31]  See Erreygers & Di Bartolomeo (2007). Nozick's (1989) contains few citations of any sort, making it difficult to be sure whether he was unaware of what had been written or simply trying to keep the discussion uncluttered, perhaps in keeping with the autobiographical character of the book.

'cruel' to some degree does not make anything obvious about its cruelty *relative* to other taxes. Ultimately, it is hard to escape the sense that there is something a bit precious about regarding inheritance taxation as cruel just because of any proximity it has to the event of death.[32]

The cruelty objection *does* get harder to dismiss in cases where inheritance involves the transfer of certain hard assets that have some important status within the family. Appeals to such cases are frequently found in contemporary political narratives. Family farms are a stock example, much used in political narratives used to undermine inheritance taxes. The point usually emphasized is that farms may have a high financial value that is out of proportion with the annual return gained from selling their output. A family that has lived on its farm for generations, while never having gained much in the way of liquid revenues, may be forced to sell their farm to pay inheritance taxes calculated on its market value, which may be much larger than the annual returns it generates. Such cases have been especially prominent in the narratives of countries without a history of very large concentrations of feudal land ownership.[33] The philosophical significance of such cases is not always made explicit. It may depend on the idea that hard assets are imbued with some kind of importance not shared by anonymous liquid assets like cash. This importance may be due to the way in which the identity of a family endures over time, through changes in the composition of its membership, in ways dependent on the continued possession of some asset. It might be said that the family has its own 'dynastic' well-being, distinct from that of its members, which is sometimes threatened by restrictions on intergenerational transfers.[34] Or perhaps family identity has some other moral importance, not explicated in terms of the

---

[32] Wedgwood makes a related point about the tendency of inheritors to be wealthy, and how this fact is misleadingly suppressed in political narratives (1929: 189–90).

[33] This is true of both Germany and the United States. For more background, see Beckert (2008: 56–9; 220–5). Similar points apply to Australia, where the abolition of inheritance taxes may owe something to a history of small-scale farm ownership by families rather than feudal landlords. On this, see Pedrick (1981).

[34] I borrow the phrase 'dynastic well-being' from Batchelder (2009: 11), who notes the possibility of this view but does not discuss it. Presumably, dynastic well-being, in order to be interestingly distinct from the well-being of individual family members, would need to be something more than just the sum total of its members' well-being. I am not sure whether this idea can be spelled out in a manner that would make it do the theoretical work required here.

family as a bearer of its own well-being. Philosophers working on the metaphysics of identity normally defend the claim that the identity of a whole can survive a degree of change in the identities of its parts. I am willing to grant that wealth transfers can play a role in enabling some continuity of group identity given the right kind of asset. What matters is whether this function is *necessary* for identity to endure, or otherwise indicates something that counts morally against an inheritance tax on relevant hard assets.

I don't know of any developed philosophical account of how the importance of group identity counts morally in favour of a right to bequeath tangible property to members of that same community. The closest philosophical work might be that done on the injustice done to indigenous people in Australia and elsewhere. Janna Thompson, for example, has argued that policies of cultural imperialism, in destroying languages and other practices, denied subsequent generations their cultural inheritance.[35] Although Thompson's views are plausibly about a real risk to (indeed, the partial destruction of) a group identity, they are not designed to show anything about the inheritance of property within the context of a capitalist economy. At least, language is not a hard asset, much less one that gets transferred down generations in ways that might be taxed. So it is hard to know exactly what to make of the appeal to the cruelty of inheritances taxes levied on hard assets. It is certainly not an injustice comparable to those done to indigenous peoples by European colonizers. But I will respond to it nonetheless.

There are two ways of developing proposals that accommodate special treatment for the inheritance of certain hard assets. One is to use the importance attached to the asset as grounds to motivate a right of *inheritance* rather than of bequest: the moral problem with an inheritance tax is of preventing inheritors from keeping their group identity or honouring certain obligations to each other that are in some way constitutive of what the family is *for*.[36] Another response is to treat the property in question as being owned by the family line and not by the deceased individual.[37] If this second response is right, then the case

---

[35] See Thompson (2002: 107–29).

[36] For some defence of this idea, see Penner (2014).

[37] This is an old suggestion, being representative of how property might have been thought about in historical times. Consider the remarks from Taussig on this matter: "The

against taxing inheritance (in such cases) is simply that there is no inheritance because there is no transfer of ownership between distinct parties. I don't have much to say about these proposals, but it is worth noting that their acceptance might force all sorts of revisions to the way taxation is understood. This is particularly true of the suggestion that the individualistic conception of a property right be abandoned in favour of property as something that can be possessed by a family line or some other group. If this claim is endorsed for inherited wealth, there may be pressure to explain why it should not be accepted for other practices in which property rights feature, such as the taxation of income or consumption of any such group member.

But there are reasons to resist accommodating these cases. In many regions where the inheritance tax debate has substance, the family farm is becoming a bit of a myth. Much productive industry historically controlled by family businesses is increasingly falling into the ownership of large companies. Whether or not it is a good thing for capital to be owned by large businesses rather than families, this shift does rather reduce the need to worry about the inheritance of farms and small family businesses.[38] It has also been suggested that intuitions about agriculture suffer from a sort of romanticism about the honour of working the land, in ways that look outdated in view of the technology now used.[39] Remaining examples of emotionally significant hard assets probably involve property whose market value is low enough to fall below the level of any plausible inheritance tax threshold. As I argued in chapter 6, if the case for taxing inheritance is made to rest on its role in causing economic segregation, then there is reason to believe that this threshold may be high enough to allow the transfer of valued family heirlooms. For

ancestor in early times was not so much the immediate owner of the property as the head and representative of the family which owned the property. Its devolution to the surviving members was no change of ownership, but a transfer to new representatives of the continuing owners" (1921: 267).

[38] This point has been made already, by Haslett (1994: 255–6). More could be said about the continuing practice of providing tax relief for the transfer of family firms, something that is still practised in various jurisdictions but not much discussed by philosophers or theorists. An illuminating exception, focusing on British tax policy, is Most (2014), who defends a version of the claim that family businesses might be owned by the family line rather than any specific individual member.

[39] For a fuller discussion of this attitude to land, and its force as an objection to taxing inheritance flows in assets of this sort, see Tait (1967: 91–6).

assets that are extremely valuable in financial terms, it may simply be hard to elicit the intuition that a family would be destroyed by their loss. As Murphy and Nagel claim, "the family farm is a much more sympathetic victim of the estate tax than the family stock portfolio".[40] There is room for yet more proposals for dealing with these cases. Perhaps I should be allowed to inherit the stately home if it is so dear to my heart, on condition that I not make money out of selling tickets to those wanting to look around its beautiful grounds. It is hard to make general claims about the importance of hard assets, given their variety. But the variety of proposals on offer indicates that there are ways of designing a tax scheme that can accommodate different cases in different ways, to the extent necessary.

## 7.4 Left Libertarianism and Abolition

One of the most enduring problems from Locke's political philosophy concerns how to understand his proviso on original acquisitions on land.[41] The important question has always been about what constraints should exist on the ability to come to own a previously unowned thing by mixing one's labour with it.[42] As noted in chapter 2, Locke tells us that when persons mix their labour with earthly resources, they must be sure to "leave enough and as good" behind for others to acquire. What this ultimately means or should mean is not obvious, and has been the object of much philosophical disagreement. Indeed, the difficulties and range of interpretive possibilities account for the divergence of libertarian schools of thought within the Lockean tradition. Lockeans of the 'right libertarian' sort, like Nozick, Mack, and Rothbard, tend to interpret the proviso as a fairly undemanding requirement: 'enough and as good' does not

---

[40] Murphy & Nagel (2002: 151).

[41] Whether any general problem of resource acquisition should have 'endured' in philosophical discussions of property and redistribution might be called into question, depending on how we interpret the fact that land and other 'external' resources no longer have the economic importance they had in the pre-industrial era inhabited by Locke and others. On this point, see Moller (2017).

[42] A contemporary libertarian answer to this question won't be quite the same as Locke's, which, apart from being rather indeterminate, might be inseparable from Locke's theistic commitments. For a useful discussion of this difference between Locke and contemporary Lockeans, see Waldron (2005).

have to mean 'equal and as good'.[43] Because of their debt to Paine, left libertarians have always had more to say.

Michael Otsuka offers a formulation of the proviso whereby resource acquisitions must "leave enough so that everyone else can acquire an equally advantageous share of unowned worldly resources".[44] The broad idea is that ownership of the world's resources starts off divided among all the persons who will ever exist. Otsuka realizes that this leaves room only for "miniature", even "infinitesimal" acquisitions of resources. His is one way of refining the proviso so as to retain Paine's concern that there is something problematic about the way later generations arrive too late to make the acquisitions available to their predecessors. If the world starts off commonly owned, then acquisitions will quickly start to approach the limits of what the proviso can allow.[45] After all, the future population of the world is, in principle, infinite, whereas worldly resources are apparently finite. Hillel Steiner points out that a person's ability to acquire earthly resources tends to be greater the earlier he or she lives: "[T]here is a strong likelihood of an earlier subset of self-owners exercising this liberty at the expense of the rest".[46]

The question is what exactly to do about this, particularly when it comes to the regulation of property via taxation. Left libertarians do not necessarily accept Paine's solution of a land tax, although some of them have sympathies for universal basic income of the sort discussed in 4.5.[47] If resources cannot be acquired so as to literally *leave* enough and as good, then perhaps they can be recycled: when a person dies, his or her acquisition goes back into the common stock. Here, left libertarianism revives Thomas Jefferson's claims that "the earth belongs in usufruct to the living" and "the portion occupied by an individual ceases to be his when he himself ceases to be, and reverts to society".[48] Still, it remains

---

[43] For an explicit interpretation of the proviso in this way, see Mack (2009: 63). Nozick's remarks on the permissiveness of his version of the Lockean proviso are at (1974: 178–82). For a criticism of such permissiveness, see Cohen (1995: 77–90).

[44] Otsuka (2003: 24).

[45] The idea that worldly resources 'start off' as jointly owned by all persons was probably not Locke's view, as has been noted by careful readers of Locke. See the discussion in chapter 2.

[46] Steiner (1992: 82).

[47] I shall say more about the connection between inheritance taxes and stakeholder grants in chapter 8.

[48] From Jefferson's *Letter to James Madison,* cited in Beckert (2008: 72).

unclear how literal versions of this idea might work in practice. If I acquire a load of iron ore and use it to make paper clips, do my paper clips get somehow dispersed around the world for new acquirers to pick up? Or is some effort made to degrade the metal back into something like ore and to put it back where I found it? According to Steiner, self-ownership expires along with all other ownership, meaning it is permissible for someone to acquire my corpse.[49] Still, this might not amount to a proper replenishment of the common stock. One other solution is to simply abolish freedom of bequest. This is the position taken by Otsuka:

> It would make for more sense to insist that the members of each generation ensure that, *at their deaths*, resources that are at least as valuable as those that they have acquired lapse back into a state of non-ownership. Each generation would therefore face anew a world of unowned resources that is undiminished when compared with that which faced the previous generation. The members of each generation would therefore have the same opportunity as their predecessors to acquire resources from an unowned state.[50]

*Complete* abolition may not be what Otsuka need insist on. Remember Paine's distinction between owning external things and owning the improvements one has added later on. Perhaps one can still bequeath or transfer at least some of that added value, without violating the Lockean proviso.[51] Otsuka rejects this view quite quickly, telling us that "since individuals possess only a lifetime leasehold on worldly resources, they have nothing more than a lifetime leasehold on whatever worldly resources they improve".[52] In making this claim, Otsuka may be relying on improvements being physically inseparable from the object that has been improved.[53] But there may be plenty of cases where these come apart.

---

[49] Steiner (1994: 273). See also Vallentyne (2000: 13–15).

[50] Otsuka (2003: 37).

[51] Arneson (1991) defends the claim that persons can be entitled to the value of improvements even if they lose an entitlement to the value of what was originally acquired.

[52] Otsuka (2003: 38).

[53] Otsuka (2003) relies on an analogy in a footnote, attributed to Ross Harrison, whereby one loses ownership of the paint applied to the walls of a leased apartment, once the lease ends. It is unclear why this case points to anything other than the fact that walls and paint are hard to separate from each other. (The paint doesn't produce anything extra that could be of value.) Compare a case in which I lease a field to grow grain that I then store somewhere else: intuitively, the grain is still mine when the lease ends on the field.

I will set aside various other criticisms that have been made of the left-libertarian project that do not focus on the relation between upholding the Lockean proviso and regulating inherited wealth.[54] One might start by disputing Paine's conviction that acquisition of worldly resources does a disservice to subsequent generations, even if it does restrict their opportunities to get property rights in certain physical things. Here, one might develop the view that resource acquisition is overrated. After all, one can't actually do much with an acquisition of, say, land with an oil field underneath it unless one is able to tap into consumer demand for oil and rely on all sorts of institutions and conventions necessary to bring it to market and make a profit. Doing this may be difficult, even dangerous. Such considerations suggest that interpretation of the proviso should be guided by what actually happens when resources get acquired and how the various costs and benefits tend to fall.

David Schmidtz has developed this sort of view about original acquisition in a series of writings.[55] He makes two particular points worth emphasizing here. Locke himself said that acquisition "does not lessen but increase[s] the common stock of mankind".[56] As Schmidtz puts it, initial acquisition is not a zero-sum game. Initial appropriations may enable future ones, given the opportunities created by what people do with the resources that they acquire. Some of these opportunities will fall to members of future generations. This fact is easier to see if we broaden our conception of an appropriation beyond the eighteenth-century emphasis on land appropriation. Land acquisition may well be a zero-sum game so long as planet Earth is the only place where one can mix one's labour with an external object. But much property nowadays is held in intangible things, like patents and copyright. Creation of intellectual property qualifies as original acquisition insofar as it involves creating new property rather than receiving it through transfer or exchange with its prior owner. Therefore, acquisition is to some degree

---

[54] See for example the works collected in Vallentyne & Steiner (2000b). Also Fried (2004); compare Vallentyne, Steiner, & Otsuka (2005).

[55] Most relevant here are Schmidtz (1991: ch. 2; 2008).

[56] Locke, *Second Treatise* V.37, 2009: 294. Paine's response, in effect, would have been that increasing the stock is not the same as making it common. For an evaluation of Locke's remark along similar lines, see Simmons (1992: 265). Schmidtz's view, as I understand it, is that acquisition increases the stock of that which may be subsequently acquired, which could be true even if the benefits of each acquisition accrued mainly to the person who appropriates.

a positive-sum game (though to what degree is unclear). Schmidtz's second point is that early generation acquisitions tend to make life better for subsequent generations for whom resource acquisition is no longer particularly worthwhile. The fact is that, in contemporary developed societies, there are far better ways to improve one's lot than were available to members of generations faced with vast tracts of unappropriated land and not much else. There is something odd, Schmidtz rightly suggests, about viewing ourselves as situated unfairly with respect to our ancestors, with whom we would not normally want to swap places. Maybe the game of acquisition is sufficiently 'positive sum' that there is always enough and as good left over to acquire, even if it is not land. Alternatively, maybe the benefits of past acquisitions do more than compensate those whose lives take place under conditions less conducive to acquiring but much more conducive to flourishing on the back of the labour of past generations. Schmidtz, it seems, places greater emphasis on the second point, although the two are quite compatible.

But there is another response, one that grants everything the left libertarians want to say about property and acquisition, while denying that their abolitionist stance follows from it. Here I should note that not all left libertarians advocate the abolition of intergenerational transfers. Peter Vallentyne, for example, has interpreted the right of self-ownership as grounding a power to transfer only what one has produced through one's own labour. There may be little or no power to transfer what was received either by prior inheritance or some other form of brute luck. Indeed, Vallentyne mentions the Rignano scheme as a way of modelling this distinction in tax policy—one of the scheme's rare mentions in contemporary philosophical literature.[57] It is possible to extend Vallentyne's thought to show how a Rignano scheme can help satisfy the left-libertarian goal of using the former property of dead people as an enduring supply of acquisition fodder for future members of the human race. We might simply ask: What's the rush? In the quoted passage from Otsuka above, I italicized the clause that property must revert to an unclaimed status *immediately* upon the prior owner's death. But if the point is merely to uphold the proviso, all that matters is that

---

[57] See the discussion in Vallentyne (1997: 333–4, including fn. 14). Bird-Pollan (2013) defends a similar view, on which Lockean ideas about establishing property through mixing one's labour with the world require limiting the power to transfer it to heirs.

there be a supply of unowned things constantly maintained. This is compatible with allowing the property of the recently departed to take an 'excursion' through the next couple of generations of inheritors before finding its way back into the commons. The supply of resources for reappropriation could be kept up simply by confiscating bequests that are already a few generations old. This might preserve something like the equality of opportunity that left-libertarian views, or at least Otsuka's version, consider important.

This is precisely what the Rignano scheme enables. Indeed, Rignano's own vision of the scheme as a means of securing the gradual national-ization of capital could simply be revised as the gradual return of capital to the commons. It is possible to accept a strong reading of the Lockean proviso, such that special efforts might be needed to replenish the commons using the property of dead people. But it is perfectly possible to resist the idea that the property in question must be returned to the common stock immediately. Overall, it is unclear why left libertarians need be committed to ruling out intergenerational transfers altogether rather than just long chains of such transfers.[58] I conclude, then, that left libertarians at least have the theoretical option of defending the Rignano scheme rather than abolition of inheritance, and that they can do this without revising their Lockean commitments.

## 7.5  Perpetual Savings

In chapter 2, I claimed that early liberal oppositions to primogeniture and entail depended on what are now outdated presuppositions about the close connection between ownership of an asset and responsibility for its management. The early liberals were bothered by entails partly because they squandered agricultural potential. Nowadays, there is much less connection between owning things and their everyday management. The very wealthy, upon inheriting large amounts of valuable capital, can simply hand control over to professionals in the financial industry, who

---

[58] There is one notable left-libertarian argument that I have not discussed, namely Steiner's (1994: 249–61) contention that bequest of property is incoherent. This claim depends instead on the idea that a transfer of ownership from A to B entails a correlating transfer of duties from B to A, something that is impossible when A is deceased. Steiner's position is criticized in Fabre (2001).

will make decisions as to how to invest it. The owners may then remain
wholly idle without this being bad for the productivity of their property.
Of course, financiers may make bad decisions with awful social consequences, just like owner-managers can. This might motivate substantial
reforms, like ending taxpayer-funded bailouts of failing companies and
sending financiers to prison rather than simply fining their companies.
But this has little to do with restricting the transfer of ownership. If
capital can stay productive even if it is concentrated into wealthy hands,
then why does it matter whether the hands are genetically descended
from those of previous owners?

   This observation leads to an interesting argument. Society needs a
steady supply of capital stock. Taxing inheritance will provide owners
of this capital with an incentive to consume it rather than preserve it.
Therefore, inheritance ought not to be taxed. This worry has the most
force with respect to forms of capital that can be meaningfully con-
sumed. The owner of a hard asset like a farm would be unlikely to
simply destroy it if his or her right to bequeath were taken away. More
likely the owner would sell it, which needn't be a bad thing so far as
productivity is concerned.[59] The plausible point, then, is that the
vulnerable sorts of capital are those that can be most easily spent
down, such as savings and other investments. This is especially true
of the large savings held by wealthy persons. These are sufficiently large
that the return from their capital is enough to provide them with the
income they need to live. Naturally they want to pass this on to their
heirs. Savings, of all levels, supply the capital that banks use to provide
loans. We need to remember that people do not keep their savings
stuffed under their mattresses, thereby limiting their productivity in a
manner analogous to the feudal landlords who used their estates for
hunting rather than farming. Most savings go into a bank, which
allocates them to other parties in the form of loans. Taxing inheritance
threatens to destroy this important resource, or at least reduce it to a
problematic extent. Moreover, encouraging consumption among the
wealthy may do more to trigger the expenditure cascades associated
with positional arms races mentioned in chapter 6.[60] There are various
ways of spelling out what might be bad about increased consumption,

---

[59] Recall the remarks on this from John Stuart Mill, referenced early in chapter 3.
[60] Edward McCaffery makes something very close to this point (1994: 290).

but the point is that savings ought to outlive the saver. Call this 'the argument from perpetual savings'.

A stolid proponent of the perpetual savings argument was the twentieth-century economist Barry Bracewell-Milnes, who has been rather overlooked by philosophers.[61] More recently, Edward McCaffery has defended a very similar version of the argument.[62] I treat the argument from perpetual savings as a libertarian argument because it apparently relies on an implicit classical liberal assumption that markets rather than governments provide a safer and more reliable way of directing money to where it can be best used. Private banking provides a point of contact between savers and borrowers, ensuring that savings are wisely invested. Governments could, in principle, do the same thing by way of taxing inheritances and allocating the revenues. But the classical liberal point, as noted earlier in this chapter, is that governments are simply much less good at this, for the most part.

I will begin by noting some quick responses to the perpetual savings argument that I will not develop at any length but which indicate some complexities that seem to have been overlooked by its proponents. First, humans are not like salmon: entire generations do not die, en masse, at the same time, as another generation spawns to take their place. Indeed, there has always been something misleading about talking about 'generations' when referring to a whole population rather than a single family line, since most populations contain significant numbers of people at just about every age group. The plausible reality is that, at any given time, those ageing are living alongside young people for whom death is distant enough to motivate saving. So the capital stock will show some degree of resilience just so long as there always exists some age group who are seeking to save money.

Second, it is unclear whether the concern about incentivizing savings really attaches to the taxing of intergenerational transfers rather than to progressive taxation in general. Something like the perpetual savings argument might also be employed against a highly progressive income tax, albeit more as an obstruction to saving in the first place than as an incentive to spend during old age.[63] Once again, it is important to

---

[61] I have mainly relied on Bracewell-Milnes (1997) and especially (2002). One reply by a philosopher can be found in Haslett (1997).

[62] See especially McCaffery (1994) and (2002: ch. 4).

[63] See for example Blum & Kalven (1952: 441–2).

consider comparisons between inheritance taxation and other forms of taxation. Significant taxing of inheritance, combined with some relief by way of a reduced income tax, might have a net neutral or beneficial effect on incentives to save. More generally, the point is that incentives to save are rather like incentives to produce, as Wedgwood pointed out in 1929: the extent to which an inheritance tax would incentivize the spending of personal savings might depend on the presence or absence of all sorts of other kinds of motivation.[64]

Third, there is the simple fact that the strength of any motivation to save is a contingent matter, on which it may be hard to make generalizations about the effects of taxation. Bracewell-Milnes and McCaffery are both somewhat naïve on this, though their reliance on the idea that inheritance tax depletes saving is strong enough that they might face some justificatory burden.[65] It is not clear that the right to bequeath will stimulate much saving in the first place except among those who already have substantial wealth. Proponents of stakeholder grants might point out that giving everyone a moderate cash grant early in life, with incentives to save rather than spend (such as high-interest guarantees if funds are added), might have a better effect.[66]

Fourth, the perpetual savings argument may rely on an inaccurate sense of how easy it is to 'spend down' large fortunes. Much of our everyday, small-scale consumption goes on goods or services that don't have an ongoing exchange value. If I spend some money on a can of soda, and then drink it, the wealth is gone. But it is actually quite difficult to run down a large fortune in this way. Imagine the sorts of things you would go out and buy if you were given tens or hundreds of millions to 'consume'. It is certainly possible to spend huge sums on single bottles of

---

[64] Recall the discussion in chapter 2. Blum and Kalven make a similar concession: "[P]rogression [in any form of taxation] probably tends to reduce the incentive [to work and save] somewhat, but in each case the complexity of total motivation is such that substantial offsetting influences are present" (1952: 442).

[65] Some useful work by economists on the relation between taxation and saving among the wealthy, focusing on the United States, can be found in Carroll (2000), who suggests that the tendency towards saving among the wealthy is best explained by the motive to accumulate wealth for its own sake rather than to pass it on. This may undermine the view that an inheritance tax would induce spending. See also Gale & Perozek (2001).

[66] Here I have in mind the Child Trust Fund, that was set up by the British Government in 2005 for newborn babies. It was discontinued (no new funds were created) in 2011. For discussion of its philosophical rationale, see Le Grand (2006).

wine or Scotch whisky, goods that can disappear as quickly as soda. But probably you would buy many things that remained intact and valuable many years later. Indeed, when wealthy people go on spending sprees, they tend to simply exchange their existing wealth for other wealth—they buy artwork, housing, private jets, and the like. These assets are typically included in tax office's measures of personal wealth.[67] Huge expenditures are very often better described as investments than as large-scale consumption. To the extent that this holds, it may be mistaken to think of an inheritance tax as a destroyer of wealth.

Moving on from these objections, one might imagine a variety of more egalitarian responses to the savings argument. Granting that inheritance taxes would indeed suppress savings, there might be something unjustly hierarchical about treating this fact as having moral force. In effect, the argument from savings allows wealthy rentiers to tell poor borrowers something like this:

"Poor people like you should be glad that rich people like me exist, otherwise you'd have no one to provide you with loans and nobody to invest in companies that provide you with wages. It might be people like you who *keep* me rich by paying interest on your debts that fund my income, perhaps enabling my idleness. But still, people like me make people like you more productive and better off, by possessing wealth of which you may be sold a small slice on terms agreeable to me."

There is an interesting question about whether principles permitting inequality can be debunked by evaluating them in this sort of second-personal presentation.[68] The argument from savings might be one such argument, although much depends on being able to come up with a proper explanation of exactly what sort of debunking has been achieved by these second-personal presentations. It is not entirely clear whether the sort of reactions we might have to these formulations is really evidence of the failure of the initial argument to establish a claim about justice.[69] Other egalitarian responses might draw on the way in which

---

[67] This point is made aptly by Edward Wolff (2015: 138).

[68] Here I have in mind especially Cohen (2008).

[69] Cohen, for example, concedes that the "second personal test" does not demonstrate a way in which arguments can be unsound or invalid in the sense normally used by philosophers to test the force of their arguments. Instead, he relies on the idea that the test shows when an argument is incompatible with what he calls "justificatory community". For the main argument, see Cohen (2008: 43–8). It remains unclear how important

wealthy savers may have enjoyed better brute luck than those who must instead borrow from the capital stock that wealthy persons are fortunate enough to own. I have nothing to add beyond the discussions of these views I provided in chapter 4.

Egalitarians might seek to further develop the lines of response just sketched. Certainly, the value of incentivizing saving will need to be traded off against other values—after all, if savings were all that mattered, then one could make a case for *regressive* taxation.[70] My own view is that the argument from perpetual savings is right up to a point. But contrary to what its proponents have claimed, it is not a straightforward argument for abolishing inheritance taxes. I will grant whatever presuppositions might be made about the incompetency of government institutions to accumulate savings that might be used for loans, as an alternative to private banking. But two points need to be made in response. The first is that it is possible to have too much of a good thing: savings need to be limited as well as preserved. Second, the argument does not actually require that savings need to be 'perpetual' in the strong sense required for it to have force against all forms of inheritance taxation.

Crudely speaking, we cannot *all* be savers. I do not just mean to point out the enduring fact that there will always be some people who do not earn enough to put anything aside each month. Rather, the point is that if society developed very large flows of savings, then we might find that fewer people want to be borrowers. After all, the short-term incentive to save (i.e. apart from the incentive provided by the right to bequeath) is for the ability to not *have* to borrow. This incentive endures even if one is not saving enough to live off the returns, but rather to accumulate wealth for the sake of a purchase as an alternative to taking out a loan. At any rate, really the argument from savings depends on a division of labour between savers and borrowers. It is easy to see that one way for any division of labour to be undermined is for it to become lopsided. Too many people try to crowd into one side of it, so that the labour associated with the other side simply does not get performed.

justificatory community is and what sort of test it provides of the *force* of a moral argument. The idea of justificatory community is one that has been discussed at greater length by Nicholas Vrousalis (2015: esp. ch. 5).

[70]  Blum & Kalven (1952: 443).

Let me generalize. The argument from savings overlooks the prospect that the division of labour will endure only so long as savings, and hence inheritance flows, do not become disproportionately large relative to returns from labour that will be used to pay off loans. Saving and borrowing are each collectively self-defeating, in the sense that either works only if some people do not do it but do the other instead. This is not recognized by the argument's proponents, who seem to be in implicit denial about the prospect of a rentier class. McCaffery wants to defend bequest as an incentive to work as well as to save. He even suggests that the "estate tax is quite possibly an anti-sin or virtue tax. It is a tax on *work and savings*".[71] This claim, however, is misleading. The reality is, of course, that inheritance flows are cumulative series of transfers rather than one-off transfers between a single pair of generations. Stressing the importance of *wealthier* savers is precisely to point out a class of people who will preserve their savings because they live off the returns, as opposed to middle-income savers who might eventually spend their savings in order (say) to buy a home. In this way, the argument from savings appears to depend on the existence not just of inheritance flows but of a rentier class. Whilst the idleness of rentiers might not be objectionable, it is hardly plausible to describe a tax that hits rentiers as a tax on virtue.

The emergence of excessive savings (in terms of disproportionate returns from capital) supports some sort of intervention to restore the division of labour. An inheritance tax remains an appropriate candidate for this. The idea of 'perpetual savings' is ambiguous between two things that might perpetuate in the absence of the other. First, there is the perpetuation of savings as wealth concentrated into particular family lines. Second, there is the perpetuation of a large stock of capital, identified in a merely quantitative sense, but which can be maintained without any particular family being allowed to maintain its savings perpetually. Instead, families might maintain savings for a generation or two (though they might create new savings that might be retained, as per the Rignano scheme), so long as chains of savings do not all stop and start at the same time. The second sense of 'perpetual' is sufficient to secure the goal of savings outliving the saver. The argument from savings

---

[71] McCaffery (1994: 296, emphasis mine).

just appeals to the idea that inheritance flows are valuable when they do enough to maintain the stock for productive borrowers. To assert that such flow requires long-running chains of transfers between individuals is to make a much stronger claim, one which the argument's conclusion does not require.

Perpetual savings of the weaker sort are precisely what a Rignano scheme can help to sustain. It ensures that there is *some* inheritance flow all the time, but not one that is composed of any really old flow within particular families. At the same time, the Rignano scheme does a certain amount of work towards giving everyone an incentive to be more productive. The argument from perpetual savings draws its support from the plausible point that society benefits when people save, in ways that enable other people to produce, and that taxation is not designed so as to raid the savings stock immediately. But it hardly follows that saving is all that matters. Simply defending large inheritance flows, without proper attention to the need to maintain a class of productive borrowers, misunderstands the argument that is supposed to be being made. The argument is, therefore, misrepresented if offered as a defence of absolute freedom of bequest that would maintain perpetual chains of inheritance within families. Instead, it is an argument for designing inheritance taxes in ways that preserve the stock of savings perpetually even if no family's savings are themselves perpetual. This is quite compatible with taxing old money.

# 8

# Taxation

## 8.1 On the Philosophical Evaluation
## of Tax Schemes

This final chapter attempts to connect the largely foundational agenda of
this book to how the taxation of inheritance might actually work in
practice. Here the focus is on questions about the design of tax policy,
though the problems I have chosen to address may not fit everyone's
view as to which are the most urgent in a policy context. I shall finish by
offering some thoughts about how the whole project relates to current
real-world political narratives on the moral status of restricting bequest.

It might be thought that questions relating to the design of inheritance
taxes could be tackled with the help of a more general theory of just
taxation. Unfortunately, however, no really complete theory exists, at
least not within political philosophy. Taxation is in this way quite unlike
other coercive aspects of law and policy. There exist long-standing
philosophical attempts to develop general theories of topics such as
punishment, just war, and the suppression of free speech. Both of these
topics are clearly about how the state can justly use special coercive
powers, and have been subject to long-standing philosophical analysis.
Taxation, however, lacks any such tradition of general theory building, at
least within philosophy. The fact that taxation is *coercive* tends to be
stressed by philosophers developing relatively sceptical agendas about
the legitimacy of government rather than by philosophers interested in
defending such powers. Longer works generally in favour of taxation are
often negatively oriented insofar as their aim is mainly to provide
answers to sceptics.[1] I should say that there is a healthy tradition, mainly

---

[1] Murphy & Nagel (2002), about which I say more below, is representative, as is perhaps
Ackerman & Alstott (1999). Slemrod & Bakija (2008) is a general discussion of taxation

due to legal theory and public economics, in which taxation is approached in both a generalized and a moralized way. Such work is often more hedged in terms of the willingness to take a decisive moral stance, compared to the usually strong willingness shown by political philosophers. Leading authorities in public economics, such as Joel Slemrod and Jon Bakija, are quite happy to say that "fairness is not in the end a question of economics.... [F]airness in taxation, like fairness of just about anything, involves ethical issues and value judgments that, by their nature, cannot be decisively resolved".[2] Political philosophers, though aware that disagreement tends to endure, would typically resist drawing such a concessive conclusion.

Taxation admittedly lacks the evocative drama that helps motivate discussion of topics like war and punishment. There may, however, be more illuminating explanations for why little grand theory building has evolved for taxation. Murphy and Nagel suggest that tax policy develops in the legislative chamber and during electoral campaigns, accounting for "less sophisticated discussion" compared to topics that are examined in the more careful environment of the courts, such as punishment and free expression.[3] This may be true to some extent, though it should be noted that governments do occasionally appoint independent committees of experts tasked with thinking carefully about just tax policy, whose reports may be just as lengthy and detailed as any philosophical treatise, such as that of the Meade committee that I discuss below. A more simple explanation may be that taxation has a highly fragmentary set of goals, compared to (say) institutions of criminal law and national defence. (The legal theorist Lon Fuller once called tax policy the "legal maid of all work".[4]) Taxes are used in an enormously wide range of contexts in pursuit of a similarly wide range of goals. Governments deploy taxation in a rather ad hoc fashion compared to the use of other coercive powers like military force and criminal punishment. We can quickly get a sense

---

from a largely economic perspective, but which stays consistently explicit about the moral significance of the subject matter.

[2] Slemrod & Bakija (2008: 60; see also the remarks at 307). I should add that these remarks should not be taken as evidence that the authors do not take fairness seriously, as will be clear to anyone who reads the material from which this quote has been taken. Chapter 3 of their book serves as an excellent overview of how the morality of taxation has been approached from a public economics perspective.

[3] Murphy & Nagel (2002: 3–4).     [4] Fuller (1969: 166).

of this by noting the substantial difference between using taxation for broadly paternalistic purposes (e.g. taxes on cigarettes) and using it to solve certain kinds of collective action problems, as when taxes enable the funding of public goods like coastal flood barriers. As well as being quite different from each other, these two categories each differ substantially from any use of taxation motivated by concerns about egalitarian justice, such as an inheritance tax. Taxation's various 'domains of deployment' each have their own distinctively difficult questions about justice. Even for the most uncontroversial sorts of public goods, such as law enforcement, there are serious difficulties about working out exactly how much revenue the state can justly extract and how the burden should be distributed.[5] Overall, it is very difficult to see how any plausible set of answers to these questions could be united under a grand theory of tax justice.[6]

Given the unavailability of any general theory on which I can draw, it will be most profitable to continue with the rather isolated focus on inheritance that I have stuck with throughout the bulk of this book. That said, there are some moral generalizations about taxation from which I will draw guidance at certain points in this chapter. First, there is a requirement of publicity. Tax schemes should be generally easy for people to understand, at least to the extent that citizens have some chance of working out what their tax liability is going to be when they engage in any sort of taxed activity. This point repeats some of Adam Smith's claims in his maxims of taxation that were mentioned in chapter 2.[7] In slogan form, the point is that in order for justice to be done, it must be *seen* to be done. The substance of this slogan lies in the idea (amongst others) that individual citizens should have the assurance not just that they are following the rules but that their fellow citizens

---

[5] Problems about how to 'price' public goods have been a source of encouragement for anarcho-capitalists. See for example Rothbard (1998: 164). A more balanced discussion of the philosophical problems associated with public goods has been recently provided by Anomaly (2015).

[6] The points summarized in this paragraph are ones I make at slightly greater length in Halliday (2013c).

[7] The political economists of the eighteenth and nineteenth centuries were rather more bold in making general claims about just taxation, compared to political philosophers in the past hundred years. This may be due to the fact that, prior to the twentieth century, taxation simply wasn't used in such a wide range of roles as that alluded to above and was therefore considered an easier topic to approach.

are following these rules as well.[8] Tax policy can fail to meet a publicity requirement quite easily. One way is for tax to be avoidable by some but not by others, so that taxpayers lack the assurance that all are paying their due. This problem is often correlated with sheer opacity in the tax laws. A society in which tax law is understood by few other than the best paid lawyers, serving only the wealthiest clients, is likely not to meet the publicity requirement. The importance of publicity should be qualified by noting the possibility that calls for 'simplicity' in taxation are often euphemistic. Simple tax systems are often the more regressive. Taxing the wealthy tends to be complicated largely because their financial affairs are more complex.[9] I should say that there is room for much more discussion as to how strongly we should interpret publicity requirements, since it is not plausible for every citizen to fully internalize the totality of tax law.[10] One possibility is that we are dealing with a gradation rather than a binary requirement: the more understood the law is, the better, subject to the costs of achieving this.

A second generalization is more methodological, though it draws some of its force from the publicity requirement. It should be conceded that most tax schemes are going to be heuristics that will generate a number of false positives and negatives. For example, consumption taxes on generally harmful products unfortunately burden consumers who need these products for medical or other 'nonrecreational' purposes. Income taxes often fail to impose the right burden on 'in kind' or 'fringe' benefits that an employee might receive from an employer. The state can try to eliminate this sort of fallibility by creating exemptions and other qualifications to a tax scheme, and inheritance taxes have been no exception to this. The pursuit of such strategies often comes at the expense, however, of transparency and intelligibility once the inevitably convoluted legislation has been fully written, perhaps leading to a failure to meet the publicity requirement. Large numbers of exemptions generate their own (sometimes worse) sets of false positives and negatives. Attempts to develop complex legislation might be more easily hijacked

---

[8] Here I am working with the idea of publicity associated with the work of John Rawls. See for example the remarks in his (2001: 120–2).

[9] Here I follow Ackerman & Alstott (1999: 102).

[10] A much fuller discussion can be found in Lon Fuller's landmark treatment of what he called "the internal morality of the law". See his (1969: esp. 44–94).

by antidemocratic forces in the form of particular sorts of lobbying and campaign funding. Very likely no tax law will be perfect, but we may see this as an inevitable consequence of meeting the publicity requirement. Approaching tax proposals as heuristics rather than as exalted philosophical principles immune to counterexamples is the right approach at this stage of the inquiry. Here, I agree with Barbara Fried's remark that "any administrable tax base will be, at best, a second-best vehicle for achieving a just distribution of tax burdens".[11] Counterexamples can play a role in comparisons, but it is better to assess heuristics against each other than against some absolute ideal standard.[12]

## 8.2 Avoidance through Gifts: The Problem of Selecting the Right Tax Base

I'll start with what might be the most frequently voiced worry about trying to restrict intergenerational transfers by taxing at the point of bequest. This is the worry that a restriction on the right to bequeath will simply motivate donors to seek an alternative form of wealth transfer. Consider Hayek's claim that "without this outlet [of freedom of bequest], men would look for other ways of providing for their children".[13] But it is worth asking exactly what these other ways might be. Bequest, as I have said, is the final act of parental partiality (or any other sort of partiality). The most obvious alternative is the earlier act of transferring wealth at some point prior to one's death, by way of giving gifts. If an inheritance tax stimulates this kind of behaviour, then it may be considered a failure. Call this problem 'the avoidance objection'.

Grappling with this objection requires addressing several questions about what economists call 'substitution effect'. Without much argument, Hayek suggests that parents prevented from making wealth transfers would resort to nepotism, and that "this would cause a waste of resources and injustice much greater than is caused by the inheritance of property".[14] Here, Hayek overlooks several questions. One is whether a substitution effect would be such a bad thing. A second is whether a substitution effect would really be very pronounced, in the event of stiffer

---

[11] See Fried (2000: 385).
[12] For more on the ideal/nonideal distinction, see Valentini (2012).
[13] Hayek (1960: 80).     [14] Hayek (1960: 80).

taxes being placed on large intergenerational transfers. A third is whether any careful design of the tax scheme might mitigate or dampen any substitution effect. We shouldn't be as hasty as Hayek in concluding that a substitution effect is both bad and inevitable. By 'substitution', we may mean a switch from bequests to *inter vivos* giving, or we may be interested in a substitution from wealth transfers in general to some other sort of practice.

I'll deal with the first question quickly. In effect, the issue here is of whether *inter vivos* wealth transfers are in some way more desirable than bequests. If they are, then an inheritance tax might be considered successful if it encourages a shift from the latter sort of transfer to the former. Over the years, some authors seem to have held this view. Hugh Dalton, for example, suggested that pressure to switch from bequeathing to *inter vivos* giving might reduce the vain "desire of rich men to die visibly rich" while benefitting children.[15] There are certainly interesting questions about the threat of disinheritance as a source of power that parents sometimes have over adult children. This may be more true now than in Dalton's day: recall the data cited in section (1.3), which suggests that some adult children will not be able to buy their own home until the death of their parents. If we're worried about parental powers of this sort, then this may be one reason to favour a state that provides certain forms of support for free, including assistance with home ownership, so that young people do not have to depend on their parents. At the same time, arguments made earlier in this book prevent me from any really strong endorsement of a substitution effect towards *inter vivos* giving. The most major diagnostic claim in this book has been that inheritance flows need to be constrained because of their role in allowing distributive inequality to replicate itself. It is likely that even a moderate shift towards *inter vivos* giving would make such replication even *worse*, because it would mean that inheritors received wealth earlier in life, further enhancing their capacity to confer advantage onto their own children, through the various informal practices that have important segregating effects.

The second question is about how strongly the avoidance objection should be formulated in the first place. Many who consider the objection seem to assume that donors have only a very weak preference for

---

[15] Dalton (1920: 326). See also the remarks in Tait (1967: 141), who gestures at a similar position without endorsing it.

bequeathing over *inter vivos* giving. James Meade, for example, writes as if an inheritance tax will motivate a switch to *inter vivos* transfers almost automatically.[16] A similar outlook is conveyed in the following remarks from Milton and Rose Friedman:

> When the law interferes with people's pursuit of their own values, they will try to find a way around. They will evade the law, they will break the law, or they will leave the country. Few of us believe in a moral code that justifies forcing people to give up much of what they produce to finance payments to persons they do not know for purposes they may not approve of. When the law contradicts what most people regard as moral and proper, they will break the law—whether the law is enacted in the name of a noble ideal such as equality or in the naked interest of one group at the expense of another. Only fear of punishment, not a sense of justice and morality, will lead people to obey the law.[17]

Meade and the Friedmans held very different outlooks about economics and justice more generally, though they apparently agree that a preference for bequest over gifting is very weak. They do not, however, explain why they think this.[18]

Current tax theorists have worked harder to dig up some evidence on the strength of the bequest motive compared with the gift motive. Their findings are worthy of some remarks. Importantly, existing tax law in many jurisdictions already permits a nontrivial amount of untaxed *inter vivos* gifting. It is not difficult for individual people to become aware of this, and its exercise doesn't make the act of tax reporting significantly more complex or expensive. And yet a large fraction of taxpayers, even elderly ones, forgo the option of untaxed gifts in favour of bequest later on.[19] So evidence suggests that the preference for bequeathing over gifting appears to be stronger than one might expect. Another piece of evidence is that parental longevity has increased in recent decades, leading to inheritance being received later in life. If parental motivations were strongly directed at benefitting children, it would make sense for parents to favour *inter vivos* transfers, given that bequests may occur too

---

[16] Meade (1964: 54–5).    [17] Friedman & Friedman (1980: 145).

[18] Meade seems to suggest that if donors *can* avoid the tax, then they *will* avoid it, to the extent that "the whole operation becomes farcical" (1964: 55). The passage from the Friedmans is also puzzling in a further way. It suggests (in the last two sentences) that a sense of justice can move people to break the law but not to obey it. If this is really what is meant, it seems like a strange asymmetry.

[19] For some accessible discussions of relevant data, see Poterba (2001) and McGarry (2013).

late in heirs' lives to be as beneficial as they once were.[20] It may be that people simply do not pay proper attention to recent increases in life expectancy. At any rate, there is no evidence of a substantial switch from bequeathing to gifting. Relatedly, there is the contingent but extremely robust fact that people cannot predict the time of their death. This creates the existence of what tax theorists call 'accidental bequest': Some people simply die when they were expecting to live longer. The prospect of paying a large inheritance tax does not increase one's ability to predict the time of death, and a desire to hang on to wealth to pay for old age may suppress a shift to *inter vivos* transfers. Taken together, these considerations cast doubt on the assumption that any preference for bequeathing over gifting is weak enough that an inheritance tax will simply convert bequests into early *inter vivos* transfers.

This evidence comes with qualifications. The data has been gathered during an era of relatively low inheritance taxation. It is one thing to discover that many parents refrain from utilizing tax-free options to transfer wealth, but quite another thing to suggest that this option would remain unused in the face of a substantial increase in the tax liability of bequests. Tendencies of increased longevity also come with an increase in the costs of ageing, such as payment for medical care and specialized housing. Rational expectation of an expensive retirement may be part of what discourages *inter vivos* transfers to adult offspring. That said, the costs involved are probably absolute, and thus subject to an upper limit. For wealthy families, the costs of aging represent a still small fraction of the overall fortune. Much the same goes for accidental bequest. Uncertainty about when the end will come may encourage donors to hang on to a certain absolute amount, but those possessing large fortunes may still be induced to pass on whatever extra they have by the prospect of a large tax on any posthumous transfers. All in all, these points suggest that a substitution effect may be larger for donors who simply have more wealth to spare.

Though its strength is hard to measure, the avoidance objection cannot be dismissed. A tax on bequests would likely have some significant substitution effect, resulting in avoidance through *inter vivos* transfers. All prior uses of 'inheritance tax' that I have made in this book

---

[20] See Ackerman & Alstott (1999: 36). The authors later concede that there remains a problem about some degree of avoidance in the face of large inheritance taxes (83).

suppress this ambiguity as to whether the tax base is the donor or the beneficiary end of the transfer, though this does not affect the force of any arguments defended (or opposed) earlier in this book. Now is the time to pay closer attention to these differences and to address the question of whether an inheritance tax can be broadened so as to include all intergenerational wealth transfers in its base. The traditional base of an inheritance tax is a dead person's 'estate', i.e. what wealth he or she possesses at the time of death, perhaps adjusted for any outstanding debts. It is perfectly possible, in principle, to include whatever transfers a donor makes prior to death, by way of a gift tax. (To save words, I'll use 'gift tax' to refer to whatever tax treats gifts *and* an estate as its base.) Another option is to tax wealth transfers at the receipts end rather than at the donor end. The idea of a receipts tax (sometimes known as an accessions tax) is that inheritance gets declared as part of its beneficiary's taxable income, with the total wealth of the donor ignored, thereby also making irrelevant the distinction between estates and other gifts. So, broadening the base by converting an estate tax into either a gift tax or a receipts tax will make a big difference, assuming it can be made to work, to the force of the avoidance objection. Tax avoidance essentially involves taking some asset out of the scope of the relevant tax base. So long as gifts or receipts are taxed at a similar enough rate, *inter vivos* gifting won't be an effective avoidance strategy for the taxation of intergenerational transfers because such transfers remain within the range of the tax base.[21]

A number of philosophers have defended receipts taxes over the years, in large part precisely because they see them as a good way to address the avoidance objection.[22] Gift taxes seem to be defended less often. This is probably because there seem to be independent advantages of taxing the beneficiary end of wealth transfers instead of the donor end. One is that receipts taxes tend to do a better job of encouraging the fragmentation of large fortunes than estate taxes. Again, if income taxes are progressive, then spreading an estate among a large number of beneficiaries will result

---

[21] This may require a calculation of liability that takes into account a beneficiary's cumulative lifetime income and total wealth rather than just his or her annual income. On this, see Meade (1964: 57).

[22] See for example Haslett (1994: 257–61), Meade (1964: 56–7), Murphy & Nagel (2002: ch. 7), White (2008), and, for an extremely brief endorsement, Rawls (2001: 160–1). For an important discussion of the estates/receipts distinction from a legal perspective, see Batchelder (2009). A more concise relative of this paper is Batchelder (2007).

in lower tax liability than bequeathing the entire estate to just one person.[23] Further plausibility may come from the way in which taxing receipts creates opportunity for ingenuity at the point of policy design. In the 1970s, Meade chaired a report that recommended a particularly elaborate receipts tax called the Progressive Annual Wealth and Accessions Tax (PAWAT).[24] A core element of this proposal is that tax liability be made an increasing function of the amount of time that a person holds wealth. The PAWAT works by taxing the receipt of inheritances at increasingly higher rates, the younger the recipient at the time of inheriting. The recipient will get a rebate if he or she passes the wealth on relatively soon. Deathbed transfers from grandparents to infant grandchildren would thus incur more tax than transfers that are more 'horizontal' in terms of the relative ages of the parties involved.

The PAWAT embodies a version of 'progressivity over time', albeit one related to the age of the parties giving and receiving rather than the age of the fortune being transferred, as per the Rignano scheme discussed earlier in this book.[25] But the intention behind it is really one of making a transfer tax behave a bit more like an annual wealth tax: liability is increasingly sensitive to how many years the wealth has been held, and will be expected to be held, by the person whose receipts are taxed.[26] The PAWAT has some specific problems, some of which pertain to details of the proposal that I will not spell out here.[27] I mention it mainly to give an

---

[23] Holding fixed the incomes of the beneficiaries: bequeathing many fragments of an estate to a number of wealthy beneficiaries may incur more taxation than bequeathing all of it to one relatively poor recipient.

[24] Meade (1978: esp. 320–30). This report has become quite well known among tax theorists interested in discussing the morality of inheritance.

[25] The PAWAT can also be viewed as a more aggressive alternative to the heavier tax liability imposed on generation-skipping transfers in the US. (The PAWAT is more aggressive just because it attends to the age gap, whereas the tax on generation-skipping does not do this.) The practice in the US is sometimes described in connection with the importance of breaking up hereditary class structures, e.g. in Batchelder (2009: 79).

[26] The PAWAT is, however, stronger than a standard annual wealth tax in one important respect: the assumption that a recipient will retain the transferred wealth for a number of years means that the liability does not decrease if the fortune dwindles due to bad luck or if it is spent on any sort of consumption, something that an annual wealth tax would normally recognize with a reduction in liability.

[27] For a philosophically sophisticated critique, see Eric Rakowski's remarks on the PAWAT as part of his longer discussion of wealth taxes and social justice (2000: 334–47). Rakowski nicely separates the hidden problems with the Meade report's proposal from its enduring attractions.

impression of the sort of proposals that might be offered when exploiting the potential of receipts taxation to tackle the avoidance objection. The broader question of age sensitivity as a feature of wealth transfer taxation probably deserves more of an extended philosophical examination than it has so far had in the literature.

There are general problems, too, with broadening the tax base beyond estates, whether this is done by identifying its scope with gifts or receipts. As I mentioned earlier, the fact that bequests are 'institutionally constituted' makes them very difficult to hide. An advantage of an estates tax is that deaths need to be registered before any bequests can be enabled. Thus, the authorities generally have a way of finding out when a person has died and can more easily take steps to levy taxation on his or her estate. Bequests can't happen without some action by legal firms of a sort that the state can monitor relatively easily. Gift giving will often be much easier to conceal, irrespective of whether tax liability is imposed at the donor or the recipient end of the transfer. This may vary somewhat with the nature of the assets being transferred. Giving someone a house might be a harder transfer to hide than giving cash, just because hard assets are more difficult to hide in the first place, particularly ones that are sometimes physically occupied by their owner. Gift recipients may be quite prepared to lie about their pretax income in general. While tax evasion carries a threat of punishment that avoidance does not, this may not always deter people. Some jurisdictions suffer from a 'culture' of tax avoidance or noncompliance among their citizens.[28] In cases of very wealthy families, government failure extends to practices of allowing wealth to be based offshore, in tax havens, where bequests and gifts both might be processed.[29]

## 8.3 The Rignano Scheme as an Anti-Avoidance Device

There is no theoretical reason why a Rignano scheme cannot be formulated as a tax on receipts rather than estates. This is because the Rignano scheme is ultimately an idea about how to calculate the rate of

---

[28] For some more discussion of tax avoidance as a challenge for social justice, see Alarie (2015).

[29] For discussion of tax havens and such problems, see Brock (2009: 125–30, 136–40). A comprehensive discussion of global tax competition can be found in Dietsch (2015).

inheritance taxation, and tax rate and tax base are different from each other. A Rignano scheme is really just any form of wealth transfer tax that links liability to the length of any series of transfers of which the taxed transfer (gift or bequest) is the latest member, or more weakly, to consistent presence of wealth up the family line of the parties whose finances are included in the tax base. It is possible to talk coherently of a series of bequests by way of a chain of successive transfers, but also of a series of receipts that may accrue to successive generations of recipients irrespective of who the donor(s) might be. A Rignano scheme may work as the liability parameter of a gift tax insofar as attention is paid to the donor's prior inheritance or receipts, whereas it could also work as a receipts tax by ignoring the donor's history and instead attending to the history of receipts up a recipient's family line, including receipts that have already accrued to that recipient. Of interest here is whether a Rignano scheme adds anything to the problem of tackling the avoidance objection.

Most interesting may be that a Rignano scheme allows tax liability to vary in a way that is the inverse of its variation if the tax rate is standardly progressive, i.e. a matter solely of the financial value of what is transferred. Here's how this difference obtains: when transfers are taxed in a traditionally progressive fashion, their tax liability starts off low (perhaps zero) and becomes larger as the amount transferred itself becomes larger. Progressivity over time works the other way: marginal liability to taxation decreases as a given transfer gets *larger*, not smaller. This is because it is the older 'portion' of the donor's fortune that is taxed first. The per-dollar rate starts off high, until such a point as the transfer exceeds whatever amount the donor received by way of prior inheritance. Progressive taxation works in reverse. It taxes the first transferred dollar at a lower rate than the nth transferred dollar. As such, the per-dollar rate decreases as a given transfer grows in size.

Although the basic idea here works in the same way in the case of receipts and gift taxes, it is worth repeating the explanation for both cases to avoid confusion. Suppose we have a gift tax with the donor's wealth serving as the tax base. Assuming that a donor is passing on an amount that has already been transferred down the family line for some number of iterations, any transfer he or she makes will be taxed at a high rate *first*, that is up until it reaches the point that the amount being transferred exceeds what the donor has inherited, at which the marginal tax rate is relaxed. If a donor has inherited, say, one million dollars, then he or she will have to donate *more* than one million before his or her gifts get into the lowest tax bracket associated with newly produced wealth. The low tax rate 'kicks in' only once an amount has been reached that exceeds the older amounts of the donor's fortune. Consequently, donors need to give up more wealth to actually achieve the intended receipt, compared with how much they must give up on traditionally progressive taxation. In this way, the Rignano scheme tests a parent's generosity to a greater extent than traditionally progressive taxation. Of course, much depends on how the liability rates differ according to the age of a fortune, measured by the number of prior intergenerational transfers up the donor's family line. Rignano himself proposed that fortunes transferred twice already should incur a 100 per cent tax rate the next time. A donor who wants to give a gift to heirs but who has inherited one million dollars that was already inherited (jointly) by his or her parents, must therefore give *more than one million* before the recipient actually receives anything after tax. This may, for various reasons, be an unduly extreme rate of taxation for third-generation transfers, but it aptly illustrates the way in which a Rignano scheme differs from progressive taxation by taxing gifts at a rate that starts high and can be 'overcome' only given a very strong motive to part with one's wealth by way of gifts.

Things are slightly different for a receipts tax. Here, the idea would be that *inter vivos* transfers would be taxed in ways sensitive to the receipts of the parents (and grandparents) of the *beneficiary*. If a beneficiary's parents had jointly received one million dollars, then *any* donor wishing to enrich this beneficiary would have to provide more than one million dollars before reaching the smallest tax bracket. Again, without saying anything specific about the rates involved, it is easy to see again that the gift motivation is tested by liability starting off high and becoming low only if a sufficiently large gift is coughed up. In this way, a Rignano scheme reduces the incentive to engage in *inter vivos* transfers by broadening the base to gifts, in ways that allow the rate to be calculated by attending to the history of transfers up the family line of either the donor or the recipient. It is clear that the case of a receipts tax makes for a slightly different way of doing things. First, it means that receipt of wealth may be taxed at a high rate even if all the wealth has been newly produced by the party donating it, just so long as there is a presence of wealth up the family line of the recipient. How appropriate this is may decide whether it is better to implement a Rignano scheme as part of a gift tax or a receipts tax, setting aside other reasons that might exist for preferring either of these alternatives.

I do not have anything elaborate to say about whether the egalitarian foundation for the Rignano scheme can prove decisive in settling these questions about the tax base. Suffice it to say that any answer will depend on whether what matters most is the history of wealth in the donor's family line or the recipient's family line. Very often these will coincide, just because donors are often parents or grandparents. But the two can come apart, as when a donor has a rich history of wealth and the recipient does not, or vice versa. If the sociological foundations of chapters 5 and 6 are solid, then it is likely that receipt of money by persons whose parents and grandparents were wealthy does more to entrench social inequality than receipts by persons from humble backgrounds made by donors who happen to be passing on old money. In short, receiving wealth makes a difference depending on how long one's family have already possessed wealth, not simply on how long the wealth was possessed by whoever donated it, in the event that the donor is from another family line. This converges with the earlier suggestion that what matters may be the continued presence of some *level* of wealth in a family line for much of a certain period of time rather than the narrower idea of the continued transfer of the *same* wealth down this family line being maintained at all times. To the extent that this holds, there is a case for integrating a Rignano scheme with a receipts tax. Indeed, to do so may be a way of incentivizing gifts made by members of historically wealthy families to members of historically impoverished families with whom they are not biologically related. From the point of view of social equality, such transfers may present no objections.

## 8.4 Charitable Bequests

So far, this book has been about inter*generational* transfers. These occur when bequests are made to *persons*. In political philosophy, discussion of inheritance has always seemed to put bequests of this sort at the forefront. But we are all familiar with bequests made to charities or other organizations, which count as persons in a legal sense but not in the physiological sense. Such bequests can have moral significance and bear on the design and evaluation of any inheritance tax scheme.

One important point about the moral significance of charitable bequests can be made quite quickly. Opponents of inheritance tax sometimes point out that taxes on intergenerational transfers have never raised much revenue.[30] This claim overlooks the possibility that low revenue is a sign of the tax's role in stimulating higher levels of charitable bequests. It is a crude fallacy to say that because a tax raises little revenue, it must therefore have failed in its moral objectives, particularly if charitable donations are something we want to encourage. I'll leave aside the claim about whether an inheritance tax could, never-theless, generate substantial revenue under the right conditions. Suffice it to say that the main agenda of this book—that restricting inheritance flows helps reduce the persistence of social inequality—does not actually depend on such taxes being great revenue generators either.

At the level of intuition, it seems as if there is something morally worthy about bequeathing to charities, and that this right should be protected by way of some sort of tax break.[31] Some jurisdictions tax bequests to (human) persons at a lower rate when some fraction of the estate is bequeathed to charity.[32] Empirical studies of the bequest motive suggest that whereas members of low-income groups tend to make charitable donations while alive, wealthy donors show a tendency to wait until they are dead, when charitable bequests are often large.[33] If it is true that wealthy donors prefer giving to charity at the point of death, then it may be that taxing bequests to biological persons could induce more charitable giving at death.

Nowadays, charitable bequest is looked upon kindly but is hardly thought to represent any sort of inescapable requirement. In nineteenth-century America, there was something of an ethos whereby bequeathing large amounts to family members was looked down upon, given the potential for advancing social life through bequests made to the right sort of organizations.[34] This view received some eloquent defences

---

[30] For example, by McCaffery (1994: 282).

[31] See for example Haslett (1986: 139).

[32] The United Kingdom, for example.

[33] For discussion of some evidence, see Joulfaian (2001).

[34] Historians of US tax law often emphasize America's lack of a feudal past as having an important bearing on attitudes towards inherited wealth in the century or so after its founding. For general discussion see Beckert (2008) and Chester (1998). The position of inheritance taxes in contemporary America suggests something of a shift in attitudes over time; see Graetz & Shapiro (2005).

by members of America's industrial elite. Representative here was Andrew Carnegie, who believed that bequeathing wealth to family members was the "most injudicious" way of exercising freedom of bequest. Carnegie's claims were markedly different from common contemporary claims that often merely esteem wealthy donors, as if bequeathing great wealth to a worthy cause is an act of generosity rather than obligation. Carnegie disagreed, strongly enough to say "the man who dies rich dies disgraced".[35] In part, these thoughts drew on a rather astute understanding of the ills of social segregation. Here I find it helpful to quote Carnegie's remarks in full:

> We assemble thousands of operatives in the factory, in the mine, and in the counting-house, of whom the employer can know little or nothing, and to whom the employer is little better than a myth. All intercourse with them is at an end. Rigid castes are formed, and, as usual, mutual ignorance breeds mutual distrust. Each caste is without sympathy for the other, and ready to credit anything disparaging in regard to it.[36]

The segregating tendencies of mass industrial employment had become more apparent during the industrial era in which Carnegie lived. Adam Smith's pin 'factory' is described as containing no more than "ten persons"—enough people to fit into the same pub after clocking off.[37] Workers who slave away in a big city factory probably have more to gain from free access to parks and swimming pools than an agricultural labourer of pre-industrial times. This accounts for certain constraints that Carnegie adds to the obligation to bequeath. It was important that charity be properly directed so as not to have "pauperizing tendencies".[38] Hence, alongside parks and swimming pools, Carnegie favoured provisions for universities, public libraries, and hospitals, and opposed its use in funding "alms". Carnegie was not calling for a rise in inheritance taxes,

---

[35] Carnegie (1889a: 664).

[36] Carnegie (1889a: 654). Here Carnegie's remarks resemble some of Mill's in the discussion of the lot of the labouring classes. See especially Mill's approval of "the civilizing and improving influences of association" preferable to systems of production involving "hostile interests and feelings" between workers and their employers (2004: IV.vii.14). Mill's claims, like Carnegie's, can be read as expressing a commitment to the values of social integration within systems of industrial production.

[37] Smith, *WN* I.i.3, 1999a: 109–10 For a comment on Smith, see Fleischacker (2004: 11). The nature of large-scale postindustrial employment raises concerns about justice that go well beyond what I have here alluded to. For more, see Anderson (2017).

[38] Carnegie (1889b: 685).

but commenting on how very wealthy individuals ought morally to behave in such a way as to render taxation unnecessary. Of course, people do still give to charity, and some wealthy individuals do emulate Carnegie's efforts. Perhaps sadly, the ethos of Carnegie's times is no longer as strong as it was, and this fact might count in favour of relying on taxation even if this is regarded as second best to such an ethos.[39] It might be added that taxation may have some ethos-generating power.

Ultimately, whether the law should protect charitable bequests depends on what charitable status actually amounts to and when it can be conferred on a legal person. It is perfectly possible, and appropriate, to approach charity law as a moralized subject matter drawing on social egalitarian concerns such as those discussed earlier in this book. On any plausible view, it may turn out that many contemporary charities are not fit for purpose. Nowadays, charity law is a capacious category that admits all sorts of organizations, some of which have better moral credentials than others. Some charitable organizations might actually work in ways that create or exacerbate injustices. Reflection on this should call into question the charitable status given to entities like expensive private schools in countries like Britain, or at least motivate a revision of its terms. Generalizing, the point is that if inheritance taxes are meant to combat economic segregation, then this will have implications for what sort of entities should count as charities, or at least whether charitable status should always include the possibility of being made a beneficiary of large bequests, tax free.

I will not try to do the work here of developing a theory of charity law. Good work has recently been done elsewhere, which might be usefully adapted to illuminate further the morality of protecting charitable bequest.[40] The conclusion here is that inheritance taxes probably should leave substantial exemptions for charitable bequests. The set of such bequests could, however, prove to have quite a narrow range of legitimate beneficiaries.

---

[39] For more from Carnegie, see West (1908: 196–8), also Chester (1982: 54–5). The ethos of Carnegie's generation of American industrialists is sympathetically discussed in Beckert (2008: 174–9), Chester (1976: 87–92), and McCloskey (2006: ch. 47). McCloskey displays some optimism that the capitalist ethos of Carnegie's peer group may be a more robust feature of market society.

[40] See especially the lengthy discussion in Harding (2014).

# 8.5  Why Not a Wealth Tax?

It is sometimes said that political philosophy has allowed itself to become disproportionately concerned with inequalities of income rather than of wealth.[41] There are signs that this is starting to change, as philosophers respond to the emergence of large wealth inequalities of the sort highlighted by Thomas Piketty.[42] Piketty's own view is that large individual wealth holdings ought to be taxed.[43] Of course, one might think that this can be overcome by just taxing large inheritances at rates proportionate to the very high rates of return that large fortunes enjoy during the interim periods. (Recall, for example, Rignano's favouring of 100 per cent rates for third-generation inheritances.) Nevertheless the idea of a wealth tax is worth discussing and allows some interesting questions to be raised. I shall not manage to do justice to this topic, and to the associated complexity surrounding the distinction between stocks and flows. But I will attempt to explain how wealth taxes and inheritance taxes perhaps shouldn't be approached as different candidates for pursuing precisely the same moral goals.

If wealth is understood as returns from capital rather than labour, then it may count as 'unearned income' in the sense that, like inheritance, it is a 'passive' sort of income. There are a variety of ways of developing this observation into a moral objection, particularly if returns to capital are starting to displace returns to labour. Here it is worth going back, again, to John Stuart Mill:

Suppose that there is a kind of income which constantly tends to increase, without any exertion or sacrifice on the part of the owners: those owners constituting a class in the community, whom the natural course of things progressively enriches, consistently with complete passiveness on their own part. In such a case it would be no violation of the principles on which private property is grounded, if the state should appropriate this increase of wealth, or part of it, as it arises. This would not properly be taking anything from anybody; it would merely be applying an accession of wealth, created by circumstances, to

---

[41] This concern is raised by Brian Barry (2005: ch. 14), who goes on to make several points about the moral significance of wealth.

[42] See for example Ingrid Robeyn's (2017) discussion of "limitarianism", a view on which there are moral reasons for limiting the wealth of individuals.

[43] Annual wealth taxes may be necessary to end "an endless inegalitarian spiral and to control the worrisome dynamics of global capital concentration" (Piketty 2014: 515).

the benefit of society, instead of allowing it to become an unearned appendage to the riches of a particular class.[44]

These remarks could just as easily have been made in the twenty-first century as in the middle of the nineteenth. The hint is in the way in which unearned income has a tendency to "constantly" increase if nothing is done to regulate it. Importantly, large concentrations of private wealth tend to endure only because they can be transferred down a family line. Indeed, Piketty is very explicit in blaming inheritance flows as an enabler of wealth inequality over time.

If the moral case for taxing wealth draws its force partly from the idea of entitlements to passive income being relatively weak, then any case for a wealth tax over an inheritance tax may depend more on practicalities than any particular point about what justice requires. Whatever the root of Piketty's normative complaint, part of his case for this claim is that the annual rate of return on large wealth has now become so large that it is likely to outstrip the effects of any transfer taxes levied on inheritance and other intergenerational transfers that may occur years apart. The rentier society that Piketty predicts for the twenty-first century may not, however, be as objectionable as the old feudalism.[45] Prior to the twentieth century, annual returns from capital were relatively low. A low rate of return on a large estate would mean that an inheritance tax could break up the problem of excessive concentration by fragmenting the estate in question. Indeed, the enforcement of legal entail was partly about preventing this from happening, as noted in chapter 2. Piketty's worry is that fragmentation can't be secured by taxing inheritance when rates of annual return become as high as they are now becoming. This is because the growth of fortunes between occasions of intergenerational transfer will 'outstrip' the work done by an inheritance tax.[46] Capital's value

---

[44] Mill (2004: V.ii.27). Mill's proposal resembles a capital gains tax insofar as it applies to returns to wealth rather than to wealth that might be massive but for some reason not deliver a return in the year in question. A wealth tax, strictly speaking, makes no such exception.

[45] Some critics say that Piketty errs in overlooking these differences. See especially Deidre McCloskey's (2014) assessment of Piketty's views. These criticize him for, among other things, focusing narrowly on physical capital to the exclusion of human capital and associated benefits. Compare Pressman (2016).

[46] Piketty is not the first to have noticed this; a very similar point was made by Alan Tait (1967: 86–90). Here, Tait is comparing the rate of return on capital in the US and UK between the 1880s and 1960s with the inheritance tax rates used in those countries during

grows so much between iterations of bequest that the fragments of large family fortunes are even larger than whatever single mass was inherited last time round. Piketty's solution is to tax fortunes much more frequently, though at only "moderate" rates, by way of a periodic (e.g. annual) wealth tax.

Again, though, my sense is that there is not good reason to try to pick a single winner between taxing flows of inheritance and taxing stocks of wealth. For sure, wealth taxes and inheritance taxes may have some advantage over the other. Here are some possible advantages of taxing inheritance, or at least bequests: Once again, the act of bequest has to happen somewhere. It cannot be hidden away, dispersed around the world like wealth can. A person cannot die in many countries at once, even if he or she spent his or her life hiding his or her wealth in many countries at once. People have to rely on the legal apparatus of their country of residence *and* that of their heirs' residence to process their estates, and this apparatus can quite easily include the mechanisms for taxing any bequests. This means that even if tax havens exist, a state can deny that a recently deceased citizen was a resident of whatever small island if he or she spent most of his or her life in the state's own territory. Inheritance taxes may suffer less from the problem of placing a value on nonliquid wealth stocks. Wealth very often grows by way of capital appreciation that is hard to precisely measure. If it can be measured, imposing a tax liability on its bearer may be very hard to meet without selling the asset. As noted in chapter 7, this point is often stressed with respect to family farms and businesses. This is somewhat less of a problem for transfer taxes, since the recipient cannot typically be said to face huge disruptions to his or her life if part of the asset needs to be sold (though again, recall the possible exceptions discussed in section 7.3).

On the other hand, wealth taxes may have their advantages. A global wealth tax of the sort favoured by Piketty may provide a valuable opportunity for international governmental cooperation, which could have valuable side effects. But Piketty's concerns are motivated by the enormous wealth of only a very small minority. I would like to note that a

this period. The rest of Tait's book discusses various other aspects of wealth taxation. Fleischer (2017) is a more recent discussion of wealth taxes, which emphasizes various contrasts with wealth transfer taxes.

concern about economic segregation can endure apart from, and even in the absence of, any reasons for being concerned about concentrations of wealth that become excessive enough to survive the occasional reduction made by taxing any transfers. The idea of economic segregation applied in this book does not have such an exclusive preoccupation with the very top of the wealth distribution. Economic segregation can occur between groups of which neither counts as a rentier class. Consequently, there may be a division of labour between taxes for the super-rich and taxes for those who merely have significant wealth (the upper middle classes). An inheritance tax and a proposed wealth tax might, therefore, complement each other while nevertheless serving different purposes. To assess the inheritance tax by its effects on the super-rich is, therefore, to assess it too narrowly, even if part of its defence might come from its effects on the very top of the wealth distribution. In summary, if a wealth tax can be achieved, then that will possibly advance social justice in ways compatible with the main claims defended in this book. But the case for inheritance taxes remains in spite of whatever (perhaps forceful) case can be made for taxing stocks of massive wealth rather than their flows.

## 8.6 Hypothecation

In a discussion that I have used several times in this book, Walter Blum and Harry Kalven wrote that "if there is any disadvantage in employing taxation as a means of lessening economic inequality it is that the process tends to conceal precisely what is being done about redistribution".[47] In other words, whatever taxation is being used for, and wherever it is being levied, nobody really gets to see what happens to the funds. Such opacity might be morally objectionable, perhaps a violation of the publicity requirement noted earlier in this chapter. Those who think that citizens ought to know where their taxes are going call for the introduction of what economists call *hypothecation*. This is the practice of earmarking specific tax revenues for expenditure on specific policies.

Something ought to be said about hypothecation in the case of taxing inheritance. There is a long, although not wholly continuous tradition of viewing inheritance tax revenues as appropriate for solving certain

---

[47] Blum & Kalven (1952: 488).

problems. This extends at least as far back as Thomas Paine's idea that every person has a natural inheritance right in some share of land. Land tax revenues should be used to redistribute from parties for whom this right has been satisfied to those for whom it has not, in the form of a stakeholder grant. Contemporary defences of stakeholder grants often retain this commitment to hypothecation. Ackerman and Alstott, for example, claim that stakeholder grants should be funded exclusively by a wealth tax, and not from any wider and potentially varying combination of tax bases.[48] Some contemporary egalitarians have attempted to extend a principled justification for this sort of view. As noted in chapter 4, Ronald Dworkin attempted to ground a progressive inheritance tax in a concern to pre-empt or at least combat class hierarchy. In this way, his views share an affinity with the stakeholding project, though Dworkin was not himself one of the project's exponents. Instead, he suggests that inheritance tax revenues could be spent on funding access to higher education and other institutional reforms aimed at reducing whatever he might have had in mind by "class distinctions".[49] There would be no special difficulty about implementing hypothecation for any sort of inheritance tax, relative to implementing it for other taxes. The Rignano scheme is perfectly compatible with it, as is any other proposal for calculating inheritance tax liabilities. (Generally, how to calculate liability can be kept independent from how to allocate revenue.)

Hypothecation rarely occurs in the real world simply because governments don't like surrendering their ability to decide where to spend money. But some familiar examples exist, such as the television licence in the UK, which funds the BBC, and Australia's medicare levy, which funds its universal healthcare provision. Theoretical discussion of hypothecation has raised some doubts about whether there can be any principled case for it. It seems natural, from a theoretical point of view, to ask why it matters that the revenue for the grant come from this specific tax, as if there would be something defective about any grant funded in some other way. There may be other problems. Julian Le Grand, for example, has identified the sheer improbability of revenue collected being in the region of the amount needed to fund the earmarked policy. Now, for some policies this might not matter, as the revenue collected

---

[48] Ackerman & Alstott (1999: 95).    [49] Dworkin (2003: 186–92).

might be a plausible measure of how much the earmarked policy is actually worth. Maybe the BBC's budget *should* vary with how many people are willing to pay the licence fee, assuming that there is some nonarbitrary way of setting the fee in the first place.[50] However, in a case where higher education subsidies are supposed to come from inheritance tax revenues, it would be normal for the revenues to provide either an excess or a shortfall. Le Grand points out that, in such cases, there would be strong pressure either to allocate the excess to other urgent policies elsewhere or to call on other sources of tax revenue to make up the shortfall.[51] And once this is done, the commitment to hypothecation has been abandoned. As to proposals about inheritance in particular, Matthew Clayton has recently argued that if the motivations for taxing inheritance are broadly egalitarian, then revenues may justly be allocated to any particular egalitarian policy.[52] To this, one might plausibly add that the revenues could be used on any of the various government services, such as the construction of coastal flood barriers or other public goods.

My own sympathies lie with Le Grand and Clayton. The best arguments for hypothecation probably rely on the expressive power of telling taxpayers what a specific tax is being used for. Such arguments are more likely to succeed when applied to specific cases rather than taxation in general. It might be a good thing to tell people that taxes on cigarettes are being spent on healthcare provision, if that makes people more accepting of the tax and/or thwarts the attempts of special interest groups (like the tobacco industry) to lobby for their removal. The Australian medicare levy might have some credentials of this sort.[53] As noted at the chapter's outset, contexts in which taxes must be used are not all alike, and a case for hypothecation in one context needn't carry over to another.

That said, people might become more accepting of inheritance taxes if they were being spent on something particularly important. In the current political climate, where inheritance taxes are often viewed as cruel or evil, there may be some politically strategic value in hypothecating inheritance

---

[50] Recall the earlier point about the difficulty of pricing public goods.
[51] Le Grand (2003: 155–7).        [52] Clayton (2012: 114–15).
[53] I have argued elsewhere that hypothecation might be appropriate with respect to unpopular taxes on cigarettes; see Halliday (2015). Le Grand takes a somewhat similar view on the funding of state healthcare more generally (2003: 161–2).

tax revenues in the right way. It is always easier to maintain an antitax narrative with the help of rhetoric that presents governments as seeking to extract tax revenues for their own sake, as if revenues just go into a big government bank vault instead of being spent on something important. While the task of altering current political narratives about inheritance is an important one, hypothecation might be only one part of pursuing this goal. Apart from that, it can be hard to see what the theoretical goal of hypothecation really is.[54] Money is, after all, a fungible resource, which largely explains why it got invented in the first place. A fixed amount of revenues from one tax is just as good at funding a policy as the same amount of revenues from somewhere else.[55]

I'll conclude with a positive suggestion about finding a broad theoretical justification of hypothecation nonetheless. Classical liberals and libertarians are committed, broadly speaking, to the goal of 'small government' in the sense that at least includes a lowering of citizens' overall tax burden. On this view, the question might not be one of where to allocate inheritance tax revenues so much as one about how to relieve the burden imposed by other forms of taxation. I made this sort of point earlier, in 7.1, when claiming that libertarians should reject inheritance taxation only if they can find reasons to prefer other sorts of taxation. It is worth revisiting the point here because it connects with hypothecation. Broadly speaking, hypothecation may have some appeal to classical liberals insofar as it might empower citizens in a certain sense. There is some evidence that people resent taxation of the standard, nonhypothecated sort.[56] The truth in the political narratives about money being 'taken by the government' is that it is genuinely difficult for citizens to know what they are actually paying for when they get taxed, much less exercise any control over it. Many citizens hate expensive government spending (especially on things like unjust wars) but cannot do much about the fact that they've already paid for such things when taxed.

---

[54] On Dworkin's view, allocation of inheritance tax revenues to policies such as accessible education is supposed to model hypothetical insurance choices aimed at preserving some right to bequeath while securing a sort of proxy for a child's inheritance in the event that one is not wealthy enough to provide it oneself. I argued against this application of the hypothetical insurance approach in chapter 4 and do so more fully in Halliday (2015).

[55] Another objection to hypothecation is that sometimes opacity helps protect policies that might be easily justified but which nevertheless lack public support. This is pointed out by Blum & Kalven (1952: 488).

[56] Le Grand (2003: 147–52).

Hypothecation might guard against certain sorts of government failures that feature in classical liberal concerns. The practice of attaching certain taxes to certain policy expenditures goes some way towards enabling government to respond to signals provided by its 'consumers', i.e. taxpaying citizens. For example, anyone who doesn't approve of a certain government policy might avoid having to pay it by legitimately avoiding the hypothecated tax. Taxpayers in Australia who purchase private healthcare are required to pay a smaller medicare levy than those on similar incomes who stay on the state-provided alternative. However, inheritance tax is unlike levies for state-provided services insofar as there is no market-provided alternative that citizens may purchase so as to opt out. I suspect, however, that views more optimistic about markets than about governments may value hypothecation as a means of making government provision through taxation somewhat more similar to the market than it usually is.

## 8.7 The Politics of Inherited Wealth

I started this book by remarking that real-world movements can benefit from a bit of philosophical substance. Any political change benefits from having an effective way of countering the prevailing rhetoric that helps support the status quo. This point extends beyond the matter of inheritance taxes. Governments need revenue. Taxation, although coercive, is one of the more peaceful ways in which they can get it. Nevertheless, taxation is widely disliked by citizens who have to pay it. Because of this, governments are often led to find alternative strategies to get money. One that is often merely annoying is the presence of arbitrarily large fees attached to straightforward services, such as getting a new passport. A more sinister strategy is that of excessive criminalization, where increasing numbers of offences are created mainly for the purposes of extracting revenue through fines.[57] Recent events in the United States have shown how bad this can become, particularly where it interacts with oppressive racial hierarchies.[58] Of course, there is room for disagreement

---

[57] For a philosophical study of this problem, see Husak (2009).

[58] Here I have in mind the events in Ferguson, Missouri, during 2014. A report by the US Department of Justice was explicit that policing had become motivated by a need to generate revenue rather than the more constitutional goal of genuine law enforcement.

about what is to be done about this. Libertarians will likely argue that the 'need' for revenue is really a symptom of government having become too large, and that over-criminalization is enabled in part by its ability to carry out surveillance on its citizens. In some cases, these observations have plausibility. Another problem is the over-fragmentation of local government, which in effect prevents redistribution: total tax revenues may remain large, but largely confined to policy expenditure in wealthy districts. Nevertheless, the facts about how governments will try to gain revenue through coercive channels other than taxation motivate a case for combatting political narratives that crudely present taxes as an evil thing. In general, people need to be given reasons to reconsider their instinctive dislike of taxation.

I haven't provided any theoretical ideas that can do much to shape public perception of taxation in general. But the proposals discussed in this book may be of some use in raising consciousness. The attack on inheritance taxes owes much to political campaigning of a sort that successfully appeals to a certain body of the electorate. Middle-class people of the baby-boomer generation have lived through periods of economic prosperity that have allowed them to accumulate often quite valuable property, compared to what their parents enjoyed. The children of baby boomers are, by contrast, starting to suffer the effects of economic slowdowns and recessions that have made it hard for them to buy their own homes or enjoy such a high standard of living, in spite of often working longer hours. So parents want to bequeath. Politicians eager to cut inheritance taxes present them as a threat to precisely this sort of aspiration.

These narratives all have one thing in common: they deliberately and systematically conceal the significant fact that a large body of inheritance may not be newly produced wealth but simply old inheritance that has been cascading down for some time before the current generation got here. No electorate is ever likely to rally to the protection of old money, so political elites pretend that the right to bequeath is an important benefit to the masses. There is no reason why some freedom of bequest can't be granted to the wider population while being tough on the largest

Report available online: US Department of Justice, 'Investigation of the Ferguson Police Department', 4 Mar. 2015, https://www.justice.gov/sites/default/files/opa/press-releases/attachments/2015/03/04/ferguson_police_department_report.pdf, accessed 20 Dec. 2016.

ancient fortunes. This accounts for why certain figures in politics try to pretend that the distinction doesn't exist.

Rignano's distinction between accumulated and previously inherited wealth is an easy one to grasp even though the work done in this book indicates some difficulties in giving it a full defence. Progressivity over time may work very well as the sort of consciousness-raiser that is currently needed to emancipate electorates from the narrative they are fed about the moral importance of a right to bequeath and the case against restricting it. If the electorate could be made more appreciative of the fact that much inheritance flow does not transmit newly accumulated wealth, they would be less hostile to taxation schemes that targeted the older parts of the flow. In this way, the immediate social value of the Rignano scheme might not be best conveyed by any philosophical defence like the one given in this book. It may just be that the core idea of the scheme helps people see past current misrepresentations of what inherited wealth actually is.

# Bibliography

Ackerman, Bruce & Alstott, Anne. 1999 *The Stakeholder Society* (New Haven, CT: Yale University Press).

Alarie, Benjamin. 2015 "The Challenge of Tax Avoidance for Social Justice in Taxation" in H. Gaisbauer, G. Schweiger, & C. Sedmak (eds.) *Philosophical Explorations of Justice and Taxation: National and Global Issues* (New York: Springer): 83–98.

Alstott, Anne. 2007 "Equal Opportunity and Inheritance Taxation" *Harvard Law Review* 121(2): 469–52.

Alstott, Anne. 2008 "Is the Family at Odds with Equality? The Legal Implications of Equality for Children" *Southern California Law Review* 82(1): 1–44.

Alstott, Anne. 2009 "Family Values, Inheritance Law, and Inheritance Taxation" *Tax Law Review* 63(1): 123–37.

Anderson, Elizabeth. 1999 "What Is the Point of Equality?" *Ethics* 109(2): 287–387.

Anderson, Elizabeth. 2007 "Fair Opportunity in Education: A Democratic Equality Perspective" *Ethics* 117(4): 595–622.

Anderson, Elizabeth. 2010a *The Imperative of Integration* (Princeton, NJ: Princeton University Press).

Anderson, Elizabeth. 2010b "The Fundamental Disagreement between Luck-Egalitarians and Relational Egalitarians" *Canadian Journal of Philosophy* 46: 1–23.

Anderson, Elizabeth. 2012 "Equality" in David Estlund (ed.) *The Oxford Handbook of Political Philosophy* (New York: Oxford University Press): 40–57.

Anderson, Elizabeth. 2017 *Private Government: How Employers Rule Our Lives (and Why We Don't Talk about It)* (Princeton, NJ: Princeton University Press).

Anderson, Elizabeth. 2016a "Adam Smith on Equality" in Ryan Hanley (ed.) *The Princeton Guide to Adam Smith* (Princeton, NJ: Princeton University Press): 157–72.

Anderson, Elizabeth. 2016b "Thomas Paine's Agrarian Justice and the Origins of Social Insurance" in Eric Schliesser (ed.) *Ten Neglected Classics of Philosophy* (New York: Oxford University Press): 55–83.

Anomaly, Jonathan. 2015 "Public Goods and Government Action" *Politics, Philosophy & Economics* 14(2): 109–28.

Armstrong, Elizabeth & Hamilton, Laura. 2013 *Paying for the Party: How College Maintains Inequality* (Cambridge, MA: Harvard University Press).

Arneson, Richard. 1991 "Lockean Self-Ownership: Towards a Demolition" *Political Studies* 39(1): 36–54.

Arneson, Richard. 2004 "Luck Egalitarianism Interpreted and Defended" *Philosophical Topics* 32(1): 1–20.

Atkinson, Anthony. 2013 "Wealth and Inheritance in Britain from 1896 to the Present" *Centre for Analysis of Social Exclusion*, discussion paper no. 178.

Atkinson, Anthony. 2015 *Inequality: What Can Be Done?* (Cambridge, MA: Harvard University Press).

Attas, Daniel. 2006 "Fragmenting Property" *Law & Philosophy* 25: 119–49.

Barry, Brian. 2005 *Why Social Justice Matters* (Malden, MA: Polity Press).

Barry, Nicholas. 2006 "Defending Luck Egalitarianism" *Journal of Applied Philosophy* 23(1): 89–107.

Batchelder, Lily. 2007 "Taxing Privilege More Effectively: Replacing the Estate Tax with an Inheritance Tax" in J. Furman & J. Bordoff (eds.) *Paths to Prosperity: Hamilton Project Ideas on Income Security, Education and Taxes* (Washington, DC: Brookings Institution Press): 345–81.

Batchelder, Lily. 2009 "What Should Society Expect from Heirs? The Case for a Comprehensive Inheritance Tax" *Tax Law Review* 63(1): 1–111.

Beckert, Jens. 2008 *Inherited Wealth*, trans. Thomas Dunlap (Princeton, NJ: Princeton University Press).

Bird-Pollan, Jennifer. 2013 "Death, Taxes, and Property (Rights): Nozick, Libertarianism, and the Estate Tax" *Maine Law Review* 66(1): 1–28.

Birnbaum, Simon. 2012 *Social Justice, Liberalism and the Demands of Equality* (New York: Palgrave Macmillan).

Blum, Walter & Kalven, Harry. 1952 "The Uneasy Case for Progressive Taxation" *University of Chicago Law Review* 19(3): 417–520.

Bou-Habib, Paul. 2014 "The Moralized View of Parental Partiality" *Journal of Political Philosophy* 22(1): 66–83.

Bowles, Samuel & Gintis, Herbert. 2002 "The Inheritance of Inequality" *Journal of Economic Perspectives* 16(3): 3–30.

Bowles, Samuel, Gintis, Herbert, & Osborne Groves, Melissa. 2005 (eds.) *Unequal Chances: Family Background and Economic Success* (Princeton, NJ: Princeton University Press).

Bracewell-Milnes, Barry. 1997 "The Hidden Costs of Inheritance Taxation" in G. Erregyers & T. Vandevelde (eds.) *Is Inheritance Legitimate? Ethical and Economic Aspects of Wealth Transfers* (Berlin: Springer): 156–201.

Bracewell-Milnes, Barry. 2002 *Euthanasia for Death Duties: Putting Inheritance Tax Out of Its Misery* (London: Institute of Economic Affairs Monographs).

Bradley, Ben. 2009 *Well-Being and Death* (New York: Oxford University Press).

Braun, S. Stewart. 2010 "Historical Entitlement and the Practice of Bequest: Is There a Moral Right of Bequest?" *Law & Philosophy* 29(6): 695–715.

Braun, S. Stewart. 2016 "Liberty, Political Equality, and Wealth-Transfer Taxation" *Journal of Applied Philosophy* 33(4): 379–95.

Brennan, Geoffrey. 2005 "'The Myth of Ownership' by Liam Murphy and Thomas Nagel: A Review Essay" *Constitutional Political Economy* 16(2): 207–19.

Brennan, Jason. 2012 *Libertarianism: What Everyone Needs to Know* (New York: Oxford University Press).

Brennan, Jason & Tomasi, John. 2012 "Classical Liberalism" in D. Estlund (ed.) *The Oxford Handbook of Political Philosophy* (New York: Oxford University Press): 115–32.

Brighouse, Harry. 2005 *On Education* (London: Routledge).

Brighouse, Harry & Swift, Adam. 2006 "Parents' Rights and the Value of the Family" *Ethics* 117(1): 80–108.

Brighouse, Harry & Swift, Adam. 2009 "Legitimate Parental Partiality" *Philosophy & Public Affairs* 37(1): 43–80.

Brighouse, Harry & Swift, Adam. 2014 *Family Values: The Ethics of Parent–Child Relationships* (Princeton, NJ: Princeton University Press).

Brighouse, Harry & Swift, Adam. 2015 "Advantage, Authority, Autonomy and Continuity: A Response to Ferracioli, Gheaus and Stroud" *Law, Ethics & Philosophy* 3: 220–40.

Brock, Gillian. 2009 *Global Justice: A Cosmopolitan Account* (New York: Oxford University Press).

Buchanan, James. 1976 "The Justice of Natural Liberty" *Journal of Legal Studies* 5(1): 1–16.

Buchanan, James. 1986 *Liberty, Market and State: Political Economy in the 1980s* (Brighton, Sussex: Wheatsheaf Press).

Burke, Edmund. 2014 *Revolutionary Writings* (New York: Cambridge University Press).

Carnegie, Andrew. 1889a "Wealth" *North American Review* 148(391): 653–64.

Carnegie, Andrew. 1889b "The Best Fields of Philanthropy" *North American Review* 149(397): 682–98.

Carroll, Christopher. 2000 "Why Do the Rich Save So Much?" in J. Slemrod (ed.) *Does Atlas Shrug? The Economic Consequences of Taxing the Rich* (Cambridge, MA: Harvard University Press).

Chan, Tak-Win & Boliver, Vikki 2013 "The Grandparents Effect in Social Mobility: Evidence from British Birth Cohort Studies" *American Sociological Review* 78(4): 622–78.

Chester, C. Ronald. 1976 "Inheritance and Wealth Taxation in a Just Society" *Rutgers Law Review* 30: 62–101.

Chester, C. Ronald. 1982 *Inheritance, Wealth and Society* (Bloomington: Indiana University Press).

Chester, C. Ronald. 1998 "Inheritance in American Legal Thought" in R. Miller & S. McNamee (eds.) *Inheritance and Wealth in America* (New York: Plenum Press).

Christiano, Thomas. 2012 "Money in Politics" in D. Estlund (ed.) *The Oxford Handbook of Political Philosophy* (New York: Oxford University Press): 241–57.

Clark, Gregory. 2014 *The Son Also Rises: Surnames and the History of Social Mobility* (Princeton, NJ: Princeton University Press).

Clark, Gregory & Cummins, Neil. 2015 "Is Most Wealth Inherited or Created? England, 1858–2012" *Tax Law Review* 68(3): 517–44.

Clayton, Matthew. 2012 "Equal Inheritance: An Anti-Perfectionist View" in J. Cunliffe & G. Erreygers (eds.) *Inherited Wealth, Justice and Equality* (London: Routledge): 98–118.

Cohen, G. A. 1995 *Self-Ownership, Freedom and Equality* (New York: Cambridge University Press).

Cohen, G. A. 2000 *If You're an Egalitarian, How Come You're So Rich?* (Cambridge, MA: Harvard University Press).

Cohen, G. A. 2001 "Why Not Socialism?" in E. Broadbent, *Democratic Equality: What Went Wrong?* (Toronto, ON: University of Toronto Press): 58–78.

Cohen, G. A. 2004 "Expensive Taste Rides Again" in J. Burley (ed.) *Dworkin and His Critics* (Malden, MA: Blackwell Press).

Cohen, G. A. 2008 *Rescuing Justice and Equality* (Cambridge, MA: Harvard University Press).

Cohen, Joshua. 1997 "Procedure and Substance in Deliberative Democracy" in J. Bohman & W. Rehg (eds.) *Deliberative Democracy: Essays on Reason and Politics* (Cambridge, MA: MIT Press): 407–38.

Cohen, Joshua. 2001 "Money, Politics, Political Equality" in A. Byrne, R. Stalnaker, & R. Wedgwood (eds.) *Fact and Value: Essays on Ethics and Metaphysics for Judith Jarvis Thomson* (Cambridge, MA: MIT Press): 47–80.

Cowen, Tyler. 2013 *Average Is Over: Powering America beyond the Age of the Great Stagnation* (New York: Plume Books).

Crawford, Rowena & Hood, Andrew. 2016 "Lifetime Receipt of Inheritances and the Distribution of Wealth in England" *Fiscal Studies* 37(1): 55–75.

Crisp, Roger. 2006 *Reasons and the Good* (New York: Oxford University Press).

Crompton, Rosemary. 2008 *Class and Stratification*, 3rd edition (Malden, MA: Polity Press).

Cunliffe, John. 2000 "Left-Libertarianism: Historical Origins" in P. Vallentyne & H. Steiner (eds.) *The Origins of Left-Libertarianism* (New York: Palgrave Macmillan).

Cunliffe, John & Erreygers, Guido. 2005 "Inheritance and Equal Shares: Early American Views" in K. Widerquist, M. Lewis, & S. Pressman (eds.) *The Ethics and Economics of the Basic Income Guarantee* (Aldershot: Ashgate): 55–76.

Cunliffe, John & Erreygers, Guido. 2013 "Equal Inheritance and Equal Shares: A Reconsideration of Some Nineteenth-Century Reform Proposals" in J. Cunliffe & G. Erreygers (eds.) *Inherited Wealth, Justice and Equality* (London: Routledge): 54–69.

Dalton, Hugh. 1920 *Some Aspects of the Inequality of Incomes in Modern Communities* (London: George Routledge & Sons).

Dalton, Hugh. 1936 *Principles of Public Finance*, 3rd edition (London: Routledge and Kegan Paul).

Darwall, Stephen. 1977 "Two Kinds of Respect" *Ethics* 88(1): 36–49.

de Dijn, Annelien. 2008 *French Political Thought from Montesquieu to Tocqueville* (New York: Cambridge University Press).

Dietsch, Peter. 2015 *Catching Capital: The Ethics of Tax Competition* (New York: Oxford University Press).

Dorfman, Avihay. 2010 "Private Ownership" *Legal Theory* 16(1): 1–35.

Dorling, Danny. 2015 *Inequality and the 1%*, 2nd edition (London: Verso).

Douglas, Thomas. 2015 "Parental Partiality and the Intergenerational Transmission of Advantage" *Philosophical Studies* 172(10): 2735–56.

Draper, Nicholas. 2010 *The Price of Emancipation: Slave-Ownership, Compensation and British Society and the End of Slavery* (New York: Cambridge University Press).

Duff, David. 2005 "Private Property and Tax Policy in a Libertarian World: A Critical Review" *Canadian Journal of Law and Jurisprudence* 18(1): 23–45.

Dworkin, Ronald. 2000 *Sovereign Virtue: The Theory and Practice of Equality* (Cambridge, MA: Harvard University Press).

Dworkin, Ronald. 2002 "Sovereign Virtue Revisited" *Ethics* 113(1): 106–43.

Dworkin, Ronald. 2003 "Equality, Luck and Hierarchy" *Philosophy & Public Affairs* 31(2): 190–8.

Dworkin, Ronald. 2004 "Ronald Dworkin Replies" in J. Burley (ed.) *Dworkin and His Critics* (Malden, MA: Blackwell Press): 339–50.

Dworkin, Ronald. 2006 *Is Democracy Possible Here?* (Princeton, NJ: Princeton University Press).

Ekelund, Robert & Walker, Douglas. 1996 "J. S. Mill on the Income Tax Exemption and Inheritance Taxes: The Evidence Reconsidered" *History of Political Economy* 28(4): 559–81.

Erreygers, Guido. 1998 "The Economic Theories and Social Reform Proposals of Ernest Solvay" in W. Samuels (ed.) *European Economists of the Early 20th Century, Volume 1* (Northampton, MA: Edward Elgar): 220–62.

Erreygers, Guido & Di Bartolomeo, Giovanni. 2007 "The Debates on Eugenio Rignano's Inheritance Tax Proposals" *History of Political Economy* 39(4): 605–38.

Fabre, Cecile. 2001 "The Choice-Based Right to Bequeath" *Analysis* 61(269): 60–5.

Ferracioli, Luara. 2015 "Why the Family?" *Law, Ethics & Philosophy* 3: 205–19.

Fishkin, Joseph. 2014 *Bottlenecks: A New Theory of Equality of Opportunity* (New York: Oxford University Press).

Fleischacker, Samuel. 2004 *On Adam Smith's Wealth of Nations: A Philosophical Companion* (Princeton, NJ: Princeton University Press).

Fleischer, Miranda Perry. 2017 "Not So Fast: The Hidden Difficulties of Taxing Wealth" in J. Knight & M. Schwartzberg (eds.) *Wealth: NOMOS LVII* (New York: New York University Press): 261–308.

Forcehimes, Andrew & Talisse, Robert. 2015 "Luck Libertarianism? A Critique of Tan's Institutional View" *Southwest Philosophy Review* 31(1): 187–96.

Fourie, Carina. 2015 "To Praise and to Scorn: The Problems of Inequalities of Esteem for Social Egalitarianism" in C. Fourie, F. Schuppert, & I. Walliman-Helmer (eds.) *Social Equality: On What It Means to Be Equals* (New York: Oxford University Press): 87–106.

Frank, Robert. 2008 "Should Public Policy Respond to Positional Externalities?" *Journal of Public Economics* 92(8): 1777–86.

Frank, Robert. 2011 *The Darwin Economy: Liberty, Competition, and the Common Good* (Princeton, NJ: Princeton University Press).

Freeman, Samuel. 2007 *Justice and the Social Contract: Essays on Rawlsian Political Philosophy* (New York: Oxford University Press).

Freeman, Samuel. 2011 "Capitalism in the Classical and High Liberal Traditions" *Social Philosophy & Policy* 28(2): 19–55.

Freiman, Christopher. 2014 "Analogical Arguments for Egalitarianism" *Ratio* 27(2): 222–37.

Fried, Barbara. 1999 "Who Gets Utility from Bequests?" *Stanford Law Review* 51: 641–81.

Fried, Barbara. 2000 "Compared to What? Taxing Brute Luck and Other Second-Best Problems" *Tax Law Review* 53: 377–95.

Fried, Barbara. 2004 "Left-Libertarianism: A Review Essay" *Philosophy & Public Affairs* 32(1): 66–92.

Fried, Barbara. 2005 "Begging the Question with Style: Anarchy, State and Utopia at Thirty Years" *Social Philosophy & Policy* 22(1): 221–54.

Fried, Barbara. 2011 "Does Nozick Have a Theory of Property Rights?" in R. Bader & J. Meadowcroft (eds.) *The Cambridge Companion to Nozick's Anarchy, State and Utopia* (New York: Cambridge University Press): 230–52.

Friedman, Lawrence. 2009 *Dead Hands: A Social History of Wills, Trusts, and Inheritance Law* (Palo Alto, CA: Stanford University Press).

Friedman, Milton. 1962 *Capitalism and Freedom* (Chicago: University of Chicago Press).

Friedman, Milton & Friedman, Rose. 1980 *Free to Choose: A Personal Statement* (London: Secker & Warburg).

Fuller, Lon. 1969 *The Morality of Law*, revised edition (New Haven, CT: Yale University Press).

Gale, William & Perozek, Maria. 2001 "Do Estate Taxes Reduce Saving?" in W. Gale, J. Hines, & J. Slemrod (eds.) *Rethinking Estate and Gift Taxation* (Washington, DC: Brookings Institution Press): 216–47.

Gale, William & Slemrod, Joel. 2001 "Overview" in W. Gale, J. Hines, & J. Slemrod (eds.) *Rethinking Estate and Gift Taxation* (Washington, DC: Brookings Institution Press): 1–64.

Galston, William. 2001 "What about Reciprocity?" in P. van Parijs, J. Cohen, & J. Rogers (eds.) *What's Wrong with a Free Lunch?* (Boston: Beacon Press): 29–33.

Gheaus, Anca. Forthcoming "Hikers in Flip-Flops: Luck Egalitarianism, Democratic Equality, and the *Distribuenda* of Justice" *Journal of Applied Philosophy*.

Gilbert, Geoffrey. 1997 "Adam Smith on the Nature and Causes of Poverty" *Review of Social Economy* 55(3): 273–91.

Gilens, Martin. 1999 *Why Americans Hate Welfare: Race, Media, and the Politics of Antipoverty Policy* (Chicago: University of Chicago Press).

Glackin, Shane. 2014 "Back to Bundles: Deflating Property Rights, Again" *Legal Theory* 20: 1–24.

Godwin, William. 2013 *An Inquiry Concerning Political Justice* (New York: Oxford University Press).

Goodwin, Iris. 2010 "How the Rich Stay Rich: Using a Family Trust Company to Secure a Family Fortune" *Seton Hall Law Review* 40(2): 467–516.

Graetz, Michael & Shapiro, Ian. 2005 *Death by a Thousand Cuts: The Fight over Taxing Inherited Wealth* (Princeton, NJ: Princeton University Press).

Grant, Ruth. 1987 *John Locke's Liberalism* (Chicago: University of Chicago Press).

Grey, Thomas. 1980 "The Disintegration of Property" in J. Chapman & J. Pennock (eds.) *Nomos 22: Property* (New York: New York University Press): 69–85.

Haakonssen, Knud. 1996 *Natural Law and Moral Philosophy* (New York: Cambridge University Press).

Halliday, Daniel. 2013a "Is Inheritance Morally Distinctive?" *Law & Philosophy* 32(5): 619–44.

Halliday, Daniel. 2013b "Kok-Chor Tan's *Justice, Luck and Institutions*" *Utilitas* 25(1): 121–32.

Halliday, Daniel. 2013c "Justice and Taxation" *Philosophy Compass* 8(12): 1111–22.

Halliday, Daniel. 2015 "Egalitarianism and Consumption Tax" in H. Gaisbauer, G. Schweiger, & C. Sedmak (eds.) *Philosophical Explorations of Justice and Taxation: National and Global Issues* (New York: Springer): 119–33.

Halliday, Daniel. 2016a "Inheritance and Hypothetical Insurance" in S. Sciaraffa & W. Waluchow (eds.) *The Legacy of Ronald Dworkin* (New York: Oxford University Press): 99–114.

Halliday, Daniel. 2016b "Private Education, Positional Goods, and the Arms Race Problem" *Politics, Philosophy & Economics* 15(2): 150–69.

Hamnett, Christopher. 1999 *Winners and Losers: Home Ownership in Modern Britain* (London: UCL Press).

Harding, David, Jencks, Christopher, Lopoo, Leonard, & Mayer, Susan. 2005 "The Changing Effect of Family Background on the Incomes of American Adults" in S. Bowles, H. Gintis, & M. Groves (eds.) *Unequal Chances: Family Background and Economic Success* (Princeton, NJ: Princeton University Press): 100–44.

Harding, Matthew. 2014 *Charity Law and the Liberal State* (New York: Cambridge University Press).

Haslett, D. W. 1986 "Is Inheritance Justified?" *Philosophy & Public Affairs* 15(2): 122–55.

Haslett, D. W. 1994 *Capitalism with Morality* (New York: Oxford University Press).

Haslett, D. W. 1997 "Reply to Bracewell-Milnes" in G. Erreygers & T. Vandevelde (eds.) *Is Inheritance Legitimate? Ethical and Economic Aspects of Wealth Transfers* (Berlin: Springer): 210–20.

Hayek, F. A. 1945 "The Use of Knowledge in Society" *American Economic Review* 35(4): 519–30.

Hayek, F. A. 1960 *The Constitution of Liberty* (London: Routledge).

Hirsch, Fred. 1977 *Social Limits to Growth* (London: Routledge & Kegan Paul).

Hood, Andrew & Joyce, Robert. 2017 "Inheritances and Inequality across and within Generations" *Institute for Fiscal Studies*, briefing note 192.

Hurley, Susan. 2003 *Justice, Luck and Knowledge* (Cambridge, MA: Harvard University Press).

Husak, Douglas. 2009 *Overcriminalization: The Limits of the Criminal Law* (New York: Oxford University Press).

Jones, Owen. 2012 *Chavs: The Demonization of the Working Class* (London: Verso).

Joulfaian, David. 2001 "Charitable Giving in Life and at Death" in W. Gale, J. Hines, & J. Slemrod (eds.) *Rethinking Estate and Gift Taxation* (Washington, DC: Brookings Institution Press): 350–69.

Karagiannaki, Eleni. 2015 "Recent Trends in the Size and Distribution of Inherited Wealth in the UK" *Fiscal Studies* 36(2): 181–213.

Katz, Larissa. 2008 "Exclusion and Exclusivity in Property Law" *University of Toronto Law Journal* 58: 275–315.

Keller, Simon. 2006 "Four Theories of Filial Duty" *Philosophical Quarterly* 56 (223) 254–74.

Kendrick, Leslie. 2011 "The Lockean Rights of Bequest and Inheritance" *Legal Theory* 17(2): 145–69.

Kerr, Gavin. 2016 "'Predistribution', Property-Owning Democracy, and Land Value Taxation" *Politics, Philosophy & Economics* 15(1): 67–91.

King, Eden B., Mendoza, Saaid A., Madera, Juan M., Hebl, Mikki R., and Knight, Jennifer L. 2006 "What's in a Name? A Multiracial Investigation of the Role of Occupational Stereotypes in Selection Decisions" *Journal of Applied Social Psychology* 36(5): 1145–59.

Knight, Carl. 2013 "Luck Egalitarianism" *Philosophy Compass* 8(10): 924–34.

Knight, Carl & Stemplowska, Zofia. 2011 (eds.) *Responsibility and Distributive Justice* (New York: Oxford University Press).

Kopczuk, Wojciech. 2009 "Economics of Estate Taxation: Review of Theory and Evidence" *Tax Law Review* 53(1): 139–57.

Kramer, Matthew. 1997 *John Locke and the Origins of Private Property* (New York: Cambridge University Press).

Kymlicka, Robert. 2002 *Contemporary Political Philosophy: An Introduction*, 2nd edition (New York: Oxford University Press).

Lamb, Robert. 2009 "Was William Godwin a Utilitarian?" *Journal of the History of Ideas* 70(1): 119–41.

Lamb, Robert. 2014 "The Power to Bequeath" *Law & Philosophy* 33(5): 629–54.

Lamb, Robert. 2015 *Thomas Paine and the Idea of Human Rights* (New York: Cambridge University Press).

Langbein, John. 1988 "The Twentieth-Century Revolution in Family Wealth Transmission" *Michigan Law Review* 86(4): 722–51.

Lareau, Annette. 2011 *Unequal Childhoods: Class, Race, and Family Life*, 2nd edition (Berkeley: University of California Press).

Lazenby, Hugh. 2010 "One Kiss Too Many? Luck Egalitarianism and Other-Affecting Choice" *Journal of Political Philosophy* 18: 271–86.

Le Grand, Julian. 2003 *Motivation, Agency, and Public Policy* (New York: Oxford University Press).

Le Grand, Julian. 2006 "Implementing Stakeholder Grants: The British Case" in B. Ackerman, A. Alstott, & P. van Parijs (eds.) *Redesigning Distribution* (London: Verso): 120–9.

Little, Adrian. 1999. "The Politics of Compensation: Tom Paine's *Agrarian Justice* and Liberal Egalitarianism" *Contemporary Politics* 5(1): 63–73.

Lippert-Rasmussen, Kasper. 2015 "Luck Egalitarians versus Relational Egalitarians: On the Prospects of a Pluralist Account of Egalitarian Justice" *Canadian Journal of Philosophy* 45(2): 220–41.

Lippert-Rasmussen, Kasper. 2016 *Luck Egalitarianism* (New York: Bloomsbury).

Locke, John. 2009 *Two Treatises of Government* (New York: Cambridge University Press).

Lomasky, Loren. 1987 *Persons, Rights and the Moral Community* (New York: Oxford University Press).

Mack, Eric. 1995 "The Self-Ownership Proviso: A New and Improved Lockean Proviso" *Social Philosophy & Policy* 12(1): 186–218.

Mack, Eric. 2006 "Non-Absolute Rights and Libertarian Taxation" *Social Philosophy & Policy* 23(2): 109–41.

Mack, Eric. 2009 *John Locke* (New York: Bloomsbury).

Macleod, Colin. 1998 *Liberalism, Justice and Markets: A Critique of Liberal Equality* (New York: Oxford University Press).

Macleod, Colin. 2010 "Parental Responsibilities in an Unjust World" in D. Benatar & D. Archard (eds.) *Procreation* (New York: Oxford University Press): 128–50.

Mason, Andrew. 2006 *Levelling the Playing Field: The Idea of Equal Opportunity and Its Place in Egalitarian Thought* (New York: Oxford University Press).

Mason, Andrew. 2015 "Justice, Respect, and Treating People as Equals" in C. Fourie, F. Schuppert, & I. Walliman-Helmer (eds.) *Social Equality: On What It Means to Be Equals* (New York: Oxford University Press): 129–45.

Mazumder, Bhashkar. 2005 "The Apple Falls Even Closer to the Tree Than We Thought: New and Revised Estimates of the Intergenerational Inheritance of Earnings" in S. Bowles, H. Gintis, & M. Groves (eds.) *Unequal Chances: Family Background and Economic Success* (Princeton, NJ: Princeton University Press): 80–99.

McCaffery, Edward. 1994 "The Political Liberal Case against the Estate Tax" *Philosophy & Public Affairs* 23(4): 281–312.

McCaffery, Edward. 2002 *Fair Not Flat: How to Make the Tax System Better and Fairer* (Chicago: University of Chicago Press).

McCloskey, Deidre. 2006 *The Bourgeois Virtues: Ethics for an Age of Commerce* (Chicago: University of Chicago Press).

McCloskey, Deidre. 2014 "Measured, Unmeasured, Mismeasured, and Unjustified Pessimism: A Review Essay of Thomas Piketty's Capital in the Twenty-First Century" *Erasmus Journal for Philosophy and Economics* 7(2): 73–115.

McGarry, Kathleen. 2013 "The Estate Tax and *Inter Vivos* Transfers over Time" *American Economic Review: Papers & Proceedings* 103(3): 478–83.

McNamee, Stephen & Miller, Robert. 1989 "Estate Inheritance: A Sociological Lacuna" *Sociological Inquiry* 59(1): 7–29.

McNamee, Stephen & Miller, Robert. 2009 *The Meritocracy Myth*, 2nd edition (New York: Rowman & Littlefield).

Meade, James. 1964 *Efficiency, Equality and Ownership of Property* (London: Allen & Unwin).

Meade, James. 1978 *The Structure and Reform of Direct Taxation* (London: Allen & Unwin).

Merrill, Thomas. 1998 "Property and the Right to Exclude" *Nebraska Law Review* 77: 730–55.

Mill, John Stuart. 1989 *On Liberty and Other Writings* ed. Stefan Collini (New York: Cambridge University Press).

Mill, John Stuart. 2004 *Principles of Political Economy* (New York: Prometheus Books).

Miller, David. 1998 "Equality and Justice" in A. Mason (ed.) *Ideals of Equality* (Malden, MA: Blackwell): 21–36.

Miller, David. 1999 *Principles of Social Justice* (Cambridge, MA: Harvard University Press).

Miller, Jon & Kumar, Rahul. 2007 (eds.) *Reparations: Interdisciplinary Inquiries* (New York: Oxford University Press).

Moller, Dan. 2017 "Property and the Creation of Value" *Economics & Philosophy* 33(1): 1–23.

Most, Fidelius. 2014 "In Defence of Family Firms: Why We Should Keep the Business Property Relief" (MSc Dissertation, Department of Philosophy, London School of Economics).

Mullainathan, Sendhil & Shafir, Eldar. 2013 *Scarcity: Why Having Too Little Means So Much* (New York: Times Books).

Munoz-Darde, Veronique. 1999 "Is the Family to Be Abolished, Then?" *Proceedings of the Aristotelian Society* 99(1): 37–56.

Murphy, Liam. 1998 "Institutions and the Demands of Justice" *Philosophy & Public Affairs* 27(4): 251–91.

Murphy, Liam. 2015 "Why Does Inequality Matter? Reflections on the Political Morality of Piketty's *Capital in the Twenty-First Century*" *Tax Law Review* 68(3): 613–29.

Murphy, Liam & Nagel, Thomas. 2002 *The Myth of Ownership: Taxes and Justice* (New York: Oxford University Press).

Nagel, Thomas. 1975 "Libertarianism without Foundations" *Yale Law Journal* 85(1): 136–49.

Nagel, Thomas. 1991 *Equality and Partiality* (New York: Oxford University Press).

Nagel, Thomas. 2009 "Liberal Democracy and Hereditary Inequality" *Tax Law Review* 63(1): 113–22.

Narveson, Jan. 1988 *The Libertarian Idea* (Philadelphia, PA: Temple University Press).

Narveson, Jan. 2009 "Present Payments, Past Wrongs: Correcting Loose Talk about Nozick and Rectification" *Libertarian Papers* 1(1): 1–17.

Neuhouser, Frederick. 2008 *Rousseau's Theodicy of Self-Love: Evil, Rationality and the Drive for Recognition* (New York: Oxford University Press).

Nozick, Robert. 1974 *Anarchy, State and Utopia* (New York: Basic Books).

Nozick, Robert. 1989 *The Examined Life: Philosophical Meditations* (New York: Simon & Schuster).

Okin, Susan. 1989 *Justice, Gender, and the Family* (New York: Basic Books).

O'Neill, Martin & Williamson, Thad. 2012 (eds.) *Property-Owning Democracy: Rawls and Beyond* (Malden, MA: Wiley & Sons).

Otsuka, Michael. 2002 "Luck, Insurance, and Hierarchy" *Ethics* 113(1): 40–54.

Otsuka, Michael. 2003 *Libertarianism without Inequality* (New York: Oxford University Press).

Otsuka, Michael. 2004 "Liberty, Equality, Envy and Abstraction" in J. Burley (ed.) *Dworkin and His Critics* (Malden, MA: Blackwell): 70–8.

Otteson, James. 2016 "Adam Smith and the Right" in R. Hanley (ed.) *Adam Smith: His Life, Thought, and Legacy* (Princeton, NJ: Princeton University Press): 494–511.

Overall, Christine. 2012 *Why Have Children? The Ethical Debate* (Cambridge, MA: MIT Press).

Paine, Thomas. 2000 *Political Writings* (New York: Cambridge University Press).

Parfit, Derek. 1984 *Reasons and Persons* (New York: Oxford University Press).

Parijs, Philippe van. 1992 "Competing Justifications of Basic Income" in Philippe van Parijs (ed.) *Arguing for Basic Income* (London: Verso): 3–43.

Parijs, Philippe van. 1997 "Nothing Wrong with Unearned Wealth?" in G. Erregyers & T. Vandevelde (eds.) *Is Inheritance Legitimate? Ethical and Economic Aspects of Wealth Transfers* (Berlin: Springer): 202–9.

Parijs, Philippe van. 2001 "A Basic Income for All" in J. Cohen & J. Rogers (eds.) *What's Wrong with a Free Lunch?* (Boston: Beacon Press): 3–28.

Patten, Allen. 2012 "Liberal Neutrality: A Reinterpretation and Defence" *Journal of Political Philosophy* 20(3): 245–72.

Paul, Pamela. 2008 *Parenting, Inc.: How We Are Sold on $800 Strollers, Fetal Education, Baby Sign Language, Sleeping Coaches, Toddler Couture, and Diaper Wipe Warmers—and What It Means for Our Children* (New York: Times Books).

Pedrick, Willard. 1981 "Oh, to Die Down Under! Abolition of Death and Gift Duties in Australia" *Tax Lawyer* 35(1): 113–41.

Penner, J. E. 1997 *The Idea of Property in Law* (New York: Oxford University Press).

Penner, J. E. 2014 "Intergenerational Justice and the 'Hereditary Principle'" *Law & Ethics of Human Rights* 8(2): 195–217.

Pfeffer, Fabian. 2014 (ed.) *Inequality across Multiple Generations*, special issue of *Research in Social Stratification and Mobility* 35: 1–128.

Philp, Mark. 1986 *Godwin's Political Justice* (Ithaca, NY: Cornell University Press).

Philp, Mark. 2013a *Reforming Ideas in Britain: Politics and Language in the Shadow of the French Revolution, 1789–1815* (New York: Cambridge University Press).

Philp, Mark. 2013b "William Godwin" in E. Zalta (ed.) *The Stanford Encyclopedia of Philosophy*, http://plato.stanford.edu/archives/sum2013/entries/godwin/.

Piff, Paul. 2014 "Wealth and the Inflated Self: Class, Entitlement, and Narcissism" *Personality and Social Psychology Bulletin* 40(1): 34–43.

Piketty, Thomas. 2014 *Capital in the Twenty-First Century*, trans. A. Goldhammer (Cambridge, MA: Harvard University Press).

Piketty, Thomas. 2015 "Property, Inequality, and Taxation: Reflections on *Capital in the Twenty-First Century*" *Tax Law Review* 68(3): 631–47.

Poterba, James. 2001 "Estate and Gift Taxes and Incentives for *Inter Vivos* Giving in the US" *Journal of Public Economics* 79: 237–64.

Pummer, Theron. 2016 "Whether and Where to Give" *Philosophy & Public Affairs* 44(1): 77–95.

Pressman, Steven. 2016 "The Mismeasure of *Capital*: A Response to McCloskey" *Erasmus Journal for Philosophy & Economics* 9(2): 145–66.

Rakowski, Eric. 1991 *Equal Justice* (New York: Oxford University Press).

Rakowski, Eric. 2000 "Can Wealth Taxes Be Justified?" *Tax Law Review* 53(3): 263–376.

Rawls, John. 1993 *Political Liberalism*, expanded edition (New York: Columbia University Press).

Rawls, John. 1999 *A Theory of Justice*, revised edition (Cambridge, MA: Harvard University Press).

Rawls, John. 2001 *Justice as Fairness: A Restatement* (Cambridge, MA: Harvard University Press).

Raz, Joseph. 1986 *The Morality of Freedom* (New York: Oxford University Press).

Reich, Rob. 2014 "Gift Giving and Philanthropy in Market Democracy" *Critical Review* 26(3–4): 408–22.

Reiman, Jeffrey & Leighton, Paul. 2010 *The Rich Get Rich and the Poor Get Prison: Ideology, Class, and Criminal Justice*, 9th edition (New York: Allyn & Bacon).

Rignano, Eugenio. 1919 "A Plea for a Greater Economic Democratisation" *Economic Journal* 29(115): 302–8.

Rignano, Eugenio. 1924 *The Social Significance of the Inheritance Tax*, trans. W. J. Shultz (New York: Alfred A. Knopf).

Rignano, Eugenio. 1925 *The Social Significance of Death Duties*, trans. J. Stamp (London: Noel Douglas).

Riley, Jonathan. 1996 "J. S. Mill's Liberal Utilitarian Assessment of Capitalism versus Socialism" *Utilitas* 8(1): 39–71.

Robeyns, Ingrid. 2017 "Having Too Much" in J. Knight & M. Schwartzberg (eds.) *Wealth: NOMOS LVII* (New York: New York University Press): 1–44.

Rothbard, Murray. 1998 *The Ethics of Liberty*, revised edition (New York: New York University Press).

Rothbard, Murray. 2006 *For a New Liberty*, 2nd edition (Auburn, AL: Ludwig von Mises Institute).

Rothschild, Emma & Sen, Amartya. 2006 "Adam Smith's Economics" in K. Haakonssen (ed.) *The Cambridge Companion to Adam Smith* (New York: Cambridge University Press): 319–65.

Runciman, W. G. 1967 "Social" Equality" *Philosophical Quarterly* 17(68): 221–30.

Ryan, Alan. 1984 *Property and Political Theory* (New York: Blackwell).

Ryan, Alan. 1987 *Property* (Minneapolis: University of Minnesota Press).

Sanyal, Sagar. 2012 "A Defence of Democratic Egalitarianism" *Journal of Philosophy* 109(7): 413–34.

Satz, Debra. 2007 "Equality, Adequacy, and Education for Citizenship" *Ethics* 117(4): 623–48.

Satz, Debra. 2010 *Why Some Things Should Not Be for Sale: The Moral Limits of Markets* (New York: Oxford University Press).

Savage, Mike. 2015 *Social Class in the 21st Century* (London: Penguin/Random House).

Scheffler, Samuel. 1982, repr. 1993 *The Rejection of Consequentialism*, revised edition (New York: Oxford University Press).

Scheffler, Samuel. 2003 "What Is Egalitarianism?, *Philosophy & Public Affairs* 31(1): 5–39.

Scheffler, Samuel. 2004 "Equality as the Virtue of Sovereigns: A Reply to Ronald Dworkin" *Philosophy & Public Affairs* 31(2): 199–206.

Scheffler, Samuel. 2005 "The Division of Moral Labour" *Aristotelian Society Supplementary Volume* 79: 229–53.

Scheffler, Samuel. 2015 "The Practice of Equality" in C. Fourie, F. Schuppert & I. Wallimann-Helmer (eds.) *Social Equality* (New York: Oxford University Press): 21–44.

Schemmel, Christian. 2011 "Why Relational Egalitarians Should Care about Distributions" *Social Theory & Practice* 37(3): 365–90.

Schemmel, Christian. 2012a "Luck Egalitarianism as Democratic Reciprocity? A Response to Tan" *Journal of Philosophy* 109(7): 435–48.

Schemmel, Christian. 2012b "Distributive and Relational Equality" *Politics, Philosophy & Economics* 11(2): 123–48.

Schmidtz, David. 1991 *The Limits of Government: An Essay on the Public Goods Argument* (Boulder, CO: Westview).

Schmidtz, David. 2005 "History and Pattern" in E. Frankel-Paul, F. Miller, & J. Paul (eds.) *Natural Rights Liberalism from Locke to Nozick* (New York: Cambridge University Press): 148–77.

Schmidtz, David. 2008 "The Institution of Property" reprinted with revisions in his *Person, Polis, Planet* (New York: Oxford University Press).

Schor, Juliet. 1998 *The Overspent American* (New York: Basic Books).

Schuppert, Fabian. 2015 "Being Equals: Analyzing the Nature of Social Egalitarian Relationships" in C. Fourie, F. Schuppert & I. Wallimann-Helmer (eds.) *Social Equality* (New York: Oxford University Press): 107–28.

Schwartz, Pedro. 1968 *The New Political Economy of J. S. Mill* (London: Weidenfeld & Nicholson).

Segall, Shlomi. 2013 *Equality and Opportunity* (New York: Oxford University Press).

Shelby, Tommie. 2012 "Justice, Work, and the Ghetto Poor" *Law & Ethics of Human Rights* 6(1): 69–96.

Sidgwick, Henry. 1887 *Principles of Political Economy*, 2nd edition (New York: Macmillan).

Sidgwick, Henry. 1891, repr. 2012 *Elements of Politics* (New York: Cambridge University Press).

Simmons, A. John. 1992 *The Lockean Theory of Rights* (Princeton, NJ: Princeton University Press).

Slemrod, Joel. & Bakija, Jon. 2008 *Taxing Ourselves: A Citizen's Guide to the Debate over Taxes*, 4th edition (Cambridge, MA: MIT Press).

Smith, Adam. 1978 *Lectures in Jurisprudence* (New York: Oxford University Press).

Smith, Adam. 1999a *The Wealth of Nations, Books I–III* (London: Penguin Books).

Smith, Adam. 1999b *The Wealth of Nations, Books IV–V* (London: Penguin Books).

Smith, Adam. 2009 *The Theory of Moral Sentiments* (New York: Cambridge University Press).

Sobel, David. 2012 "Backing Away from Libertarian Self-Ownership" *Ethics* 123(1): 32–60.

Sreenivasan, Gopal. 1995 *The Limits of Lockean Rights in Property* (New York: Oxford University Press).

Steiner, Hillel. 1992 "Three Just Taxes" in P. van Parijs (ed.) *Arguing for Basic Income* (London: Verso): 81–92.

Steiner, Hillel. 1994 *An Essay on Rights* (Malden, MA: Blackwell).

Stellar, Jennifer, Manzo, Vida, Kraus, Michael, & Keltner, Dacher. 2012 "Class and Compassion: Socioeconomic Factors Predict Responses to Suffering" *Emotion* 12(3): 449–59.

Stemplowska, Zofia. 2012 "Luck Egalitarianism" in F. D'Agostino & G. Gaus (eds.) *The Routledge Companion to Social and Political Philosophy* (London: Routledge): 389–400.

Stuber, Jenny. 2011 *Inside the College Gates: How Class and Culture Matter in Higher Education* (New York: Rowman & Littlefield).

Swift, Adam. 2005 "Justice, Luck, and the Family: The Intergenerational Transmission of Economic Advantage from a Normative Perspective" in S. Bowles, H. Gintis, & M. Groves (eds.) *Unequal Chances: Family Background and Economic Success* (Princeton, NJ: Princeton University Press): 256–76.

Tait, Alan. 1967 *The Taxation of Personal Wealth* (Chicago: University of Illinois Press).

Tan, Kok-Chor. 2012 *Justice, Luck and Institutions: The Site, Ground and Scope of Equality* (New York: Oxford University Press).

Tan, Kok-Chor. 2013 "Reply to Halliday" *Utilitas* 25(1): 133–5.

Taussig, Frank William. 1921 *Principles of Economics*, 3rd edition, volume 2 (New York: Macmillan).

Tawney, R. H. 1921 *The Acquisitive Society* (London: Bell & Sons).

Tawney, R. H. 1931 *Equality* (London: Allen & Unwin).

Tebble, Adam. 2001 "The Tables Turned: Wilt Chamberlain versus Robert Nozick on Rectification" *Economics & Philosophy* 17(1): 89–108.

Temkin, Larry. 1993 *Inequality* (New York: Oxford University Press).

Thompson, Janna. 2002 *Taking Responsibility for the Past: Reparation and Historical Injustice* (London: Polity).

Thrasher, John & Hankins, Keith. 2015 "When Justice Demands Inequality" *Journal of Moral Philosophy* 12: 172–94.

Tilly, Charles. 1998 *Durable Inequality* (Berkeley: University of California Press).

Tomasi, John. 2012 *Free Market Fairness* (Princeton, NJ: Princeton University Press).

Toynbee, Polly & Walker, David. 2008 *Unjust Rewards: Exposing Greed and Inequality in Britain Today* (London: Granta).

Valentini, Laura. 2012 "Ideal versus Non-Ideal Theory: A Conceptual Map" *Philosophy Compass* 7(9): 654–64.

Vallentyne, Peter. 1997 "Self-Ownership and Equality: Brute Luck, Gifts, Universal Dominance, and Leximin" *Ethics* 107(2): 321–43.

Vallentyne, Peter. 2000 "Left-Libertarianism: A Primer" in Peter Vallentyne & Hillel Steiner (eds.) *Left-Libertarianism and Its Critics* (New York: Palgrave): 1–20.

Vallentyne, Peter. 2015 "Justice, Interpersonal Morality, and Luck Egalitarianism" in A. Kaufman (ed.) *Distributive Justice and Access to Advantage: G. A. Cohen's Egalitarianism* (New York: Cambridge University Press): 40–49.

Vallentyne, Peter & Steiner, Hillel. 2000a (eds.) *The Origins of Left-Libertarianism* (New York: Palgrave).

Vallentyne, Peter & Steiner, Hillel. 2000b *Left Libertarianism and Its Critics* (New York: Palgrave).

Vallentyne, Peter, Steiner, Hillel, & Otsuka, Michael. 2005 "Why Left-Libertarianism Is Not Incoherent, Indeterminate, or Irrelevant: A Reply to Fried" *Philosophy & Public Affairs* 33(2): 201–15.

Vallier, Kevin. 2015 "A Moral and Economic Critique of the New Property-Owning Democrats: On Behalf of a Rawlsian Welfare State" *Philosophical Studies* 172(2): 283–304.

Vincent, Carol & Ball, Stephen. 2006 *Childcare, Choice and Class Practices: Middle Class Parents and Their Children* (London: Routledge).

Vincent, Carol & Ball, Stephen. 2007 "Making Up the Middle-Class Child: Families, Activities and Class Dispositions" *Sociology* 41(6): 1061–77.

Vrousalis, Nicholas. 2015 *The Political Philosophy of G. A. Cohen* (New York: Bloomsbury).

Waldron, Jeremy. 1981 "Locke's Account of Inheritance and Bequest" *Journal of the History of Philosophy* 19(1): 39–51.

Waldron, Jeremy. 1986 "Welfare and the Images of Charity" *Philosophical Quarterly* 36(145): 463–82.

Waldron, Jeremy. 1988 *The Right to Private Property* (New York: Oxford University Press).

Waldron, Jeremy. 2002 *God, Locke, and Equality: Christian Foundations in Locke's Political Thought* (New York: Cambridge University Press).

Waldron, Jeremy. 2005 "Nozick and Locke: Filling the Space of Rights" *Social Philosophy and Policy* 22(1): 81–110.

Waldron, Jeremy. 2013 "*Political* Political Theory: An Inaugural Lecture" *Journal of Political Philosophy* 21(1): 1–23.

Wedgwood, Josiah. 1929 *The Economics of Inheritance* (London: Pelican Books).

Weitzman, Susan. 2000 "*Not to People Like Us*": Hidden Abuse in Upscale Marriages (New York: Basic Books).

West, Max. 1908 *The Inheritance Tax*, 2nd edition (New York: Columbia University Press).

White, Stuart. 2003 *The Civic Minimum: On the Rights and Obligations of Economic Citizenship* (New York: Oxford University Press).

White, Stuart. 2008 "What (If Anything) Is Wrong with Inheritance Tax?" *Political Studies* 79(2): 162–71.

Williams, Andrew. 2004 "Equality, Ambition and Insurance" *Aristotelian Society Supplementary Volume* 78(1): 131–50.

Williams, Andrew. 2013 "How Gifts and Gambles Preserve Justice" *Economics & Philosophy* 29: 65–85.

Wolff, Edward. 2015 *Inheriting Wealth in America: Future Boom or Bust?* (New York: Oxford University Press).

Wolff, Jonathan. 1998 "Fairness, Respect, and the Egalitarian Ethos" *Philosophy & Public Affairs* 27(2): 97–122.

Wolff, Jonathan. 2010 "Fairness, Respect, and the Egalitarian Ethos Revisited" *Journal of Moral Philosophy* 14(3–4): 335–50.

Wolff, Jonathan. 2015 "Social Equality and Social Inequality" in C. Fourie, F. Schuppert, & I. Walliman-Helmer (eds.) *Social Equality: On What It Means to Be Equals* (New York: Oxford University Press): 209–26.

Wood, Neal. 1984 *John Locke and Agrarian Capitalism* (Berkeley: University of California Press).

Young, Iris. 1990 *Justice and the Politics of Difference* (Princeton, NJ: Princeton University Press).

Young, Iris. 2011 *Responsibility for Justice* (New York: Oxford University Press).

# Name Index

# General Index